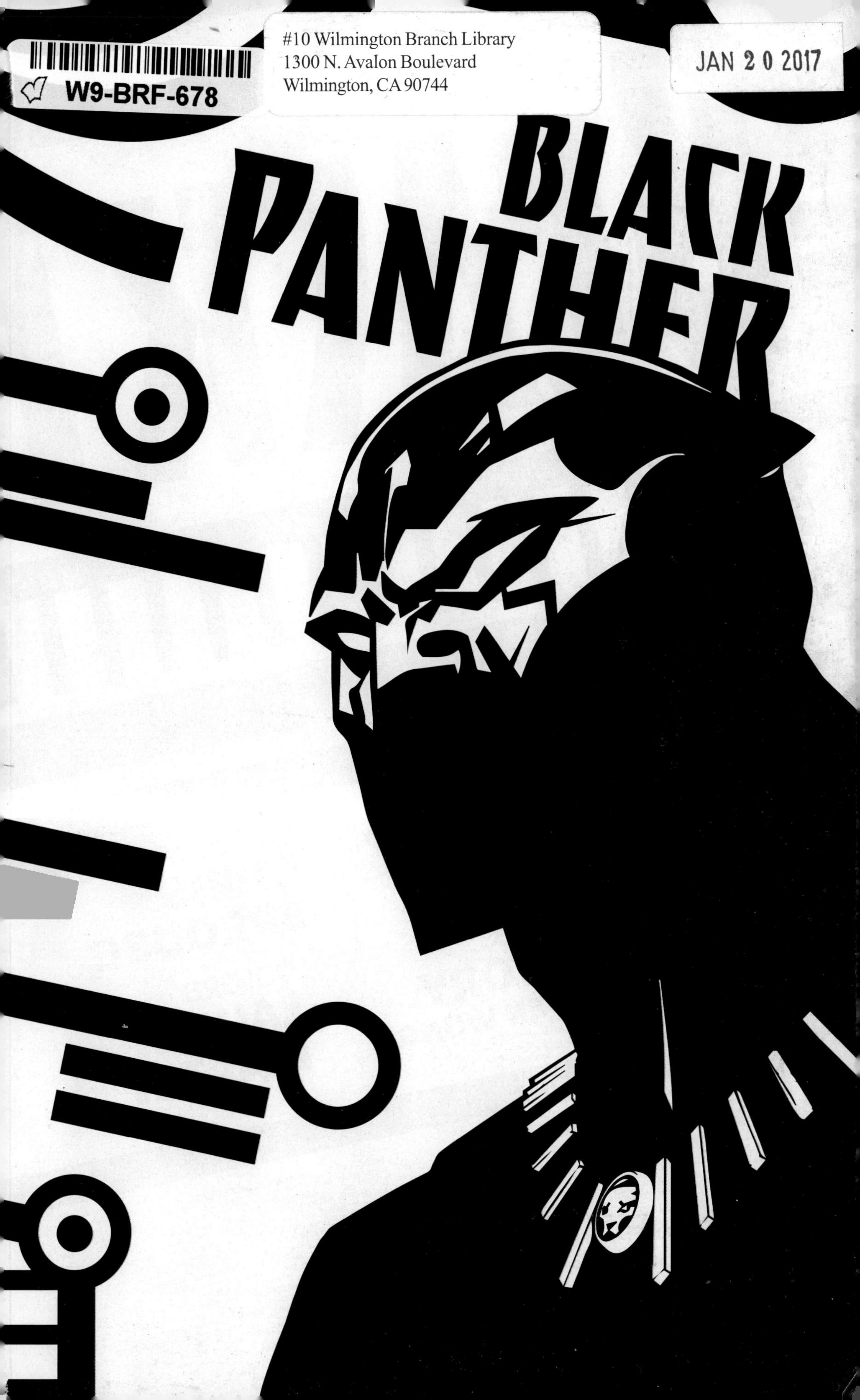
BLACK
PANTHER

BLACK

WRITER
TA-NEHISI COATES

PENCILS/LAYOUTS
CHRIS SPROUSE

INKS/FINISHES
KARL STORY
WITH **WALDEN WONG**

COLORS
LAURA MARTIN

COLLECTION EDITOR **JENNIFER GRÜNWALD**
ASSOCIATE MANAGING EDITOR **KATERI WOODY**
ASSOCIATE EDITOR **SARAH BRUNSTAD**
EDITOR, SPECIAL PROJECTS **MARK D. BEAZLEY**
VP PRODUCTION & SPECIAL PROJECTS **JEFF YOUNGQUIST**
SVP PRINT, SALES & MARKETING **DAVID GABRIEL**
BOOK DESIGNER **JAY BOWEN AND MANNY MEDEROS**

EDITOR IN CHIEF **AXEL ALONSO**
CHIEF CREATIVE OFFICER **JOE QUESADA**
PUBLISHER **DAN BUCKLEY**
EXECUTIVE PRODUCER **ALAN FINE**

BLACK PANTHER: A NATION UNDER OUR FEET BOOK 2. Contains material originally published in magazine form as BLACK PANTHER #5-8 and JUNGLE ACTION #6-7. First printing 2017. ISBN# 978-1-302-90054-0. Published by MARVEL WORLDWIDE, INC., a subsidiary of MARVEL ENTERTAINMENT, LLC. OFFICE OF PUBLICATION: 135 West 50th Street, New York, NY 10020. **Printed in the U.S.A.** ALAN FINE, President, Marvel Entertainment; DAN BUCKLEY, President, TV, Publishing & Brand Management; JOE QUESADA, Chief Creative Officer; TOM BREVOORT, SVP of Publishing; DAVID BOGART, SVP of Business Affairs & Operations, Publishing & Partnership; C.B. CEBULSKI, VP of Brand Management & Development, Asia; DAVID GABRIEL, SVP of Sales & Marketing, Publishing; JEFF YOUNGQUIST, VP of Production & Special Projects; DAN CARR, Executive Director of Publishing Technology; ALEX MORALES, Director of Publishing Operations; SUSAN CRESPI, Production Manager; STAN LEE, Chairman Emeritus. For information regarding advertising in Marvel Comics or on Marvel.com, please contact Vit DeBellis, Integrated Sales Manager, at vdebellis@marvel.com. For Marvel subscription inquiries, please call 888-511-5480. **Manufactured between 11/18/2016 and 12/26/2016 by LSC COMMUNICATIONS INC., SALEM, VA, USA.**

10 9 8 7 6 5 4 3 2 1

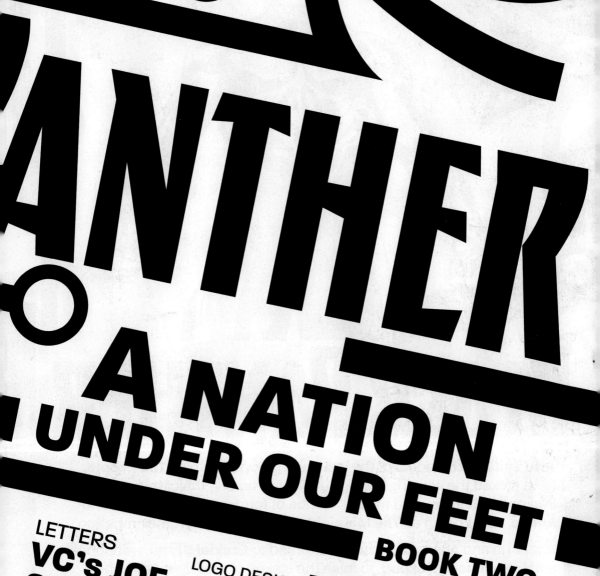

PANTHER

A NATION UNDER OUR FEET

BOOK TWO

LETTERS **VC's JOE SABINO**

LOGO DESIGN **RIAN HUGHES**

ASSISTANT EDITOR **CHRIS ROBINSON**

EDITOR **WIL MOSS**

EXECUTIVE EDITOR **TOM BREVOORT**

BLACK PANTHER CREATED BY **STAN LEE & JACK KIRBY**

BLACK PANTHER

Tetu and **Zenzi**, leaders of the insurgent group known as **The People**, have stoked the growing feelings of dissent among the citizens of Wakanda. They courted the assistance of former Dora Milaje **Ayo** and **Aneka**, now known as **The Midnight Angels**, to support their rebellion.

After Ayo and Aneka declined, Tetu turned to **Ezekiel Stane**, weaponeer and biotechnology expert, to raise the stakes of their war; Repulsor-tech suicide bombers attacked a city square, killing many innocents and severely injuring queen-mother **Ramonda**.

The situation now has King **T'Challa's** full attention, as he puts aside a very personal project: reviving his sister **Shuri** from living death. Unbeknownst to him, Shuri's mind travels the Djalia, a plane of Wakanda's collective past, present, and future. She is guided by a griot spirit who has taken the visual form of Ramonda.

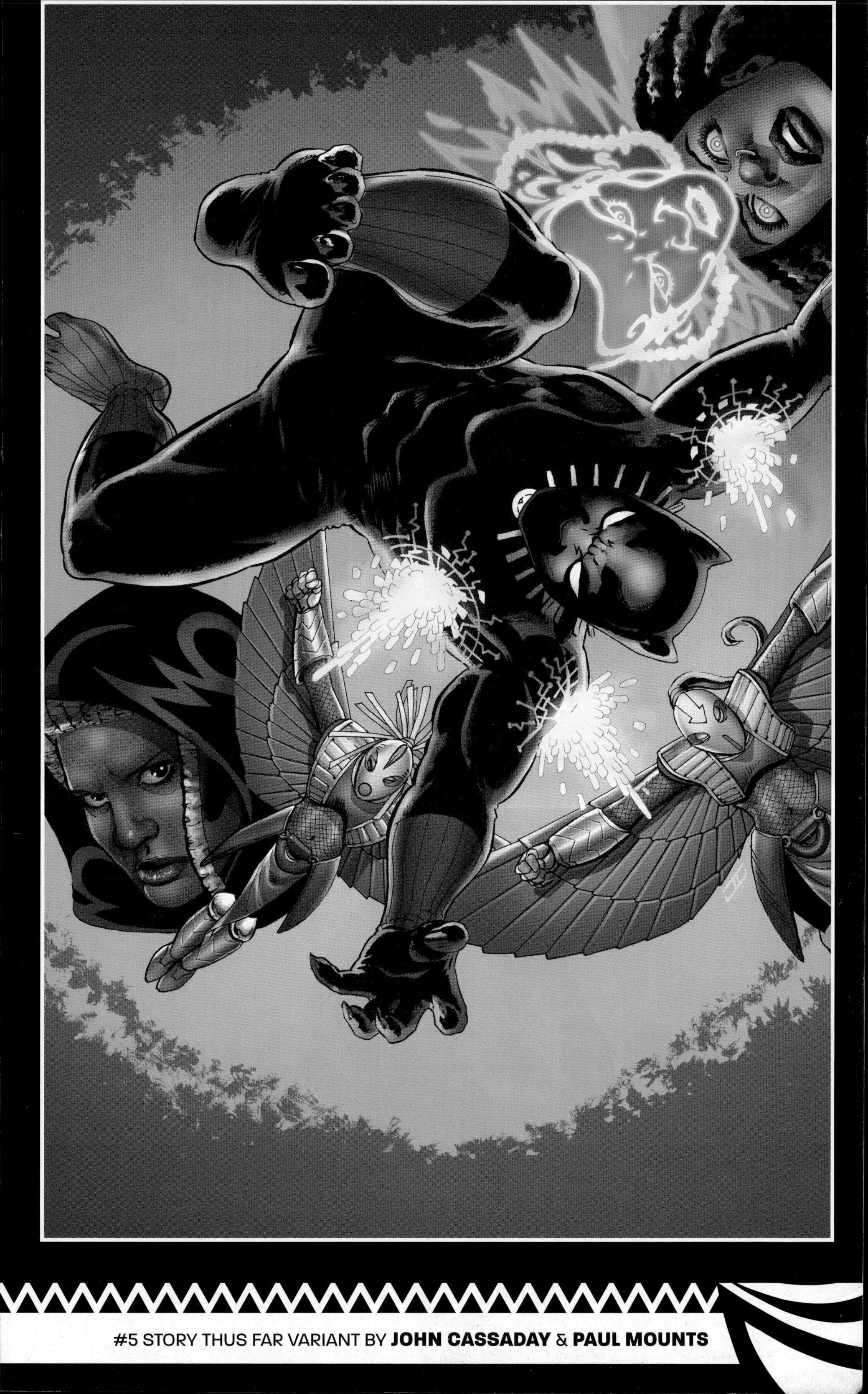

#5 STORY THUS FAR VARIANT BY **JOHN CASSADAY** & **PAUL MOUNTS**

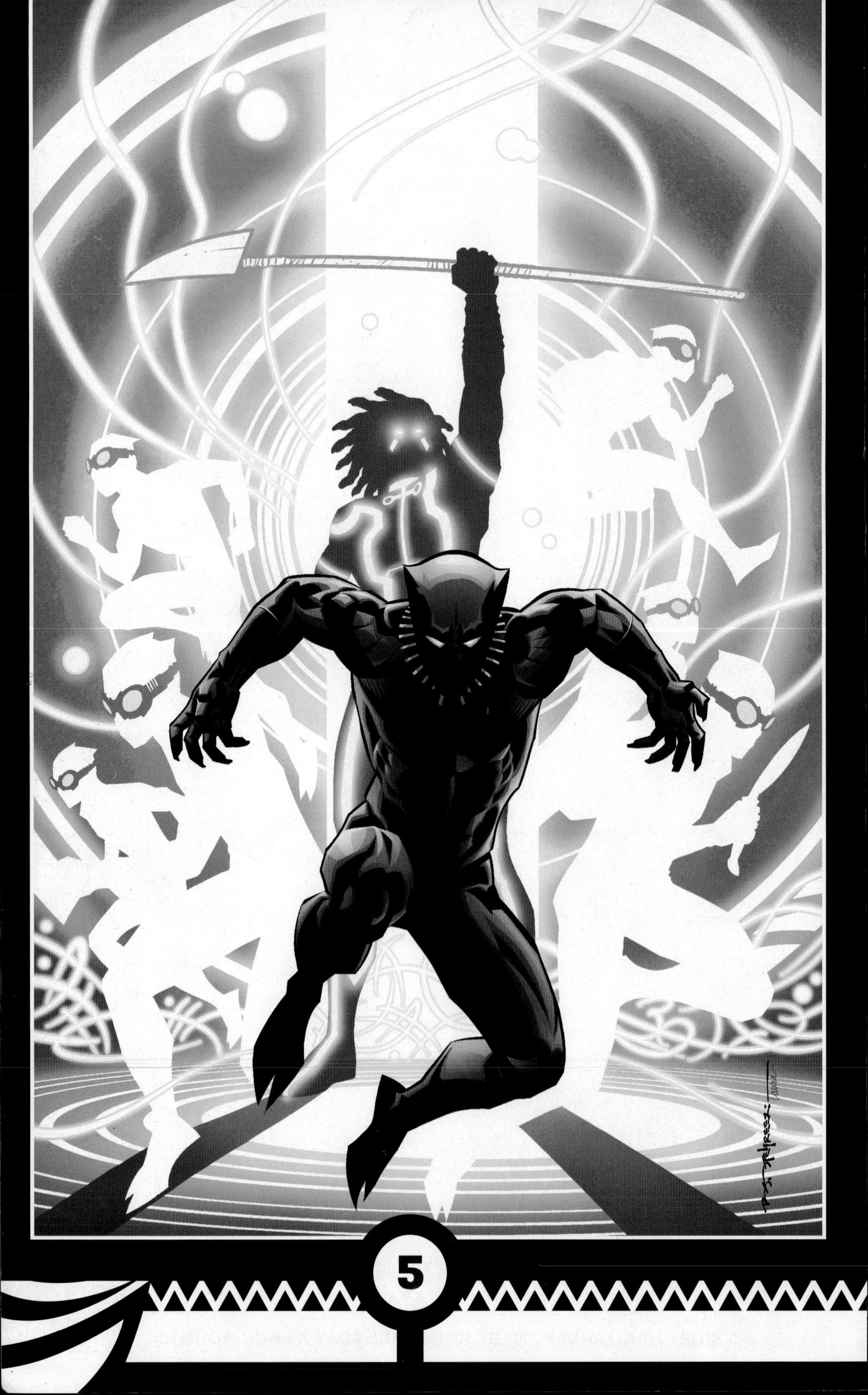

5

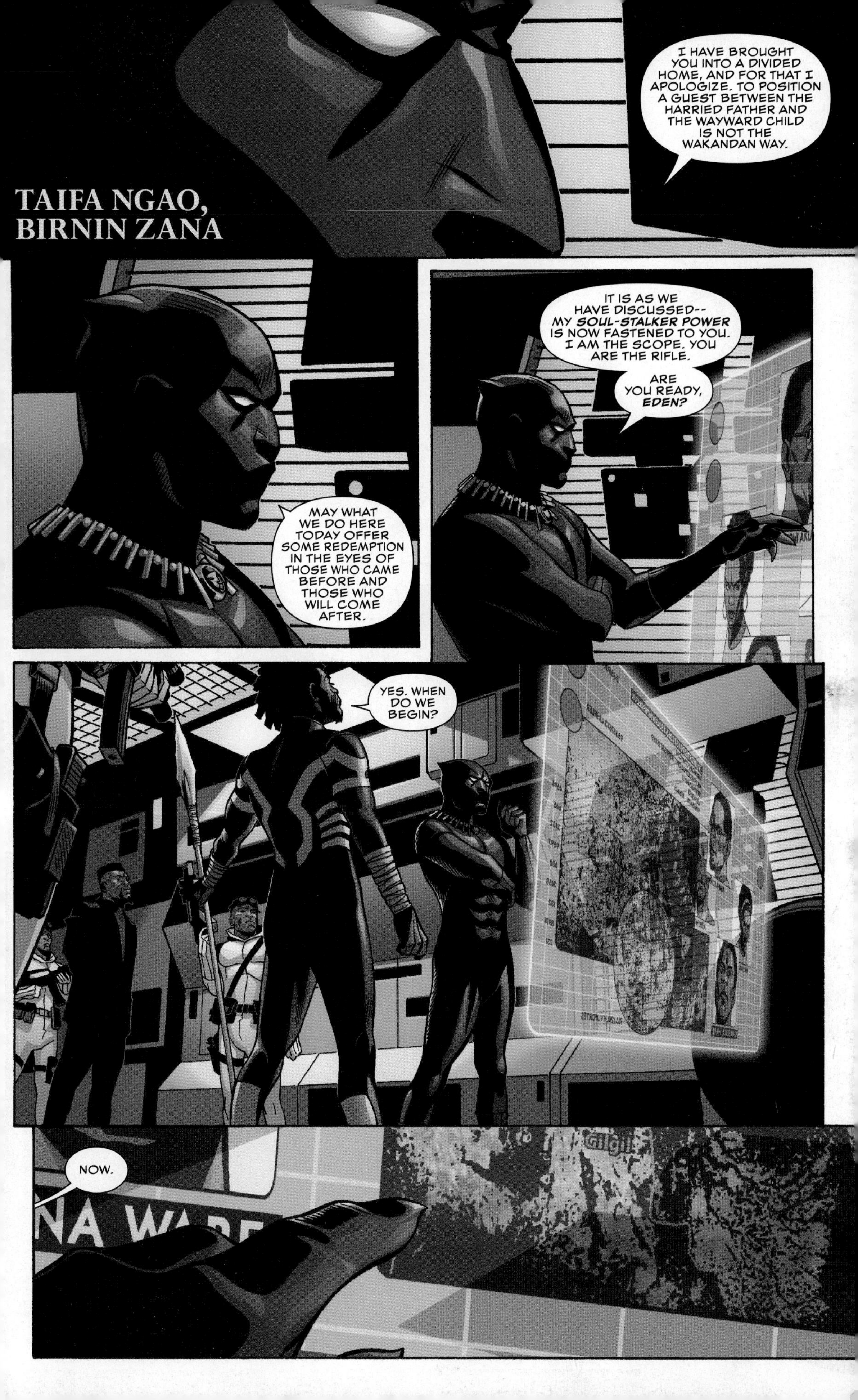
TAIFA NGAO, BIRNIN ZANA
I HAVE BROUGHT YOU INTO A DIVIDED HOME, AND FOR THAT I APOLOGIZE. TO POSITION A GUEST BETWEEN THE HARRIED FATHER AND THE WAYWARD CHILD IS NOT THE WAKANDAN WAY.
MAY WHAT WE DO HERE TODAY OFFER SOME REDEMPTION IN THE EYES OF THOSE WHO CAME BEFORE AND THOSE WHO WILL COME AFTER.
IT IS AS WE HAVE DISCUSSED-- MY SOUL-STALKER POWER IS NOW FASTENED TO YOU. I AM THE SCOPE. YOU ARE THE RIFLE.
ARE YOU READY, EDEN?
YES. WHEN DO WE BEGIN?
NOW.
Gilgil

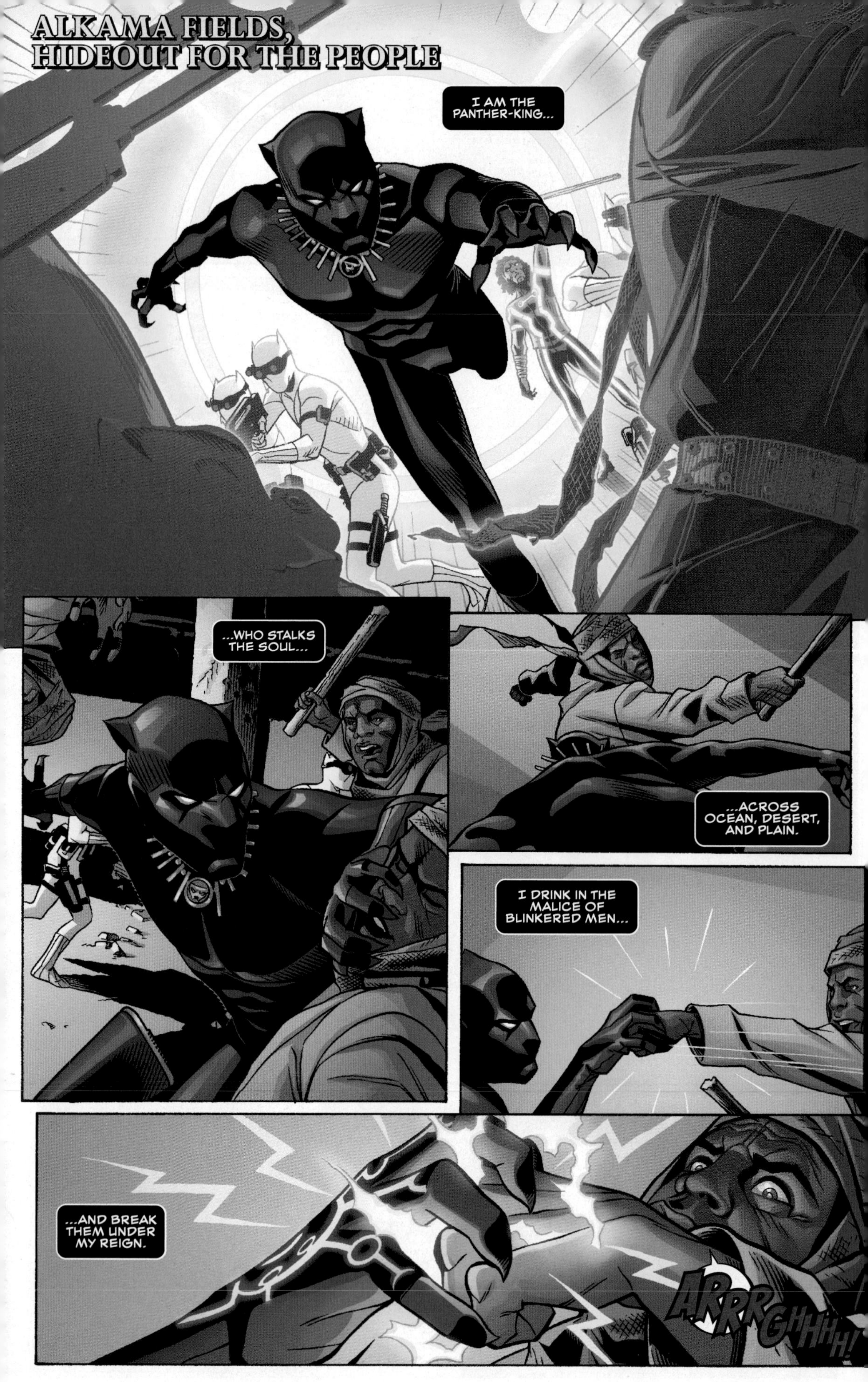
ALKAMA FIELDS,
HIDEOUT FOR THE PEOPLE
I AM THE PANTHER-KING...
...WHO STALKS THE SOUL...
...ACROSS OCEAN, DESERT, AND PLAIN.
I DRINK IN THE MALICE OF BLINKERED MEN...
...AND BREAK THEM UNDER MY REIGN.
ARRRGHHHH!

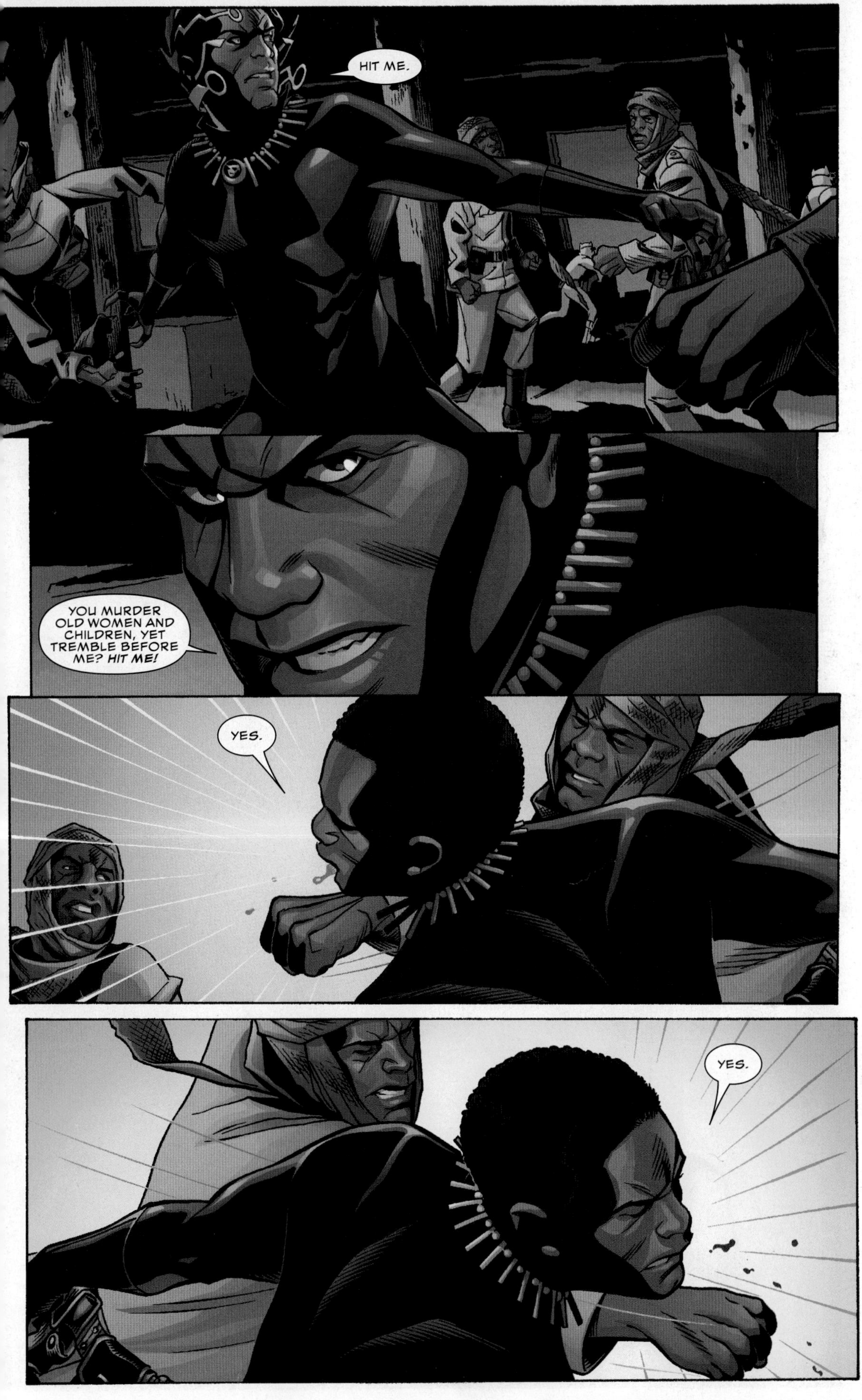
HIT ME.
YOU MURDER OLD WOMEN AND CHILDREN, YET TREMBLE BEFORE ME? HIT ME!
YES.
YES.

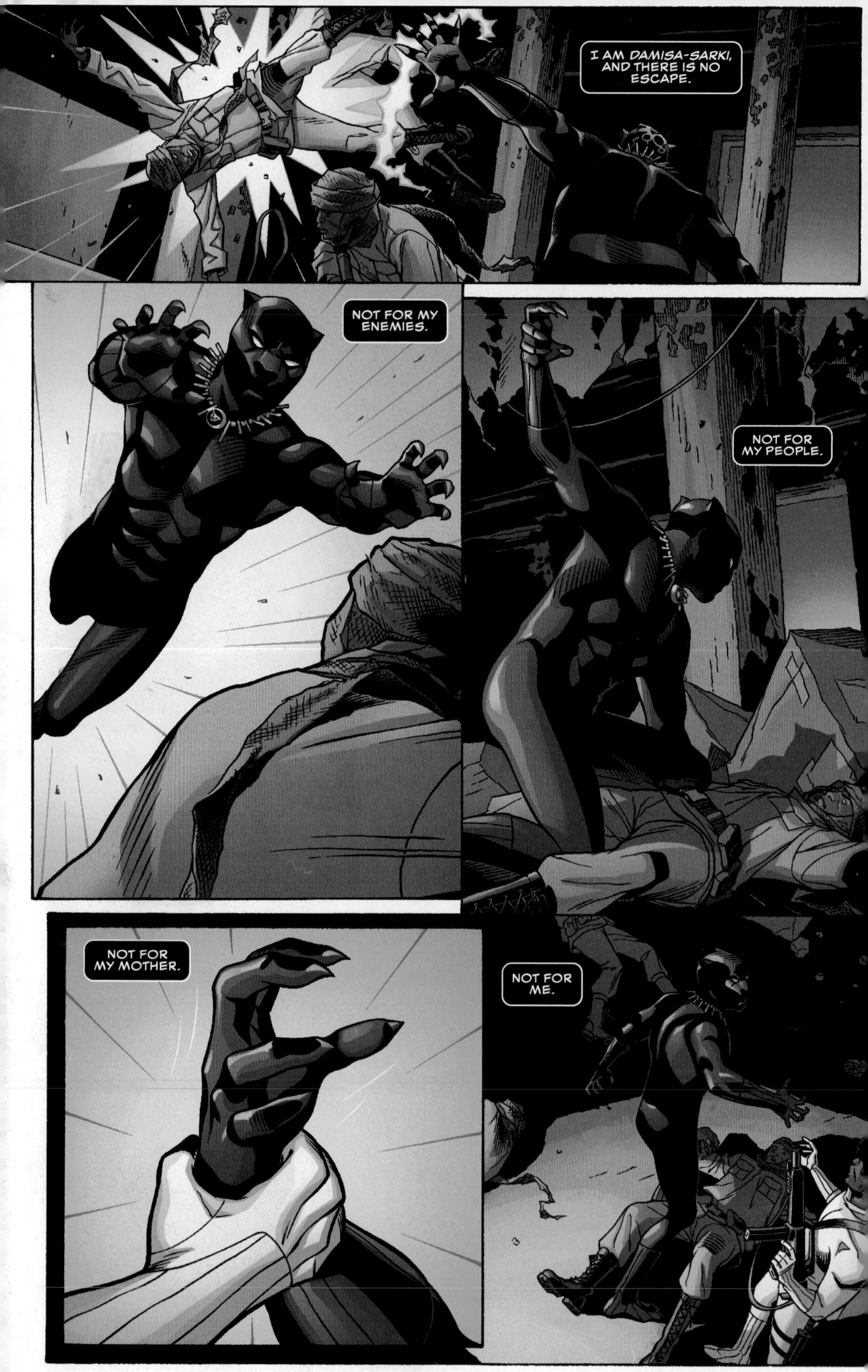
I AM DAMISA-SARKI, AND THERE IS NO ESCAPE.
NOT FOR MY ENEMIES.
NOT FOR MY PEOPLE.
NOT FOR MY MOTHER.
NOT FOR ME.

SO MUCH RAGE.
SO MUCH HATE.
SO MUCH SHAME. I
MUST MASTER ALL
OF IT. I MUST NOT
LET IT MASTER ME.

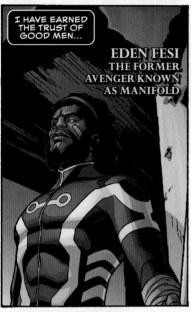

I HAVE EARNED
THE TRUST OF
GOOD MEN...

EDEN FESI
THE FORMER
AVENGER KNOWN
AS MANIFOLD

EDEN IS BRAVER THAN HE
KNOWS. ONCE, HE DIED
SO THAT THE WORLD MIGHT
LIVE. PERHAPS SOMEDAY
I SHALL TELL HIM THIS.

FOR NOW, MY
CONCERNS ARE MORE
IMMEDIATE.

THESE MEN ARE WAKANDAN, EVEN IN
REBELLION. PRIDE IN THEIR NATION
WAS EVERYTHING TO THEM. AND
WHEN THE GOLDEN CITY FELL, THEY
FELL WITH IT. NOW THEY FASHION
THEIR VERY BODIES INTO LIVING
BOMBS, FOR THEY MEASURE THEIR
LIVES IN THE BLOOD OF OTHERS.

I KNOW WHAT
HAUNTS THEM--
SHAME, HATE,
RAGE.

I KNOW WHAT SHALL
SAVE THEM. THE GOLDEN
CITY FELL. BUT WAKANDA
HAS NOT YET DIED.

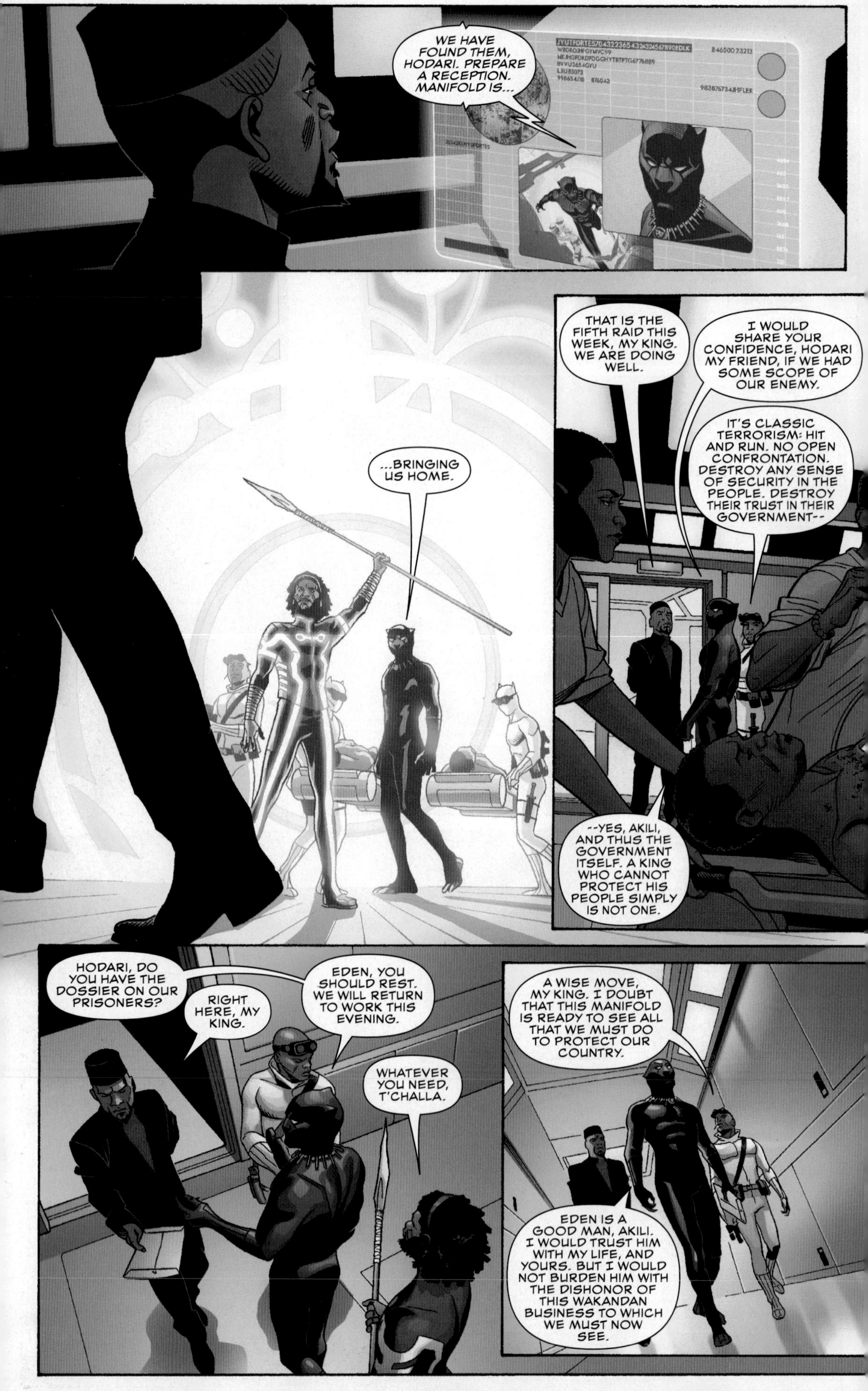

WE HAVE FOUND THEM, HODARI. PREPARE A RECEPTION. MANIFOLD IS...
...BRINGING US HOME.
THAT IS THE FIFTH RAID THIS WEEK, MY KING. WE ARE DOING WELL.
I WOULD SHARE YOUR CONFIDENCE, HODARI MY FRIEND, IF WE HAD SOME SCOPE OF OUR ENEMY.
IT'S CLASSIC TERRORISM: HIT AND RUN. NO OPEN CONFRONTATION. DESTROY ANY SENSE OF SECURITY IN THE PEOPLE. DESTROY THEIR TRUST IN THEIR GOVERNMENT--
--YES, AKILI, AND THUS THE GOVERNMENT ITSELF. A KING WHO CANNOT PROTECT HIS PEOPLE SIMPLY IS NOT ONE.
HODARI, DO YOU HAVE THE DOSSIER ON OUR PRISONERS?
RIGHT HERE, MY KING.
EDEN, YOU SHOULD REST. WE WILL RETURN TO WORK THIS EVENING.
WHATEVER YOU NEED, T'CHALLA.
A WISE MOVE, MY KING. I DOUBT THAT THIS MANIFOLD IS READY TO SEE ALL THAT WE MUST DO TO PROTECT OUR COUNTRY.
EDEN IS A GOOD MAN, AKILI. I WOULD TRUST HIM WITH MY LIFE, AND YOURS. BUT I WOULD NOT BURDEN HIM WITH THE DISHONOR OF THIS WAKANDAN BUSINESS TO WHICH WE MUST NOW SEE.

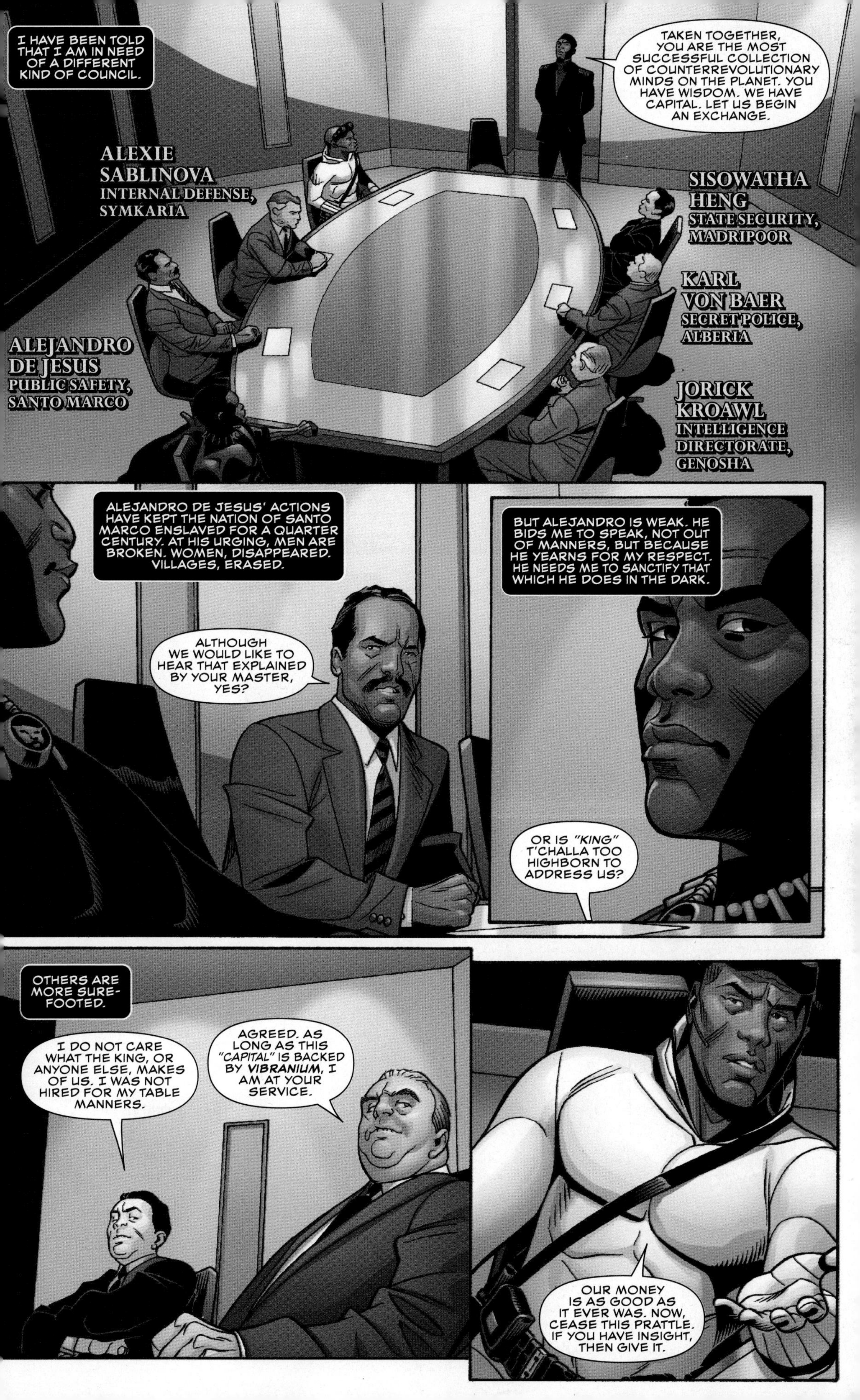

I HAVE BEEN TOLD THAT I AM IN NEED OF A DIFFERENT KIND OF COUNCIL.
TAKEN TOGETHER, YOU ARE THE MOST SUCCESSFUL COLLECTION OF COUNTERREVOLUTIONARY MINDS ON THE PLANET. YOU HAVE WISDOM. WE HAVE CAPITAL. LET US BEGIN AN EXCHANGE.
ALEXIE SABLINOVA INTERNAL DEFENSE, SYMKARIA
SISOWATHA HENG STATE SECURITY, MADRIPOOR
KARL VON BAER SECRET POLICE, ALBERIA
ALEJANDRO DE JESUS PUBLIC SAFETY, SANTO MARCO
JORICK KROAWL INTELLIGENCE DIRECTORATE, GENOSHA
ALEJANDRO DE JESUS' ACTIONS HAVE KEPT THE NATION OF SANTO MARCO ENSLAVED FOR A QUARTER CENTURY. AT HIS URGING, MEN ARE BROKEN. WOMEN, DISAPPEARED. VILLAGES, ERASED.
ALTHOUGH WE WOULD LIKE TO HEAR THAT EXPLAINED BY YOUR MASTER, YES?
BUT ALEJANDRO IS WEAK. HE BIDS ME TO SPEAK, NOT OUT OF MANNERS, BUT BECAUSE HE YEARNS FOR MY RESPECT. HE NEEDS ME TO SANCTIFY THAT WHICH HE DOES IN THE DARK.
OR IS "KING" T'CHALLA TOO HIGHBORN TO ADDRESS US?
OTHERS ARE MORE SURE-FOOTED.
I DO NOT CARE WHAT THE KING, OR ANYONE ELSE, MAKES OF US. I WAS NOT HIRED FOR MY TABLE MANNERS.
AGREED. AS LONG AS THIS "CAPITAL" IS BACKED BY VIBRANIUM, I AM AT YOUR SERVICE.
OUR MONEY IS AS GOOD AS IT EVER WAS. NOW, CEASE THIS PRATTLE. IF YOU HAVE INSIGHT, THEN GIVE IT.

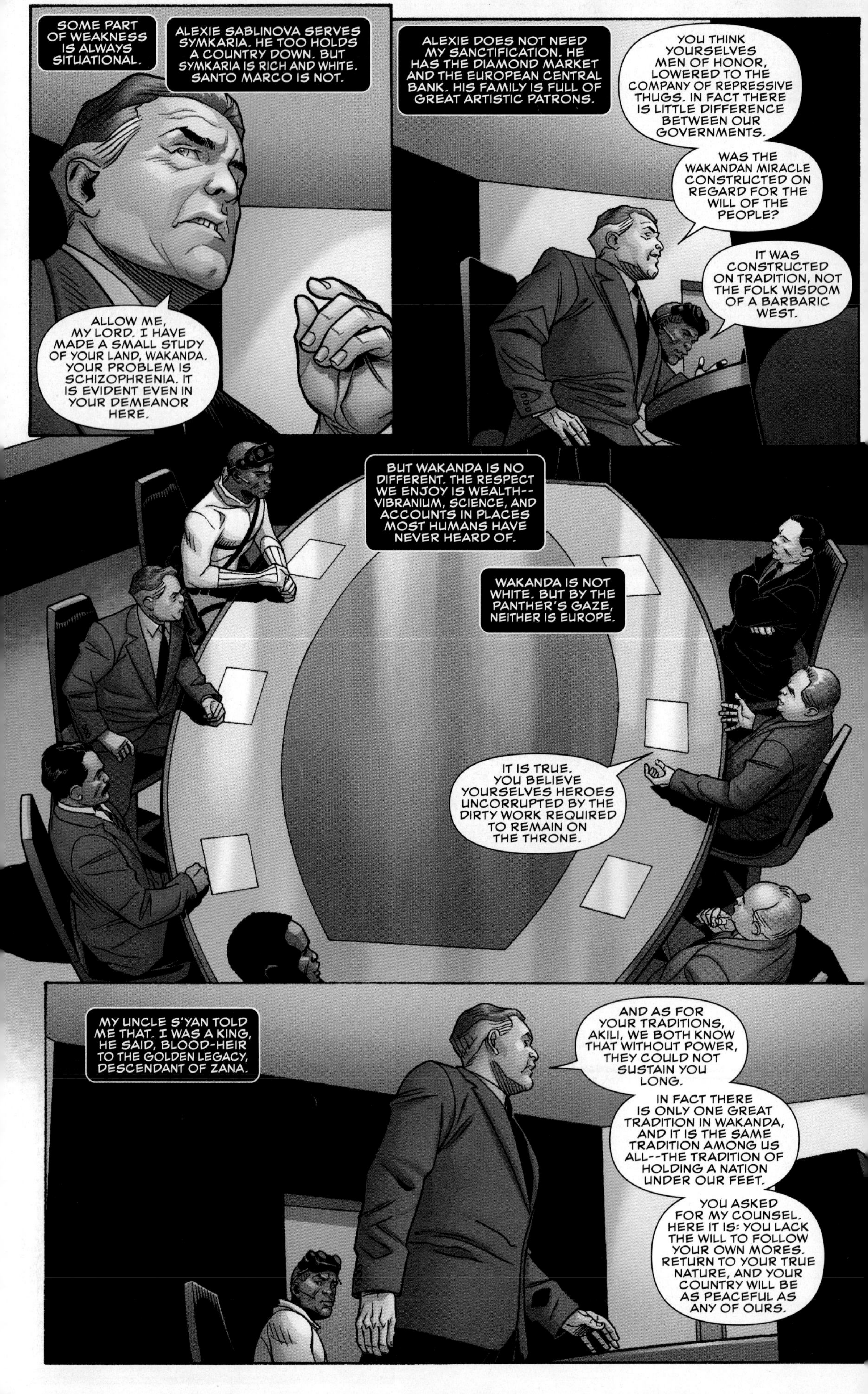

SOME PART OF WEAKNESS IS ALWAYS SITUATIONAL.
ALEXIE SABLINOVA SERVES SYMKARIA. HE TOO HOLDS A COUNTRY DOWN. BUT SYMKARIA IS RICH AND WHITE. SANTO MARCO IS NOT.
ALLOW ME, MY LORD. I HAVE MADE A SMALL STUDY OF YOUR LAND, WAKANDA. YOUR PROBLEM IS SCHIZOPHRENIA. IT IS EVIDENT EVEN IN YOUR DEMEANOR HERE.
ALEXIE DOES NOT NEED MY SANCTIFICATION. HE HAS THE DIAMOND MARKET AND THE EUROPEAN CENTRAL BANK. HIS FAMILY IS FULL OF GREAT ARTISTIC PATRONS.
YOU THINK YOURSELVES MEN OF HONOR, LOWERED TO THE COMPANY OF REPRESSIVE THUGS. IN FACT THERE IS LITTLE DIFFERENCE BETWEEN OUR GOVERNMENTS.
WAS THE WAKANDAN MIRACLE CONSTRUCTED ON REGARD FOR THE WILL OF THE PEOPLE?
IT WAS CONSTRUCTED ON TRADITION, NOT THE FOLK WISDOM OF A BARBARIC WEST.
BUT WAKANDA IS NO DIFFERENT. THE RESPECT WE ENJOY IS WEALTH--VIBRANIUM, SCIENCE, AND ACCOUNTS IN PLACES MOST HUMANS HAVE NEVER HEARD OF.
WAKANDA IS NOT WHITE. BUT BY THE PANTHER'S GAZE, NEITHER IS EUROPE.
IT IS TRUE. YOU BELIEVE YOURSELVES HEROES UNCORRUPTED BY THE DIRTY WORK REQUIRED TO REMAIN ON THE THRONE.
MY UNCLE S'YAN TOLD ME THAT. I WAS A KING, HE SAID, BLOOD-HEIR TO THE GOLDEN LEGACY, DESCENDANT OF ZANA.
AND AS FOR YOUR TRADITIONS, AKILI, WE BOTH KNOW THAT WITHOUT POWER, THEY COULD NOT SUSTAIN YOU LONG.
IN FACT THERE IS ONLY ONE GREAT TRADITION IN WAKANDA, AND IT IS THE SAME TRADITION AMONG US ALL--THE TRADITION OF HOLDING A NATION UNDER OUR FEET.
YOU ASKED FOR MY COUNSEL. HERE IT IS: YOU LACK THE WILL TO FOLLOW YOUR OWN MORES. RETURN TO YOUR TRUE NATURE, AND YOUR COUNTRY WILL BE AS PEACEFUL AS ANY OF OURS.

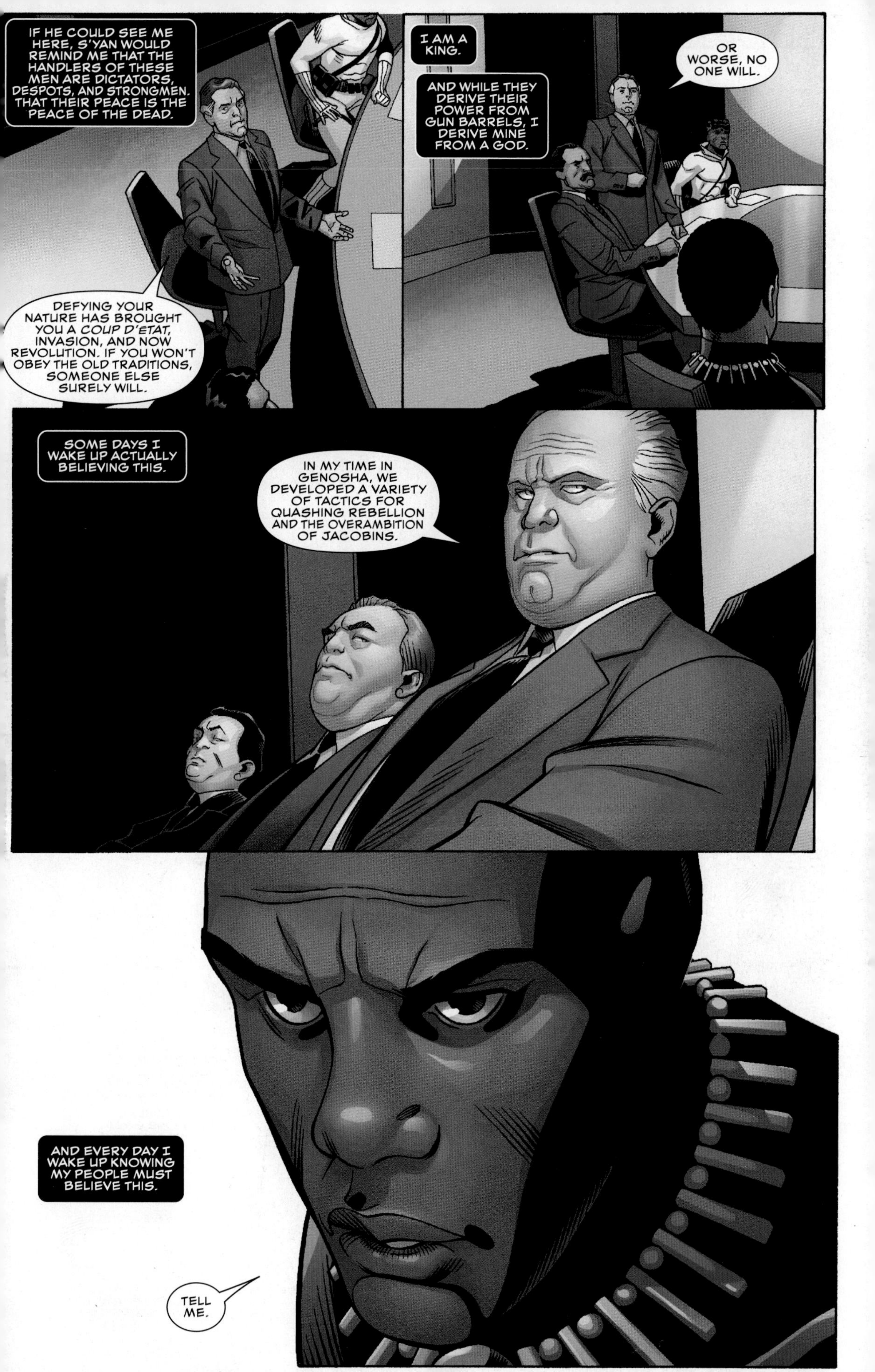
IF HE COULD SEE ME HERE, S'YAN WOULD REMIND ME THAT THE HANDLERS OF THESE MEN ARE DICTATORS, DESPOTS, AND STRONGMEN. THAT THEIR PEACE IS THE PEACE OF THE DEAD.
DEFYING YOUR NATURE HAS BROUGHT YOU A *COUP D'ETAT*, INVASION, AND NOW REVOLUTION. IF YOU WON'T OBEY THE OLD TRADITIONS, SOMEONE ELSE SURELY WILL.
I AM A KING.
AND WHILE THEY DERIVE THEIR POWER FROM GUN BARRELS, I DERIVE MINE FROM A GOD.
OR WORSE, NO ONE WILL.
SOME DAYS I WAKE UP ACTUALLY BELIEVING THIS.
IN MY TIME IN GENOSHA, WE DEVELOPED A VARIETY OF TACTICS FOR QUASHING REBELLION AND THE OVERAMBITION OF JACOBINS.
AND EVERY DAY I WAKE UP KNOWING MY PEOPLE MUST BELIEVE THIS.
TELL ME.

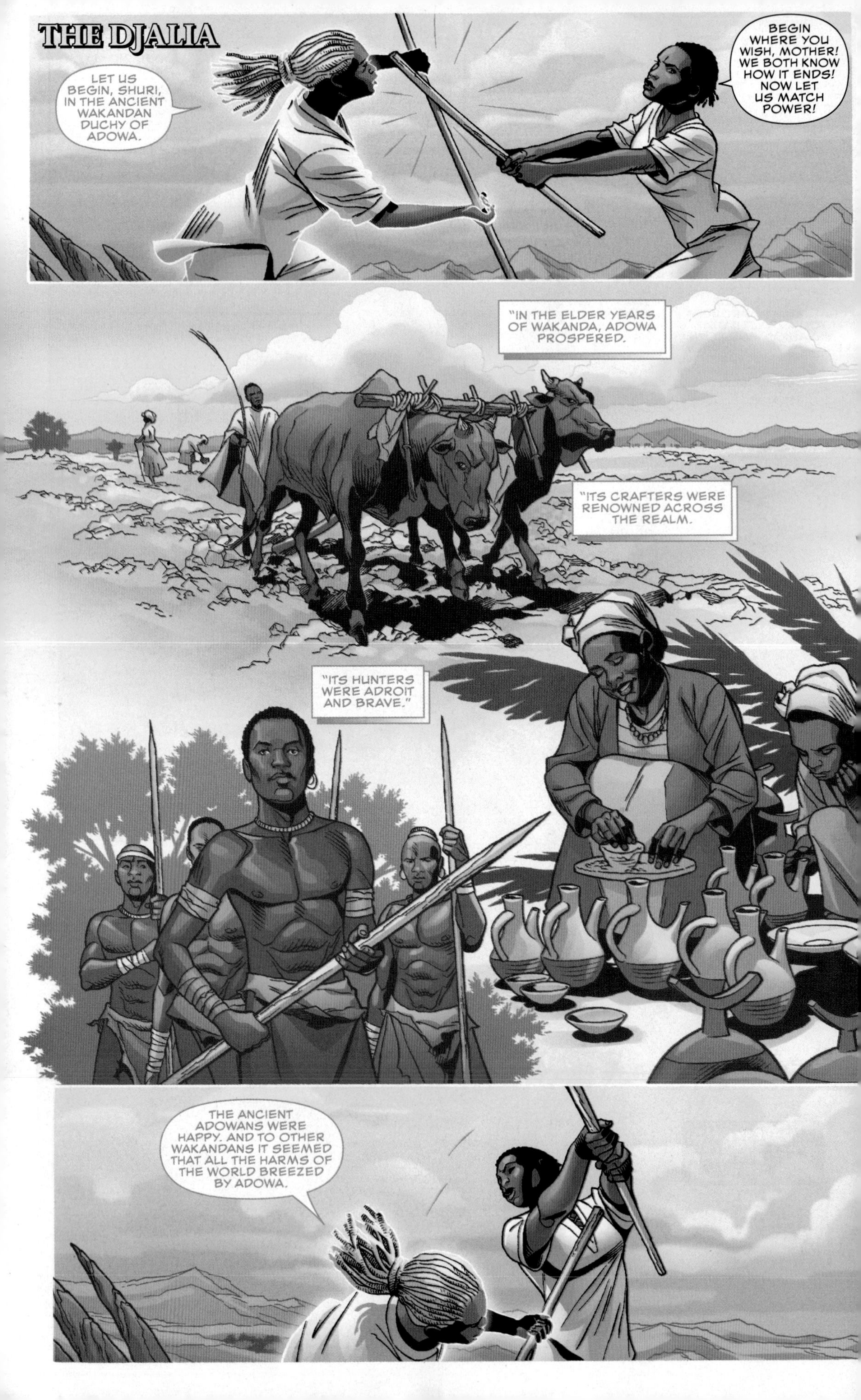
THE DJALIA
LET US BEGIN, SHURI, IN THE ANCIENT WAKANDAN DUCHY OF ADOWA.
BEGIN WHERE YOU WISH, MOTHER! WE BOTH KNOW HOW IT ENDS! NOW LET US MATCH POWER!
"IN THE ELDER YEARS OF WAKANDA, ADOWA PROSPERED.
"ITS CRAFTERS WERE RENOWNED ACROSS THE REALM.
"ITS HUNTERS WERE ADROIT AND BRAVE."
THE ANCIENT ADOWANS WERE HAPPY. AND TO OTHER WAKANDANS IT SEEMED THAT ALL THE HARMS OF THE WORLD BREEZED BY ADOWA.

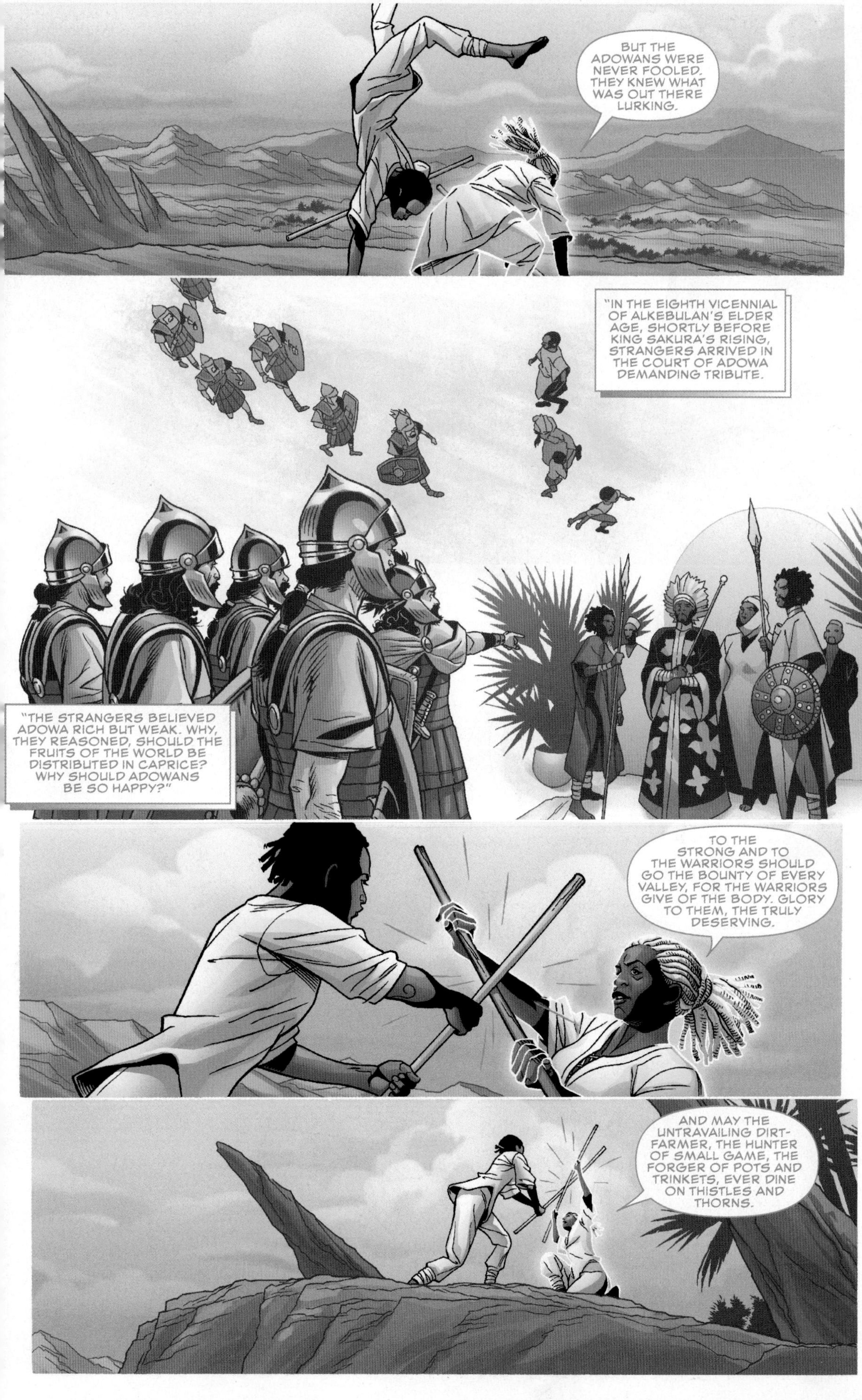
BUT THE ADOWANS WERE NEVER FOOLED. THEY KNEW WHAT WAS OUT THERE LURKING.
"IN THE EIGHTH VICENNIAL OF ALKEBULAN'S ELDER AGE, SHORTLY BEFORE KING SAKURA'S RISING, STRANGERS ARRIVED IN THE COURT OF ADOWA DEMANDING TRIBUTE.
"THE STRANGERS BELIEVED ADOWA RICH BUT WEAK. WHY, THEY REASONED, SHOULD THE FRUITS OF THE WORLD BE DISTRIBUTED IN CAPRICE? WHY SHOULD ADOWANS BE SO HAPPY?"
TO THE STRONG AND TO THE WARRIORS SHOULD GO THE BOUNTY OF EVERY VALLEY, FOR THE WARRIORS GIVE OF THE BODY. GLORY TO THEM, THE TRULY DESERVING.
AND MAY THE UNTRAVAILING DIRT-FARMER, THE HUNTER OF SMALL GAME, THE FORGER OF POTS AND TRINKETS, EVER DINE ON THISTLES AND THORNS.

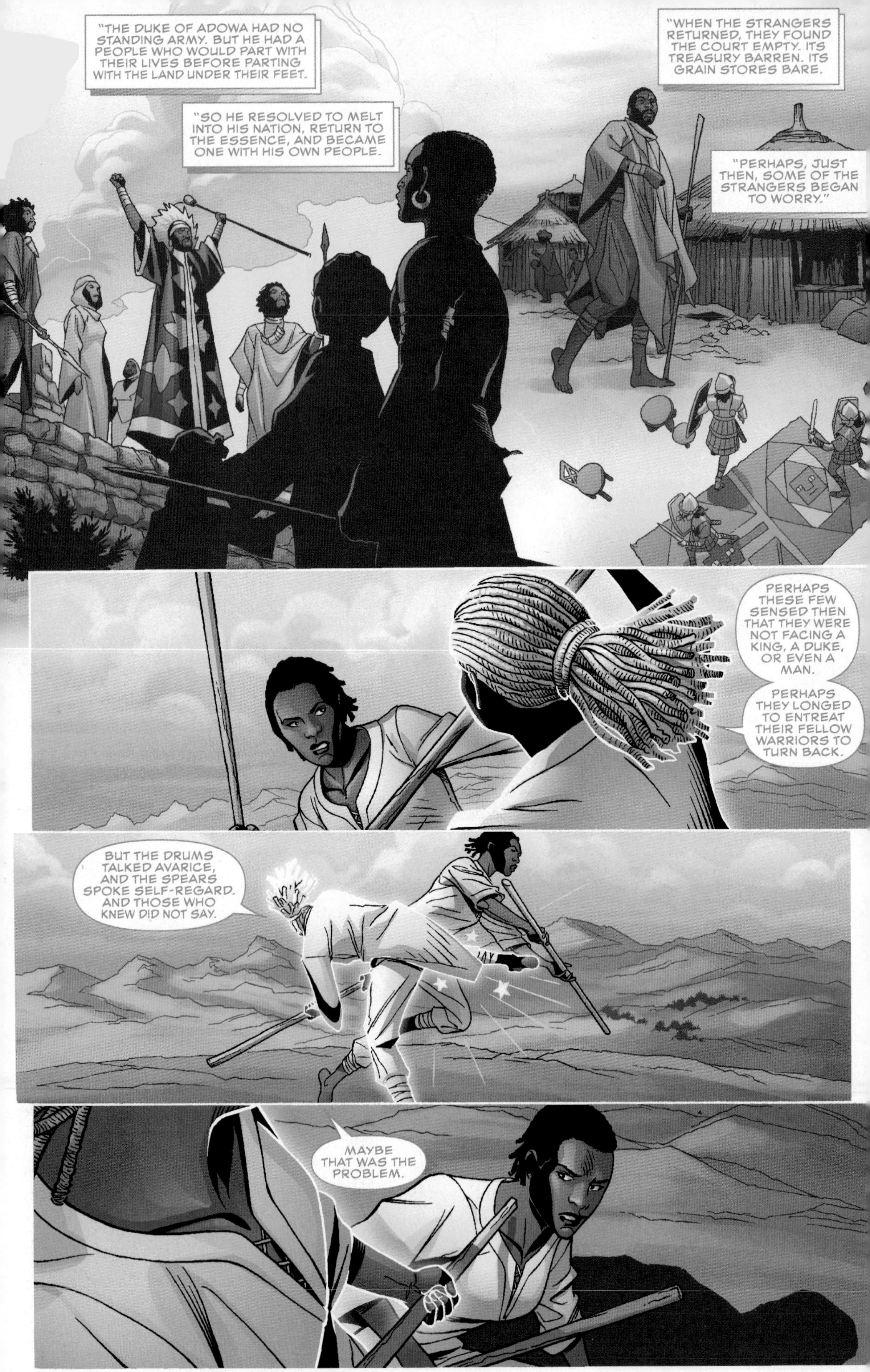
"THE DUKE OF ADOWA HAD NO STANDING ARMY. BUT HE HAD A PEOPLE WHO WOULD PART WITH THEIR LIVES BEFORE PARTING WITH THE LAND UNDER THEIR FEET.
"SO HE RESOLVED TO MELT INTO HIS NATION, RETURN TO THE ESSENCE, AND BECAME ONE WITH HIS OWN PEOPLE.
"WHEN THE STRANGERS RETURNED, THEY FOUND THE COURT EMPTY. ITS TREASURY BARREN. ITS GRAIN STORES BARE.
"PERHAPS, JUST THEN, SOME OF THE STRANGERS BEGAN TO WORRY."
PERHAPS THESE FEW SENSED THEN THAT THEY WERE NOT FACING A KING, A DUKE, OR EVEN A MAN.
PERHAPS THEY LONGED TO ENTREAT THEIR FELLOW WARRIORS TO TURN BACK.
BUT THE DRUMS TALKED AVARICE, AND THE SPEARS SPOKE SELF-REGARD. AND THOSE WHO KNEW DID NOT SAY.
MAYBE THAT WAS THE PROBLEM.

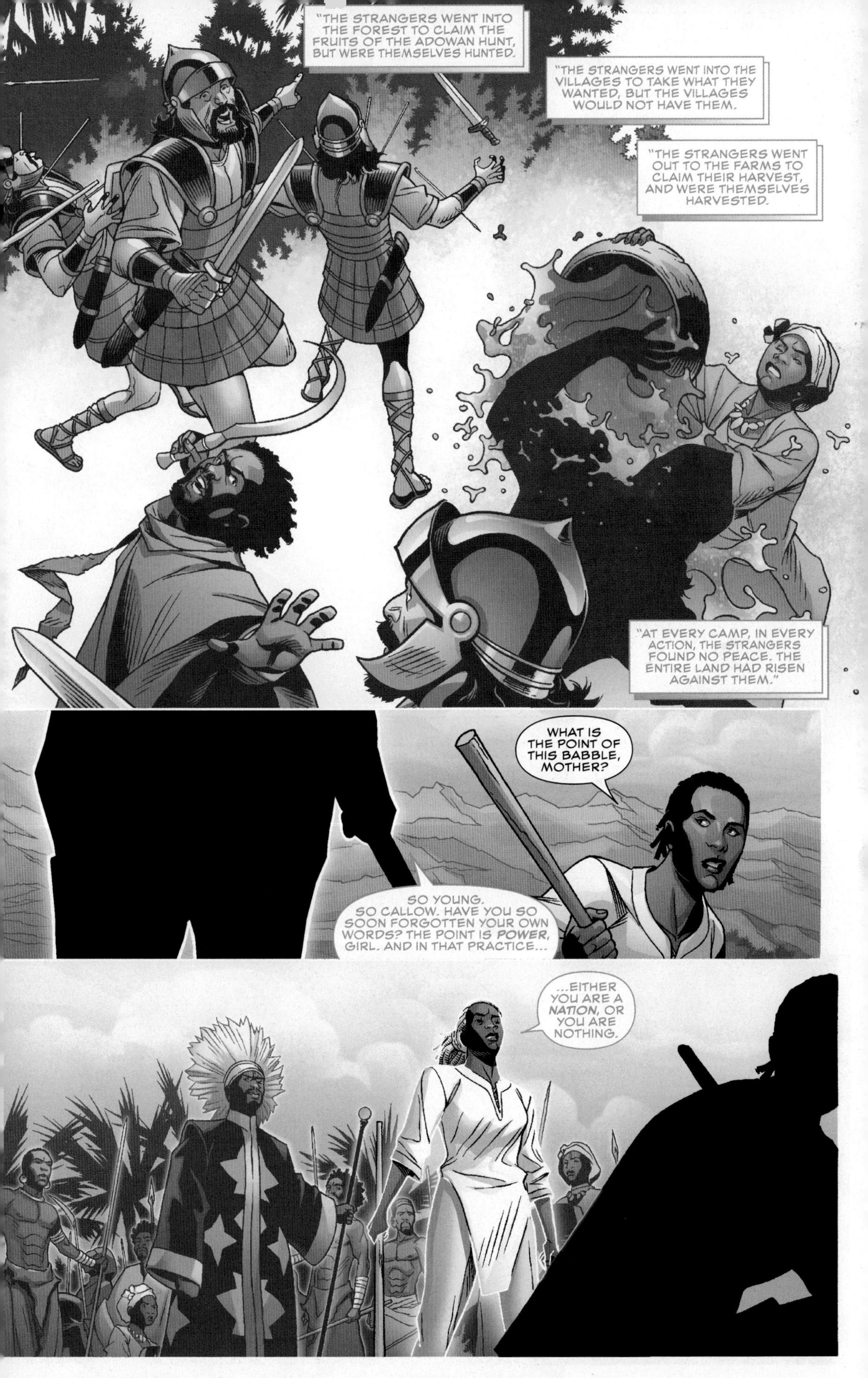
"THE STRANGERS WENT INTO THE FOREST TO CLAIM THE FRUITS OF THE ADOWAN HUNT, BUT WERE THEMSELVES HUNTED.
"THE STRANGERS WENT INTO THE VILLAGES TO TAKE WHAT THEY WANTED, BUT THE VILLAGES WOULD NOT HAVE THEM.
"THE STRANGERS WENT OUT TO THE FARMS TO CLAIM THEIR HARVEST, AND WERE THEMSELVES HARVESTED.
"AT EVERY CAMP, IN EVERY ACTION, THE STRANGERS FOUND NO PEACE. THE ENTIRE LAND HAD RISEN AGAINST THEM."
WHAT IS THE POINT OF THIS BABBLE, MOTHER?
SO YOUNG. SO CALLOW. HAVE YOU SO SOON FORGOTTEN YOUR OWN WORDS? THE POINT IS *POWER*, GIRL. AND IN THAT PRACTICE...
...EITHER YOU ARE A *NATION*, OR YOU ARE NOTHING.

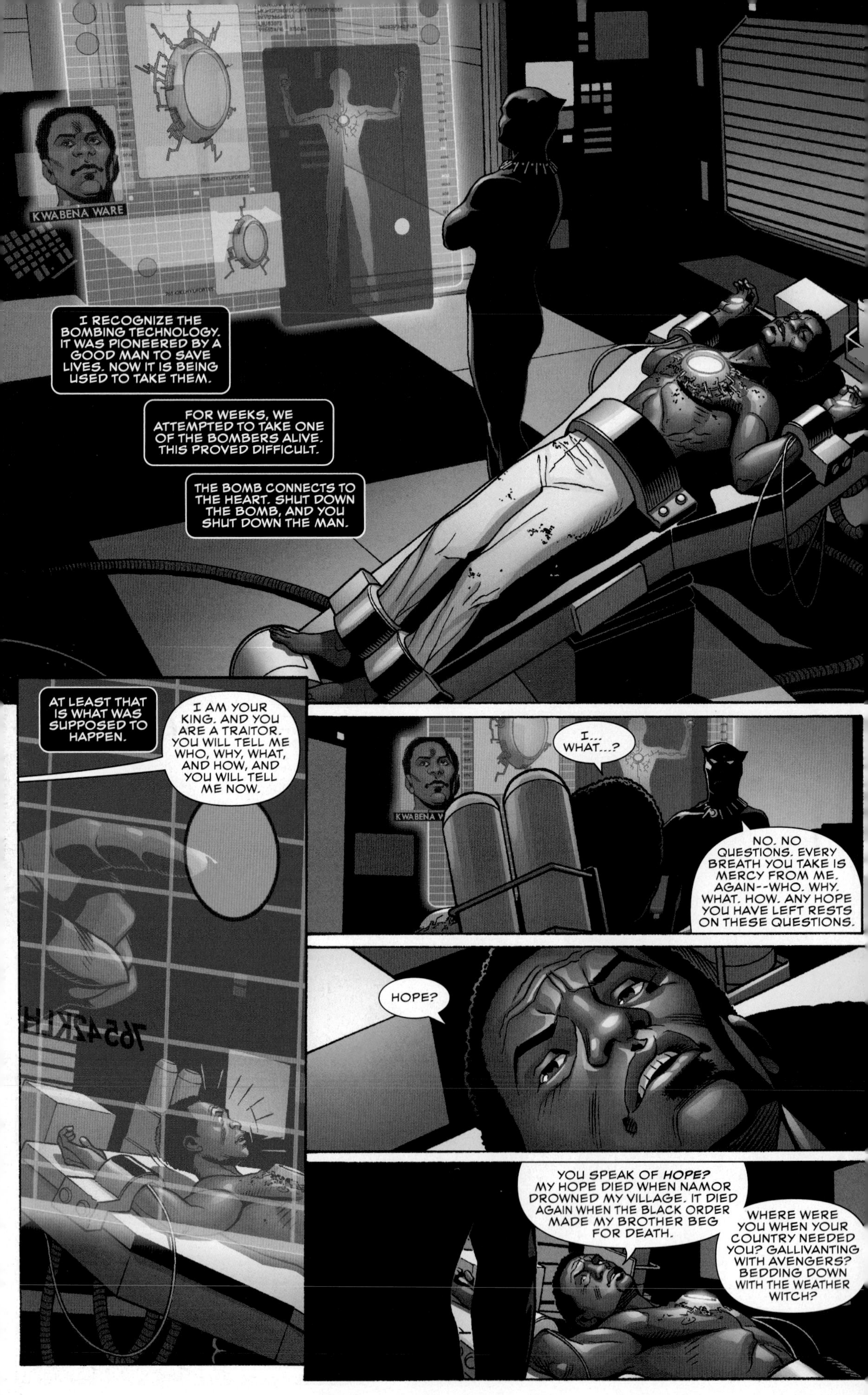
KWABENA WARE
I RECOGNIZE THE BOMBING TECHNOLOGY. IT WAS PIONEERED BY A GOOD MAN TO SAVE LIVES. NOW IT IS BEING USED TO TAKE THEM.
FOR WEEKS, WE ATTEMPTED TO TAKE ONE OF THE BOMBERS ALIVE. THIS PROVED DIFFICULT.
THE BOMB CONNECTS TO THE HEART. SHUT DOWN THE BOMB, AND YOU SHUT DOWN THE MAN.
AT LEAST THAT IS WHAT WAS SUPPOSED TO HAPPEN.
I AM YOUR KING. AND YOU ARE A TRAITOR. YOU WILL TELL ME WHO, WHY, WHAT, AND HOW, AND YOU WILL TELL ME NOW.
I... WHAT...?
NO. NO QUESTIONS. EVERY BREATH YOU TAKE IS MERCY FROM ME. AGAIN--WHO. WHY. WHAT. HOW. ANY HOPE YOU HAVE LEFT RESTS ON THESE QUESTIONS.
HOPE?
YOU SPEAK OF *HOPE?* MY HOPE DIED WHEN NAMOR DROWNED MY VILLAGE. IT DIED AGAIN WHEN THE BLACK ORDER MADE MY BROTHER BEG FOR DEATH.
WHERE WERE YOU WHEN YOUR COUNTRY NEEDED YOU? GALLIVANTING WITH AVENGERS? BEDDING DOWN WITH THE WEATHER WITCH?

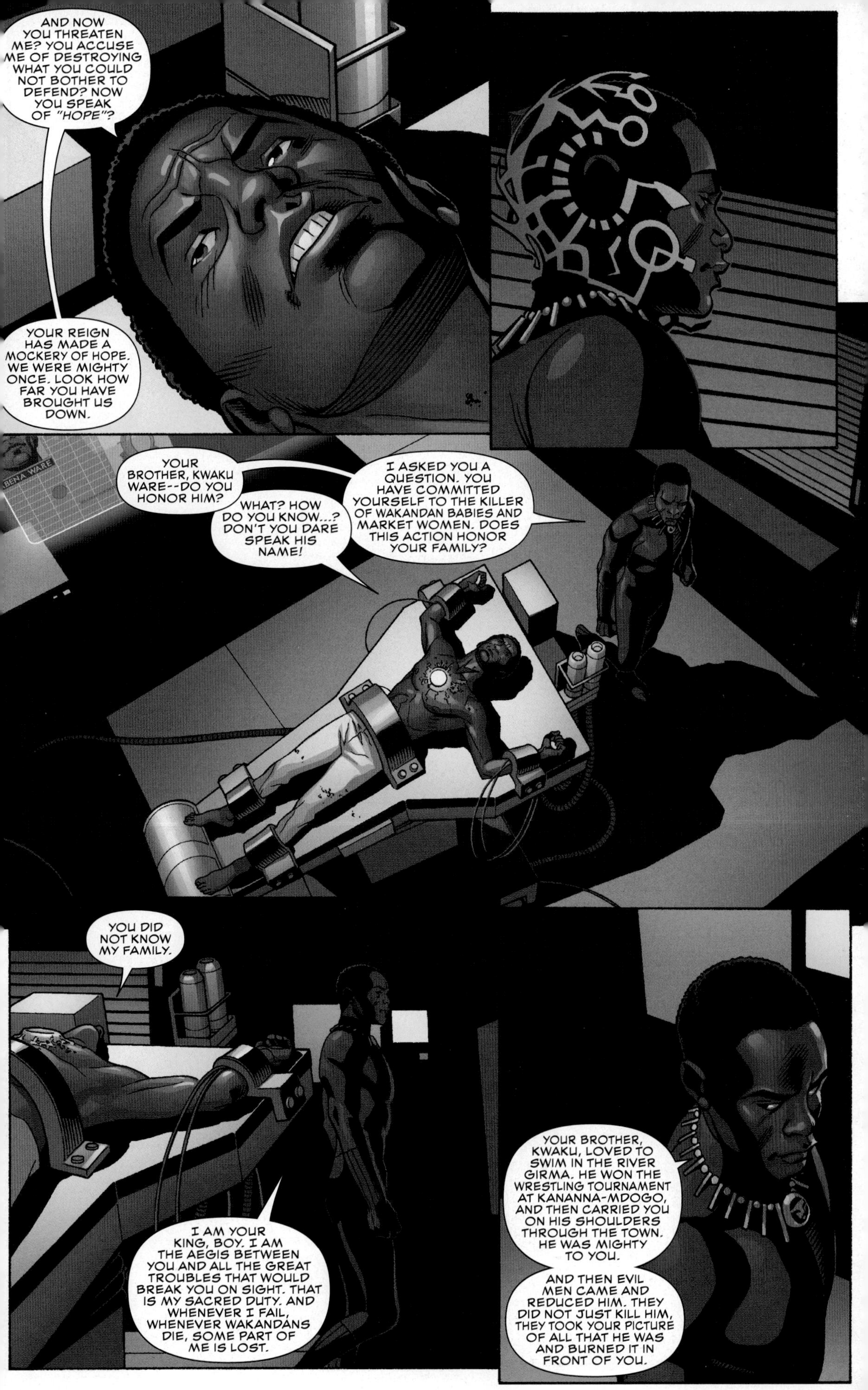
AND NOW YOU THREATEN ME? YOU ACCUSE ME OF DESTROYING WHAT YOU COULD NOT BOTHER TO DEFEND? NOW YOU SPEAK OF "HOPE"?
YOUR REIGN HAS MADE A MOCKERY OF HOPE. WE WERE MIGHTY ONCE. LOOK HOW FAR YOU HAVE BROUGHT US DOWN.
ABENA WARE
YOUR BROTHER, KWAKU WARE--DO YOU HONOR HIM?
WHAT? HOW DO YOU KNOW...? DON'T YOU DARE SPEAK HIS NAME!
I ASKED YOU A QUESTION. YOU HAVE COMMITTED YOURSELF TO THE KILLER OF WAKANDAN BABIES AND MARKET WOMEN. DOES THIS ACTION HONOR YOUR FAMILY?
YOU DID NOT KNOW MY FAMILY.
I AM YOUR KING, BOY. I AM THE AEGIS BETWEEN YOU AND ALL THE GREAT TROUBLES THAT WOULD BREAK YOU ON SIGHT. THAT IS MY SACRED DUTY. AND WHENEVER I FAIL, WHENEVER WAKANDANS DIE, SOME PART OF ME IS LOST.
YOUR BROTHER, KWAKU, LOVED TO SWIM IN THE RIVER GIRMA. HE WON THE WRESTLING TOURNAMENT AT KANANNA-MDOGO, AND THEN CARRIED YOU ON HIS SHOULDERS THROUGH THE TOWN. HE WAS MIGHTY TO YOU.
AND THEN EVIL MEN CAME AND REDUCED HIM. THEY DID NOT JUST KILL HIM, THEY TOOK YOUR PICTURE OF ALL THAT HE WAS AND BURNED IT IN FRONT OF YOU.

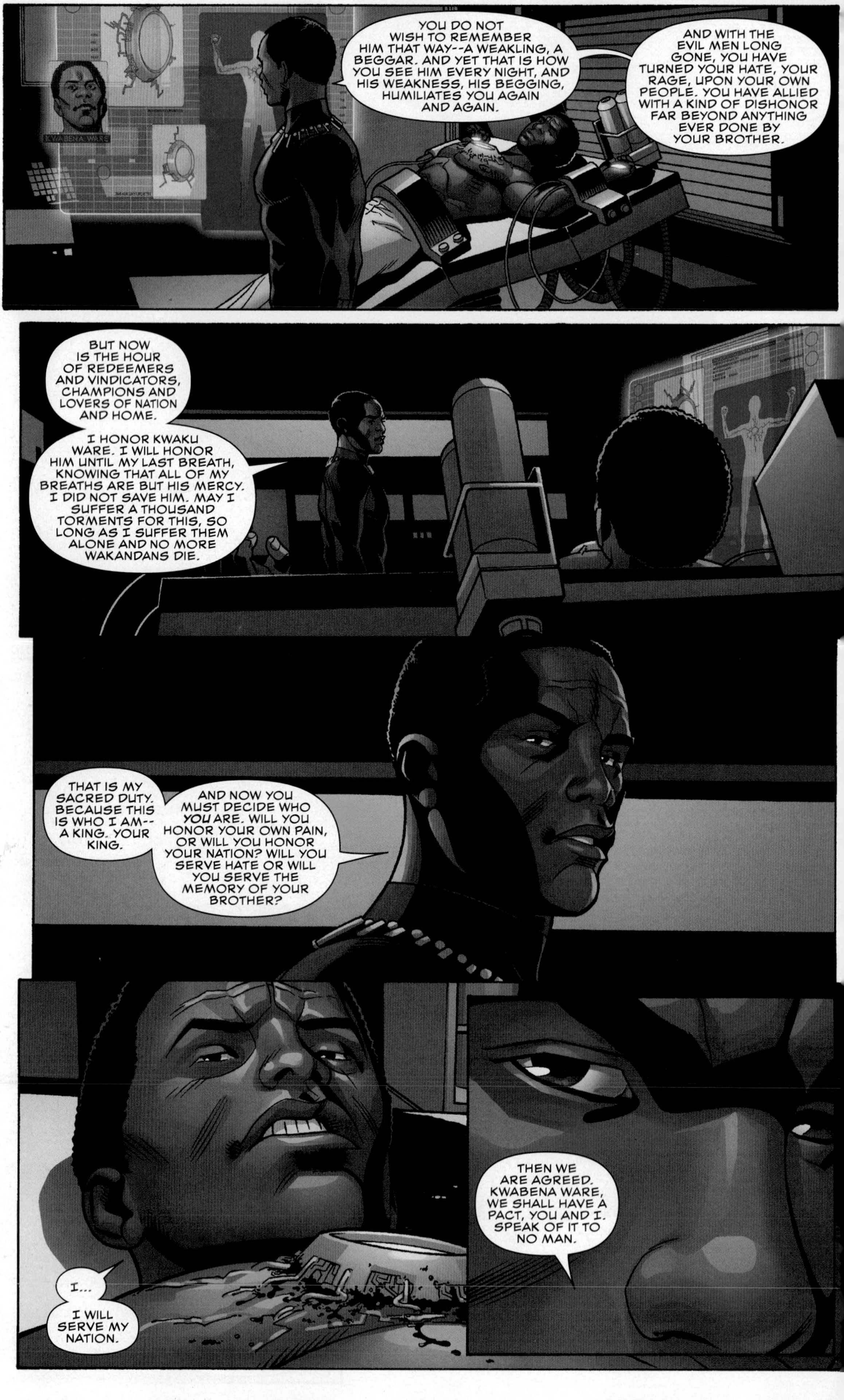
KWABENA WARE
YOU DO NOT WISH TO REMEMBER HIM THAT WAY--A WEAKLING, A BEGGAR. AND YET THAT IS HOW YOU SEE HIM EVERY NIGHT, AND HIS WEAKNESS, HIS BEGGING, HUMILIATES YOU AGAIN AND AGAIN.
AND WITH THE EVIL MEN LONG GONE, YOU HAVE TURNED YOUR HATE, YOUR RAGE, UPON YOUR OWN PEOPLE. YOU HAVE ALLIED WITH A KIND OF DISHONOR FAR BEYOND ANYTHING EVER DONE BY YOUR BROTHER.
BUT NOW IS THE HOUR OF REDEEMERS AND VINDICATORS, CHAMPIONS AND LOVERS OF NATION AND HOME.
I HONOR KWAKU WARE. I WILL HONOR HIM UNTIL MY LAST BREATH, KNOWING THAT ALL OF MY BREATHS ARE BUT HIS MERCY. I DID NOT SAVE HIM. MAY I SUFFER A THOUSAND TORMENTS FOR THIS, SO LONG AS I SUFFER THEM ALONE AND NO MORE WAKANDANS DIE.
THAT IS MY SACRED DUTY. BECAUSE THIS IS WHO I AM-- A KING. YOUR KING.
AND NOW YOU MUST DECIDE WHO *YOU* ARE. WILL YOU HONOR YOUR OWN PAIN, OR WILL YOU HONOR YOUR NATION? WILL YOU SERVE HATE OR WILL YOU SERVE THE MEMORY OF YOUR BROTHER?
THEN WE ARE AGREED. KWABENA WARE, WE SHALL HAVE A PACT, YOU AND I. SPEAK OF IT TO NO MAN.
I...
I WILL SERVE MY NATION.

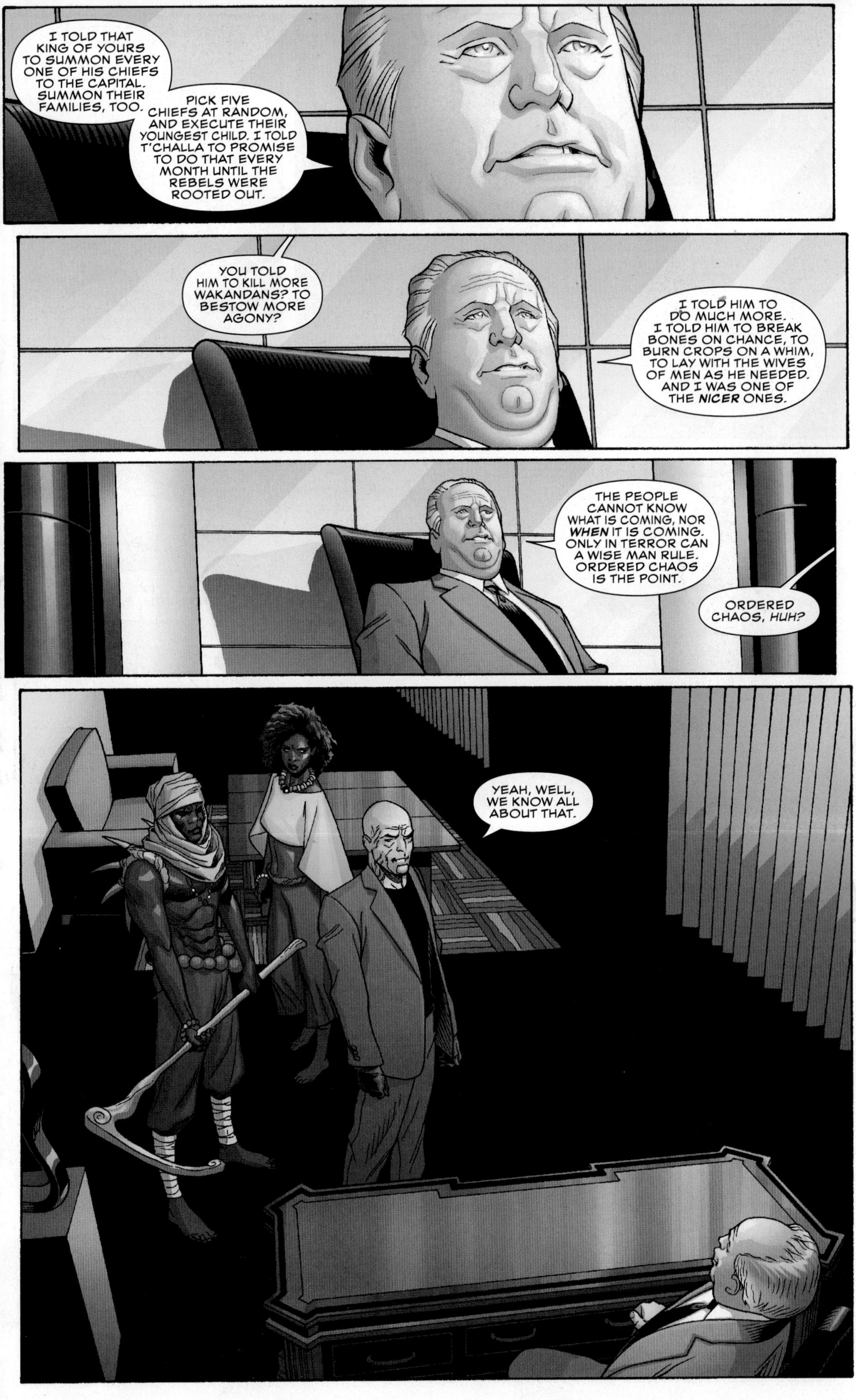
I TOLD THAT KING OF YOURS TO SUMMON EVERY ONE OF HIS CHIEFS TO THE CAPITAL. SUMMON THEIR FAMILIES, TOO.
PICK FIVE CHIEFS AT RANDOM, AND EXECUTE THEIR YOUNGEST CHILD. I TOLD T'CHALLA TO PROMISE TO DO THAT EVERY MONTH UNTIL THE REBELS WERE ROOTED OUT.
YOU TOLD HIM TO KILL MORE WAKANDANS? TO BESTOW MORE AGONY?
I TOLD HIM TO DO MUCH MORE. I TOLD HIM TO BREAK BONES ON CHANCE, TO BURN CROPS ON A WHIM, TO LAY WITH THE WIVES OF MEN AS HE NEEDED. AND I WAS ONE OF THE NICER ONES.
THE PEOPLE CANNOT KNOW WHAT IS COMING, NOR WHEN IT IS COMING. ONLY IN TERROR CAN A WISE MAN RULE. ORDERED CHAOS IS THE POINT.
ORDERED CHAOS, HUH?
YEAH, WELL, WE KNOW ALL ABOUT THAT.

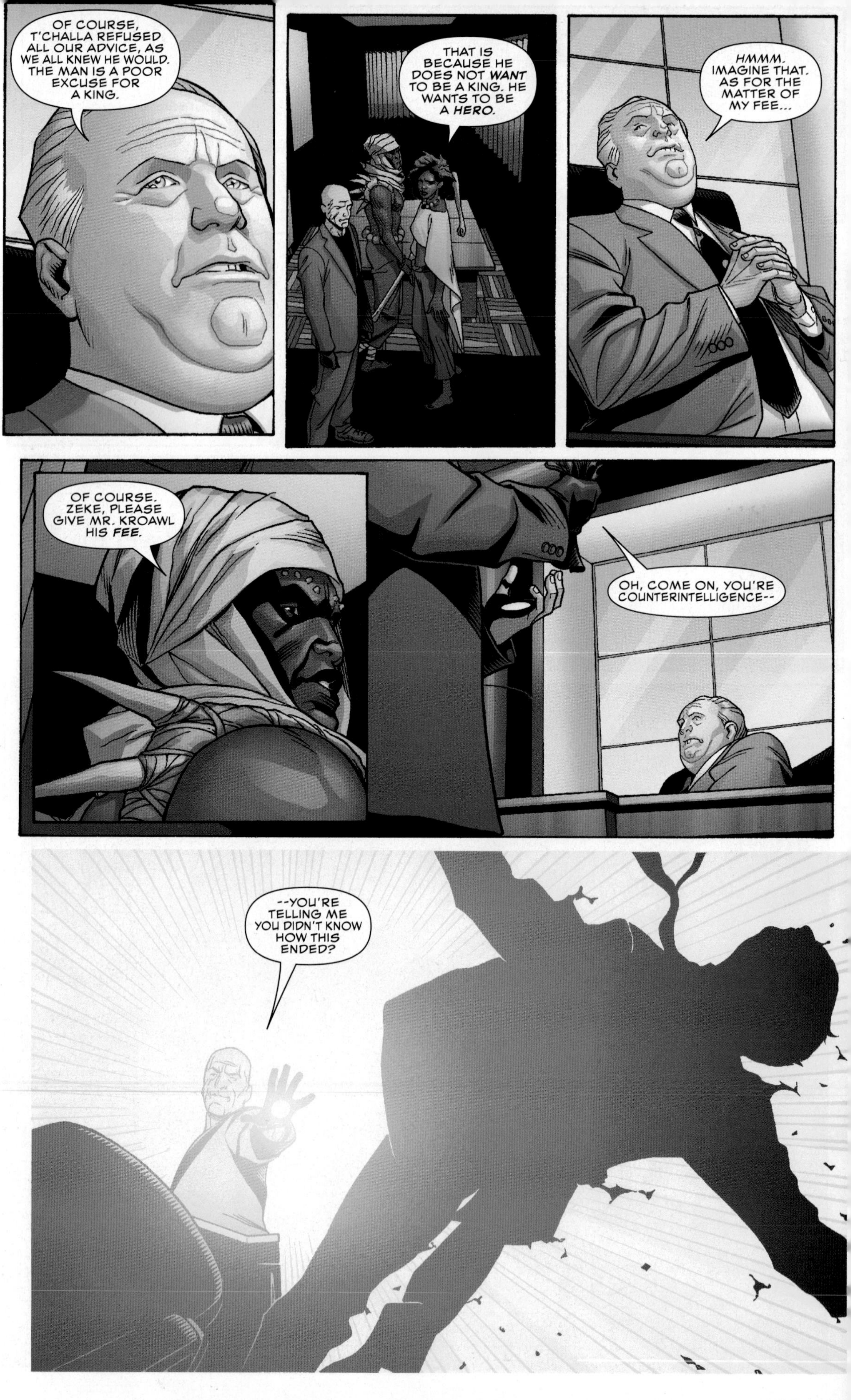
OF COURSE, T'CHALLA REFUSED ALL OUR ADVICE, AS WE ALL KNEW HE WOULD. THE MAN IS A POOR EXCUSE FOR A KING.
THAT IS BECAUSE HE DOES NOT *WANT* TO BE A KING. HE WANTS TO BE A *HERO*.
HMMM. IMAGINE THAT. AS FOR THE MATTER OF MY FEE...
OF COURSE. ZEKE, PLEASE GIVE MR. KROAWL HIS *FEE*.
OH, COME ON, YOU'RE COUNTERINTELLIGENCE--
--YOU'RE TELLING ME YOU DIDN'T KNOW HOW THIS ENDED?

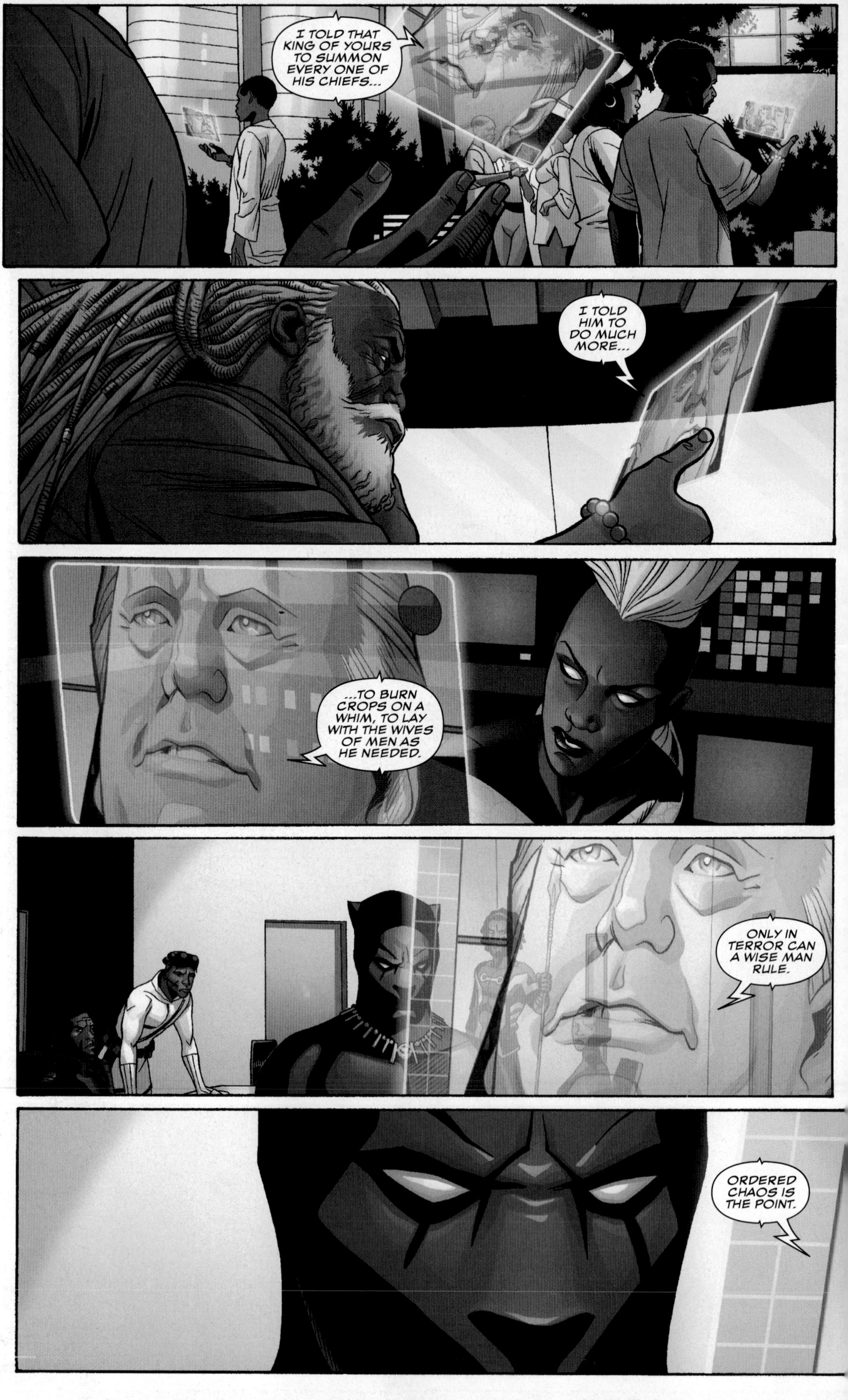
I TOLD THAT KING OF YOURS TO SUMMON EVERY ONE OF HIS CHIEFS...
I TOLD HIM TO DO MUCH MORE...
...TO BURN CROPS ON A WHIM, TO LAY WITH THE WIVES OF MEN AS HE NEEDED.
ONLY IN TERROR CAN A WISE MAN RULE.
ORDERED CHAOS IS THE POINT.

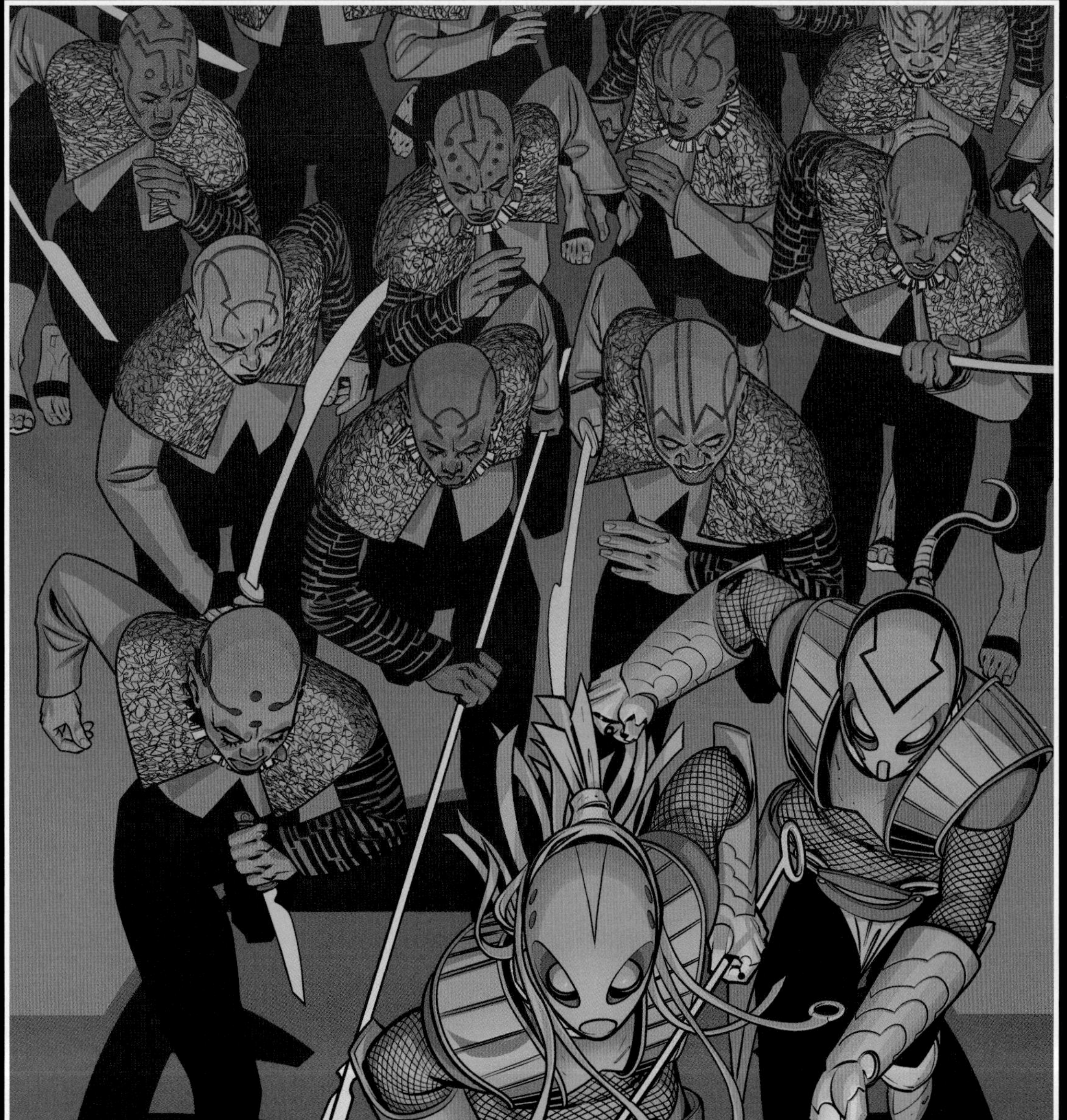

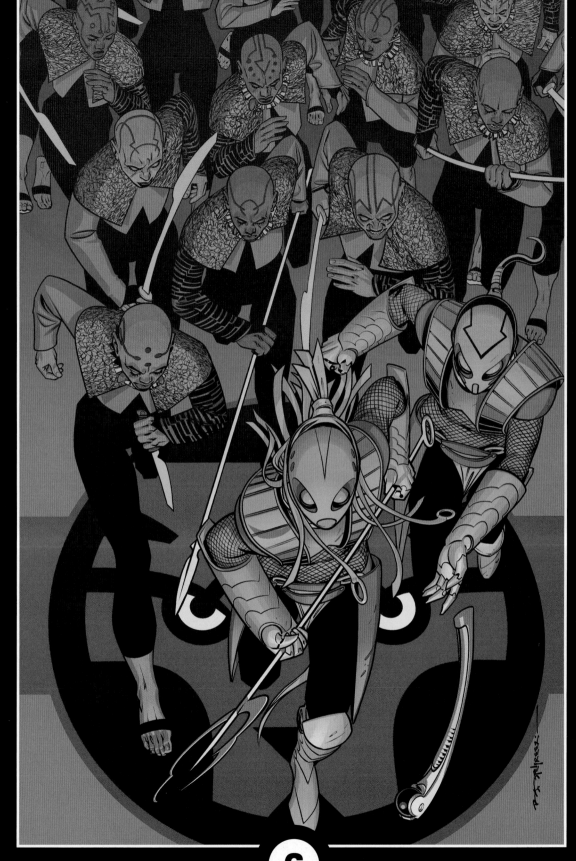

6

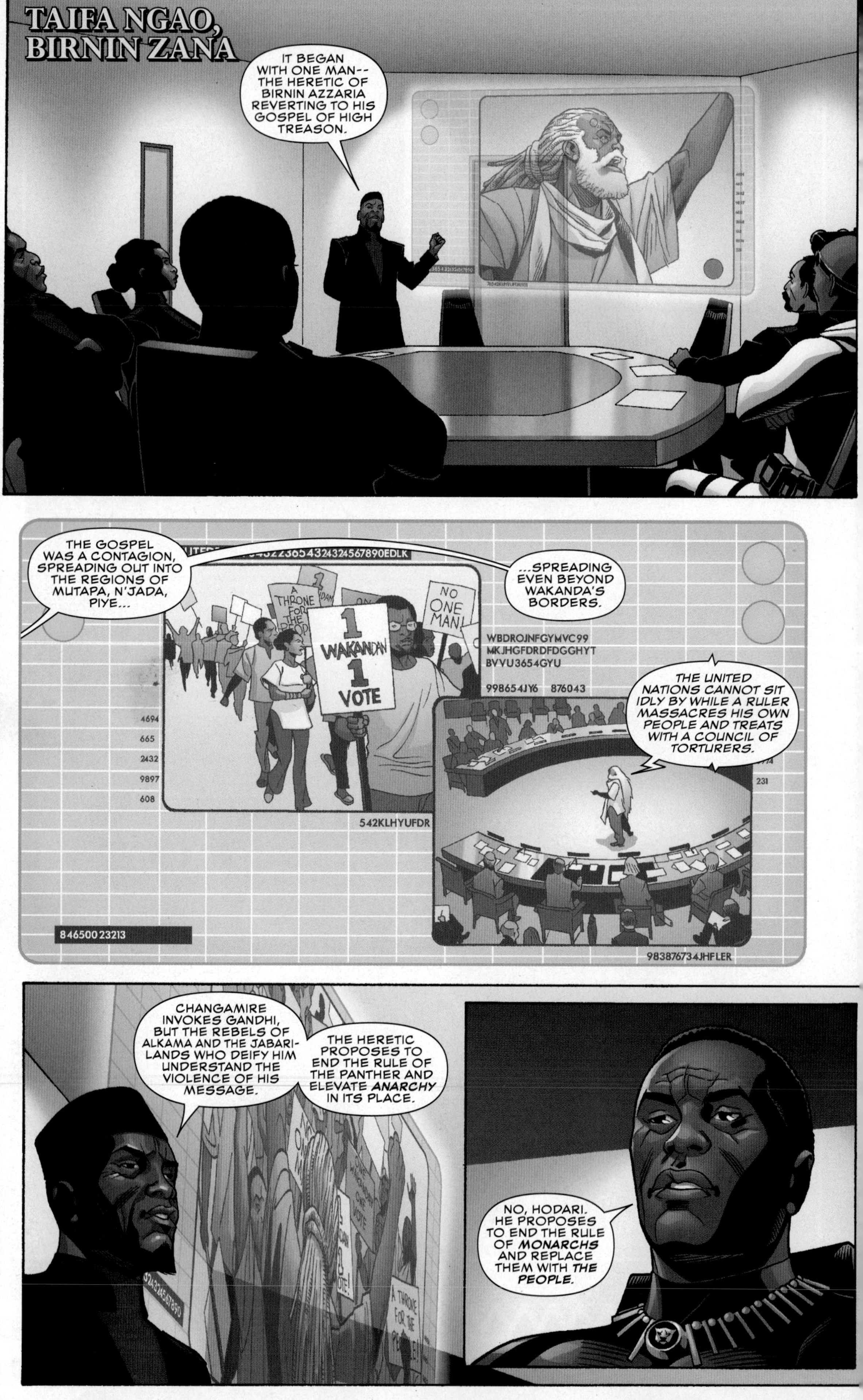
TAIFA NGAO, BIRNIN ZANA
IT BEGAN WITH ONE MAN-- THE HERETIC OF BIRNIN AZZARIA REVERTING TO HIS GOSPEL OF HIGH TREASON.
THE GOSPEL WAS A CONTAGION, SPREADING OUT INTO THE REGIONS OF MUTAPA, N'JADA, PIYE...
...SPREADING EVEN BEYOND WAKANDA'S BORDERS.
THE UNITED NATIONS CANNOT SIT IDLY BY WHILE A RULER MASSACRES HIS OWN PEOPLE AND TREATS WITH A COUNCIL OF TORTURERS.
CHANGAMIRE INVOKES GANDHI, BUT THE REBELS OF ALKAMA AND THE JABARI-LANDS WHO DEIFY HIM UNDERSTAND THE VIOLENCE OF HIS MESSAGE.
THE HERETIC PROPOSES TO END THE RULE OF THE PANTHER AND ELEVATE ANARCHY IN ITS PLACE.
NO, HODARI. HE PROPOSES TO END THE RULE OF MONARCHS AND REPLACE THEM WITH THE PEOPLE.

I HAVE STUDIED HIS WRITINGS. CHANGAMIRE BELIEVES THAT WISDOM ULTIMATELY RESTS WITHIN THE PEOPLE THEMSELVES.

RUBBISH. THE THRONE OF WAKANDA IS THE EMBODIMENT OF THE GODDESS *BAST*, AND YOU ARE HER EXALTED SERVANT.

AND YET WE FIND THIS EXALTED SERVANT POWERLESS BEFORE ALL OUR MIGHTY TROUBLES AND TREATING WITH CRAVEN THUGS.

MY APOLOGIES, KING T'CHALLA. I CONFESS I ERRED IN MY COUCIL.

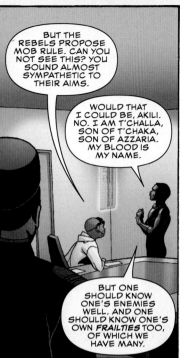

BUT THE REBELS PROPOSE MOB RULE. CAN YOU NOT SEE THIS? YOU SOUND ALMOST SYMPATHETIC TO THEIR AIMS.

WOULD THAT I COULD BE, AKILI. NO. I AM T'CHALLA, SON OF T'CHAKA, SON OF AZZARIA. MY BLOOD IS MY NAME.

BUT ONE SHOULD KNOW ONE'S ENEMIES WELL. AND ONE SHOULD KNOW ONE'S OWN *FRAILTIES* TOO, OF WHICH WE HAVE MANY.

ZEKE STANE

DESIGNATION:
Metahuman

DOMAIN:
Partis Acceleratus

AURA:
Malice

KWABENA WARE

STILL, WE ARE NOT WITHOUT OUR OWN RESOURCES. OUR MAN IS LOOSE. I HAVE HIS SCENT AND THE SCENT OF HIS MASTER.

WHEN THE TWO CROSS, WE SHALL KNOW, AND THEN I WILL ATTACK.

IN THE MEANTIME, PROCEED WITH YOUR PLANNED STRIKE IN THE JABARI-LANDS.

CHAOS IS THE AIR OF THIS REVOLT. WE WILL SMOTHER IT WITH ORDER-- *OUR ORDER.*

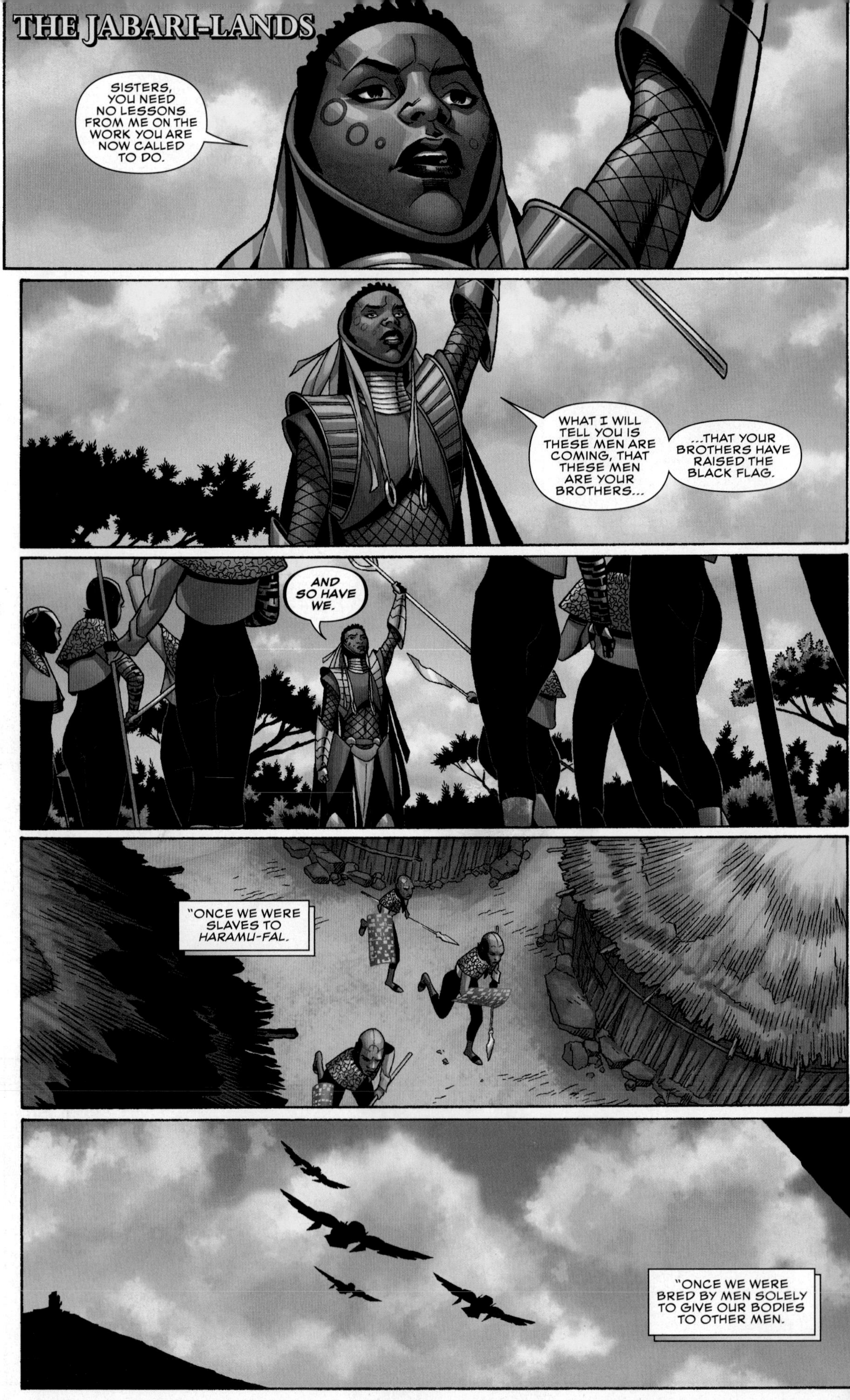
THE JABARI-LANDS
SISTERS, YOU NEED NO LESSONS FROM ME ON THE WORK YOU ARE NOW CALLED TO DO.
WHAT I WILL TELL YOU IS THESE MEN ARE COMING, THAT THESE MEN ARE YOUR BROTHERS...
...THAT YOUR BROTHERS HAVE RAISED THE BLACK FLAG.
AND SO HAVE WE.
"ONCE WE WERE SLAVES TO HARAMU-FAL.
"ONCE WE WERE BRED BY MEN SOLELY TO GIVE OUR BODIES TO OTHER MEN.

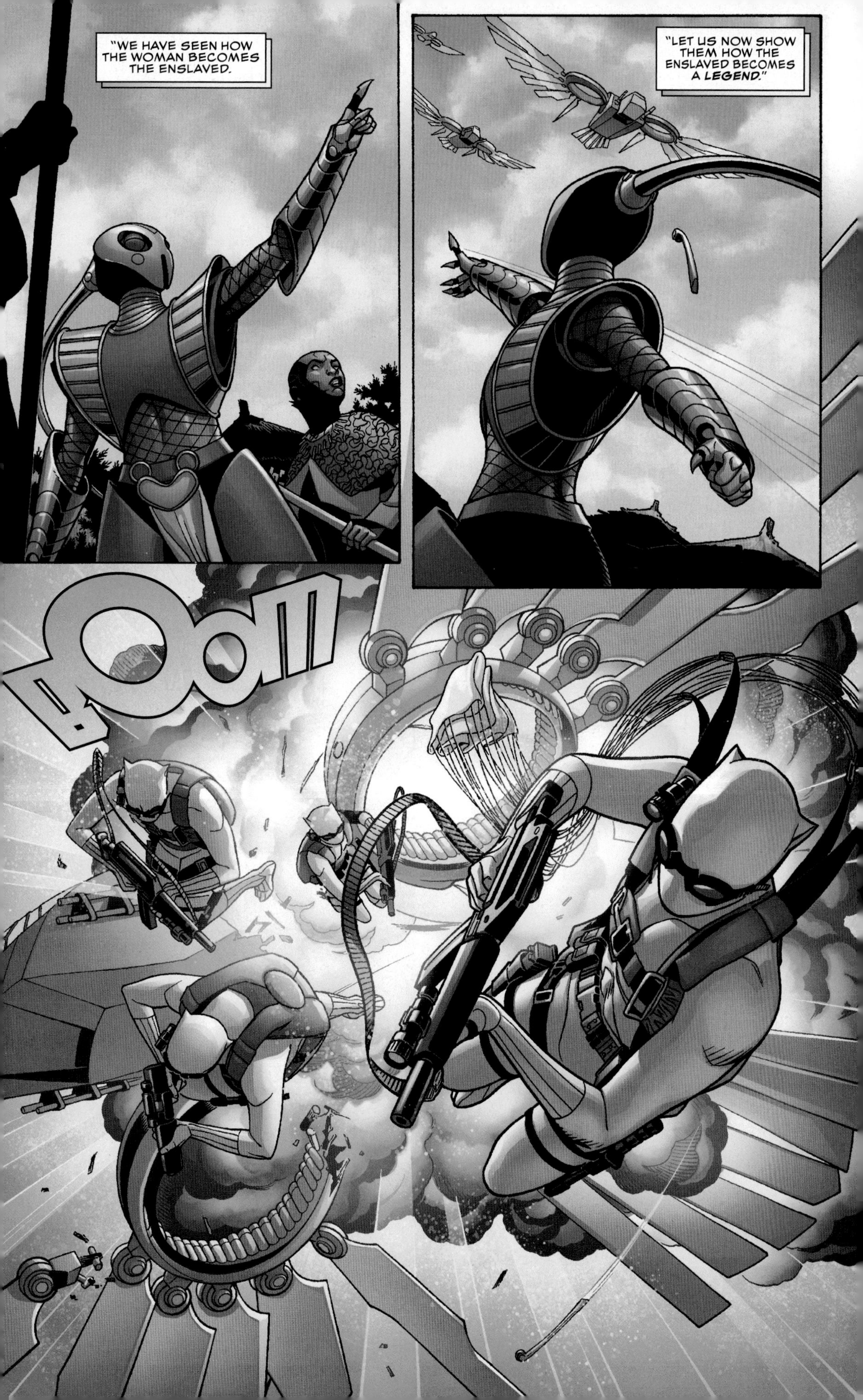
"WE HAVE SEEN HOW THE WOMAN BECOMES THE ENSLAVED.
"LET US NOW SHOW THEM HOW THE ENSLAVED BECOMES A *LEGEND*."
BOOM!

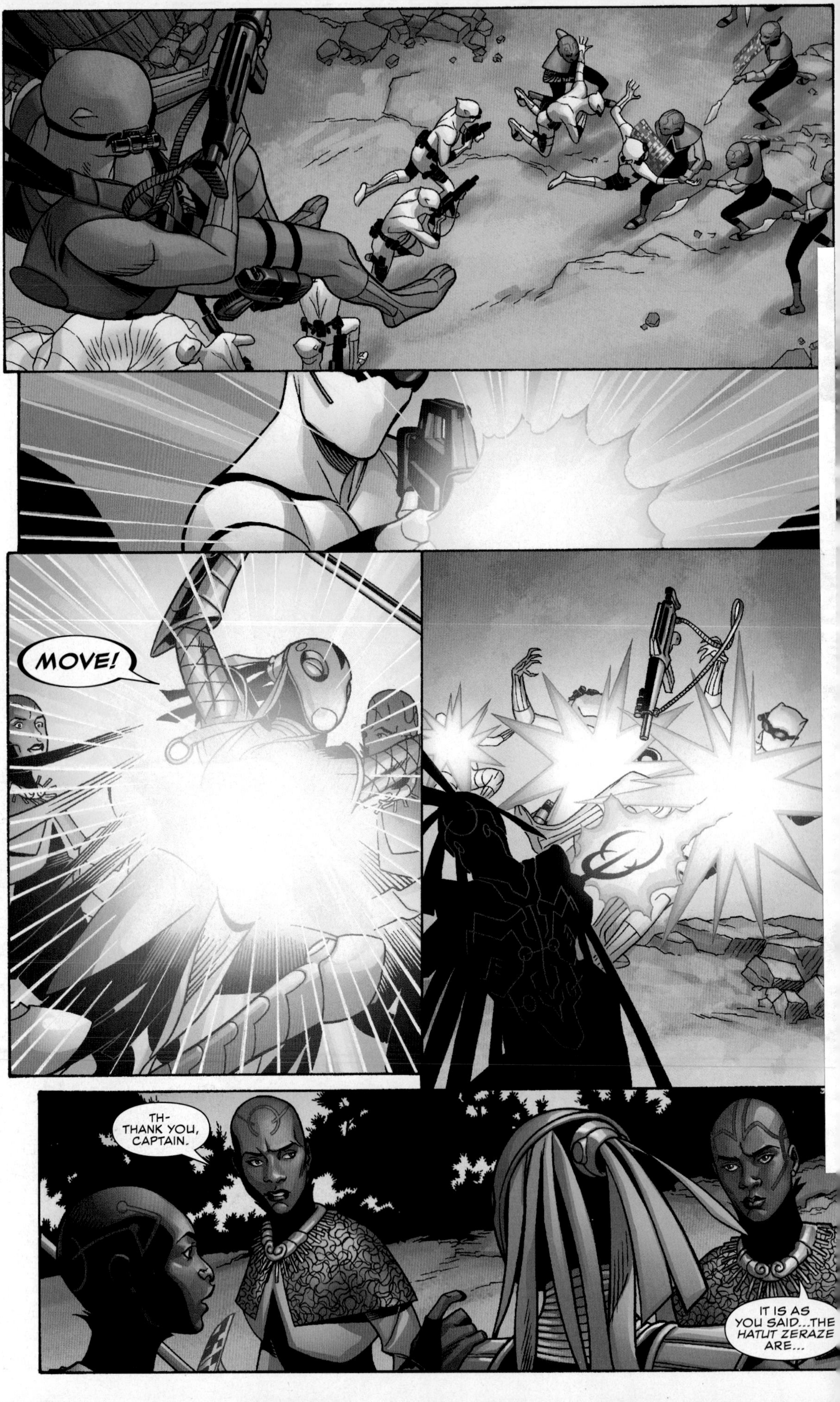
MOVE!
TH- THANK YOU, CAPTAIN.
IT IS AS YOU SAID...THE HATUT ZERAZE ARE...

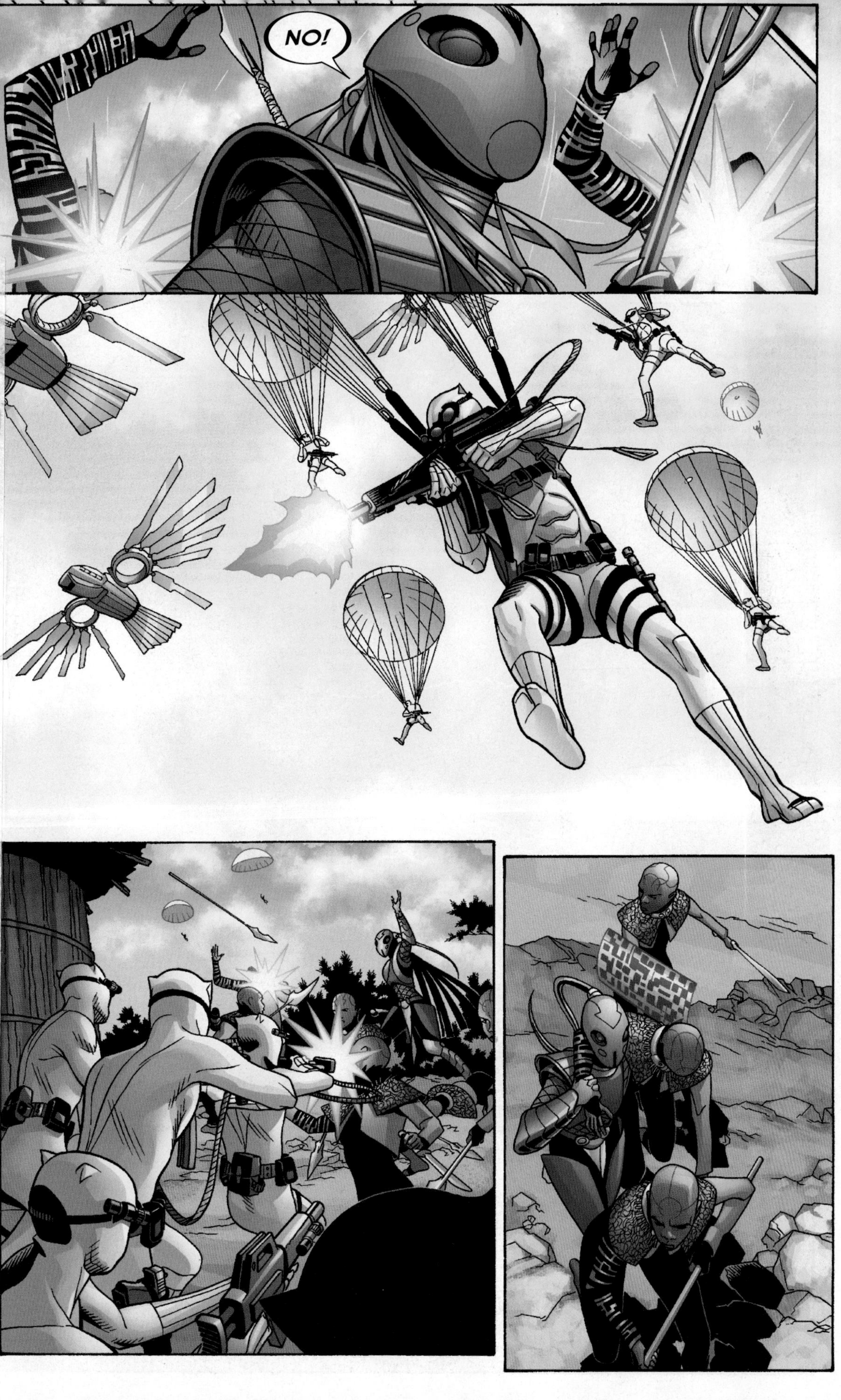
NO!

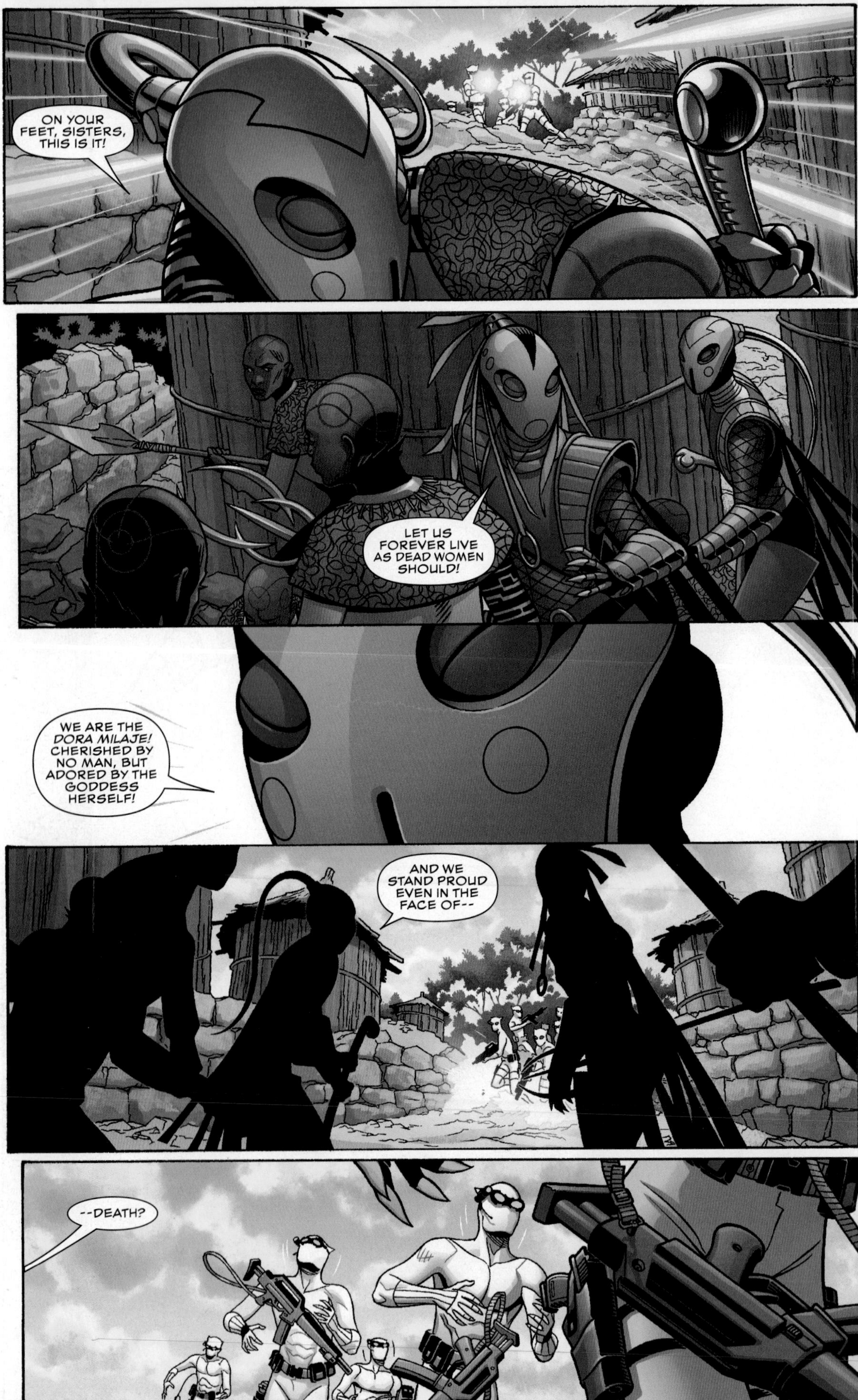
ON YOUR FEET, SISTERS, THIS IS IT!
LET US FOREVER LIVE AS DEAD WOMEN SHOULD!
WE ARE THE *DORA MILAJE!* CHERISHED BY NO MAN, BUT ADORED BY THE GODDESS HERSELF!
AND WE STAND PROUD EVEN IN THE FACE OF--
--DEATH?

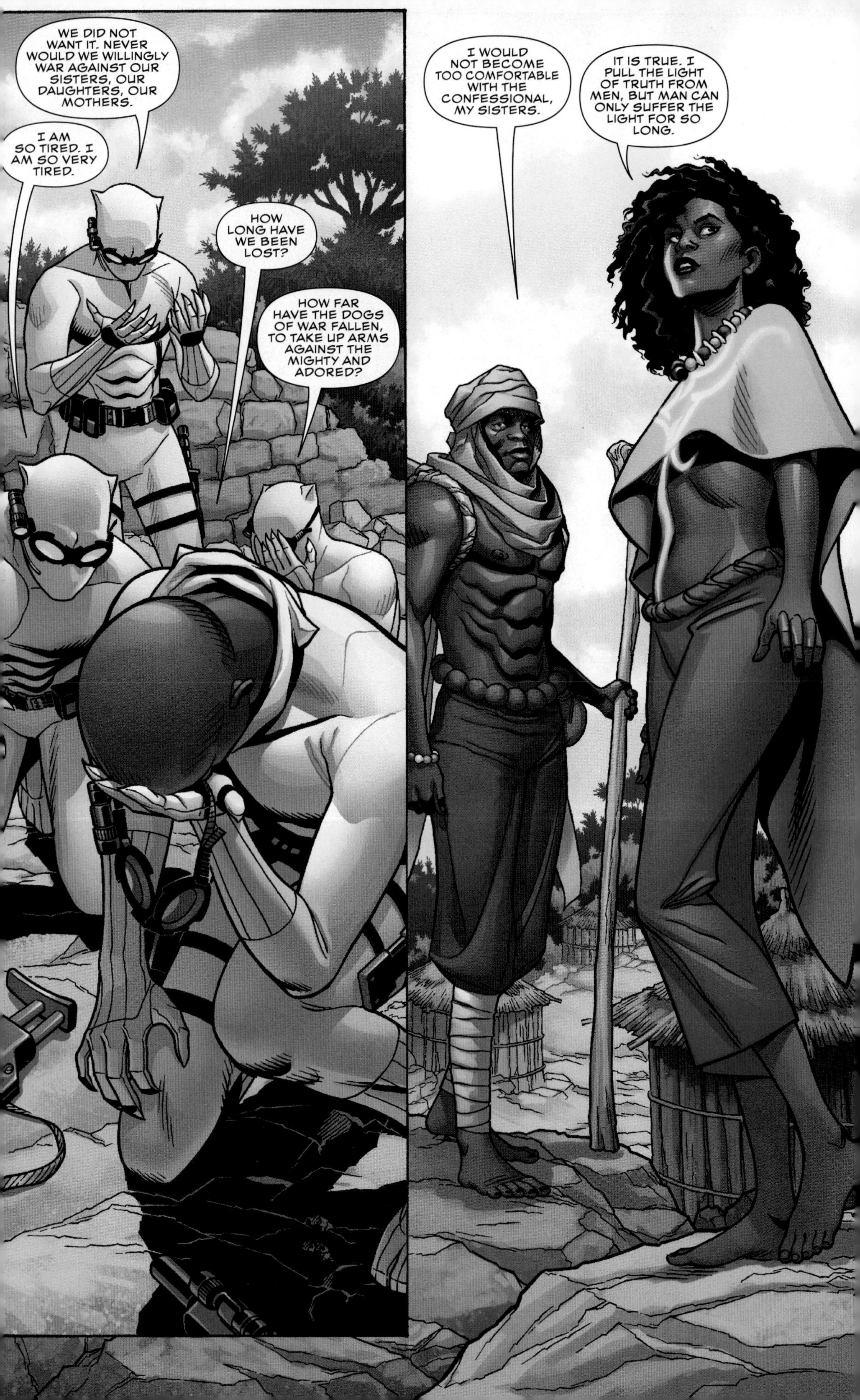
WE DID NOT WANT IT. NEVER WOULD WE WILLINGLY WAR AGAINST OUR SISTERS, OUR DAUGHTERS, OUR MOTHERS.
I AM SO TIRED. I AM SO VERY TIRED.
HOW LONG HAVE WE BEEN LOST?
HOW FAR HAVE THE DOGS OF WAR FALLEN, TO TAKE UP ARMS AGAINST THE MIGHTY AND ADORED?
I WOULD NOT BECOME TOO COMFORTABLE WITH THE CONFESSIONAL, MY SISTERS.
IT IS TRUE. I PULL THE LIGHT OF TRUTH FROM MEN, BUT MAN CAN ONLY SUFFER THE LIGHT FOR SO LONG.

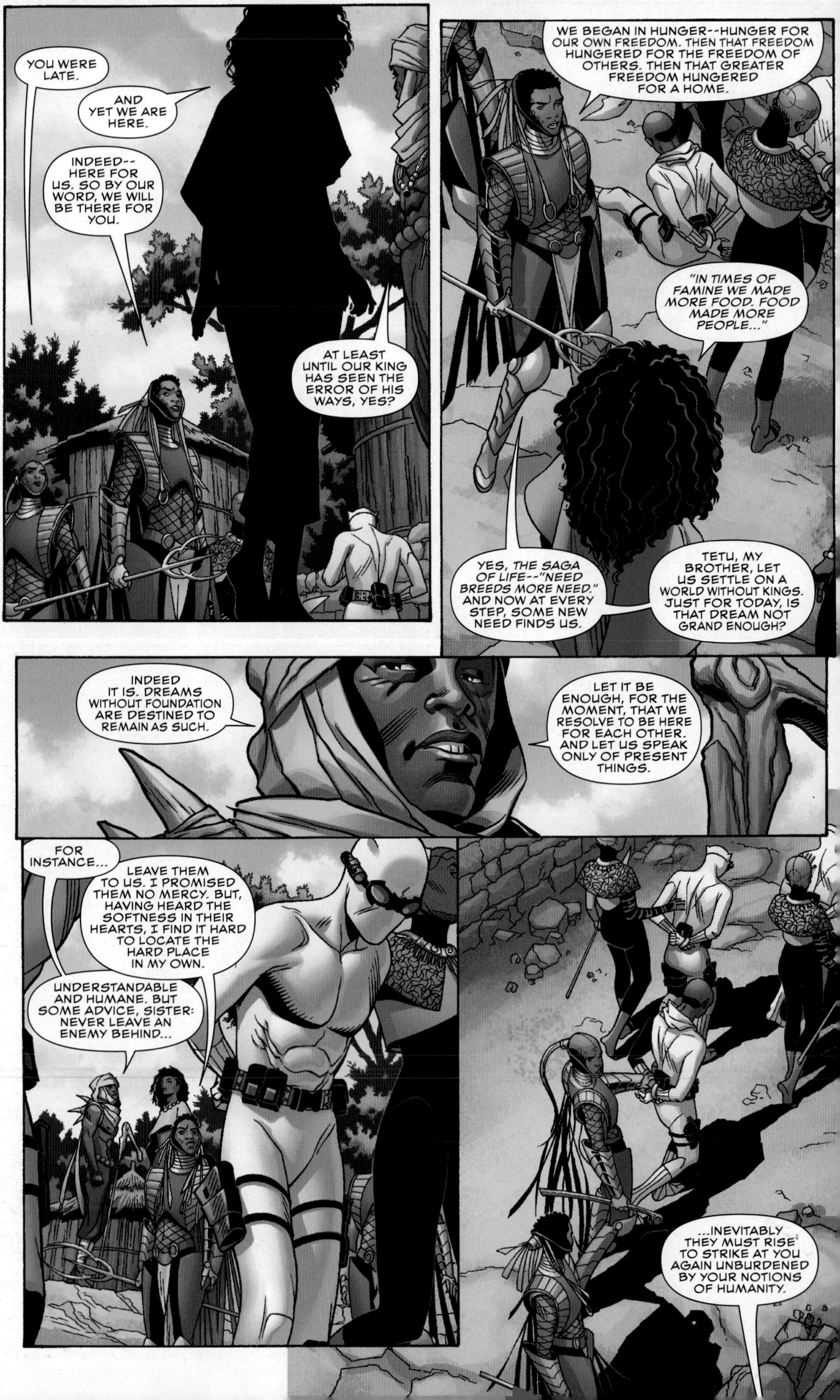
YOU WERE LATE.
AND YET WE ARE HERE.
INDEED-- HERE FOR US. SO BY OUR WORD, WE WILL BE THERE FOR YOU.
AT LEAST UNTIL OUR KING HAS SEEN THE ERROR OF HIS WAYS, YES?
WE BEGAN IN HUNGER--HUNGER FOR OUR OWN FREEDOM. THEN THAT FREEDOM HUNGERED FOR THE FREEDOM OF OTHERS. THEN THAT GREATER FREEDOM HUNGERED FOR A HOME.
"IN TIMES OF FAMINE WE MADE MORE FOOD. FOOD MADE MORE PEOPLE..."
YES, THE SAGA OF LIFE--"NEED BREEDS MORE NEED." AND NOW AT EVERY STEP, SOME NEW NEED FINDS US.
TETU, MY BROTHER, LET US SETTLE ON A WORLD WITHOUT KINGS. JUST FOR TODAY, IS THAT DREAM NOT GRAND ENOUGH?
INDEED IT IS. DREAMS WITHOUT FOUNDATION ARE DESTINED TO REMAIN AS SUCH.
LET IT BE ENOUGH, FOR THE MOMENT, THAT WE RESOLVE TO BE HERE FOR EACH OTHER. AND LET US SPEAK ONLY OF PRESENT THINGS.
FOR INSTANCE...
LEAVE THEM TO US. I PROMISED THEM NO MERCY. BUT, HAVING HEARD THE SOFTNESS IN THEIR HEARTS, I FIND IT HARD TO LOCATE THE HARD PLACE IN MY OWN.
UNDERSTANDABLE AND HUMANE. BUT SOME ADVICE, SISTER: NEVER LEAVE AN ENEMY BEHIND...
...INEVITABLY THEY MUST RISE TO STRIKE AT YOU AGAIN UNBURDENED BY YOUR NOTIONS OF HUMANITY.

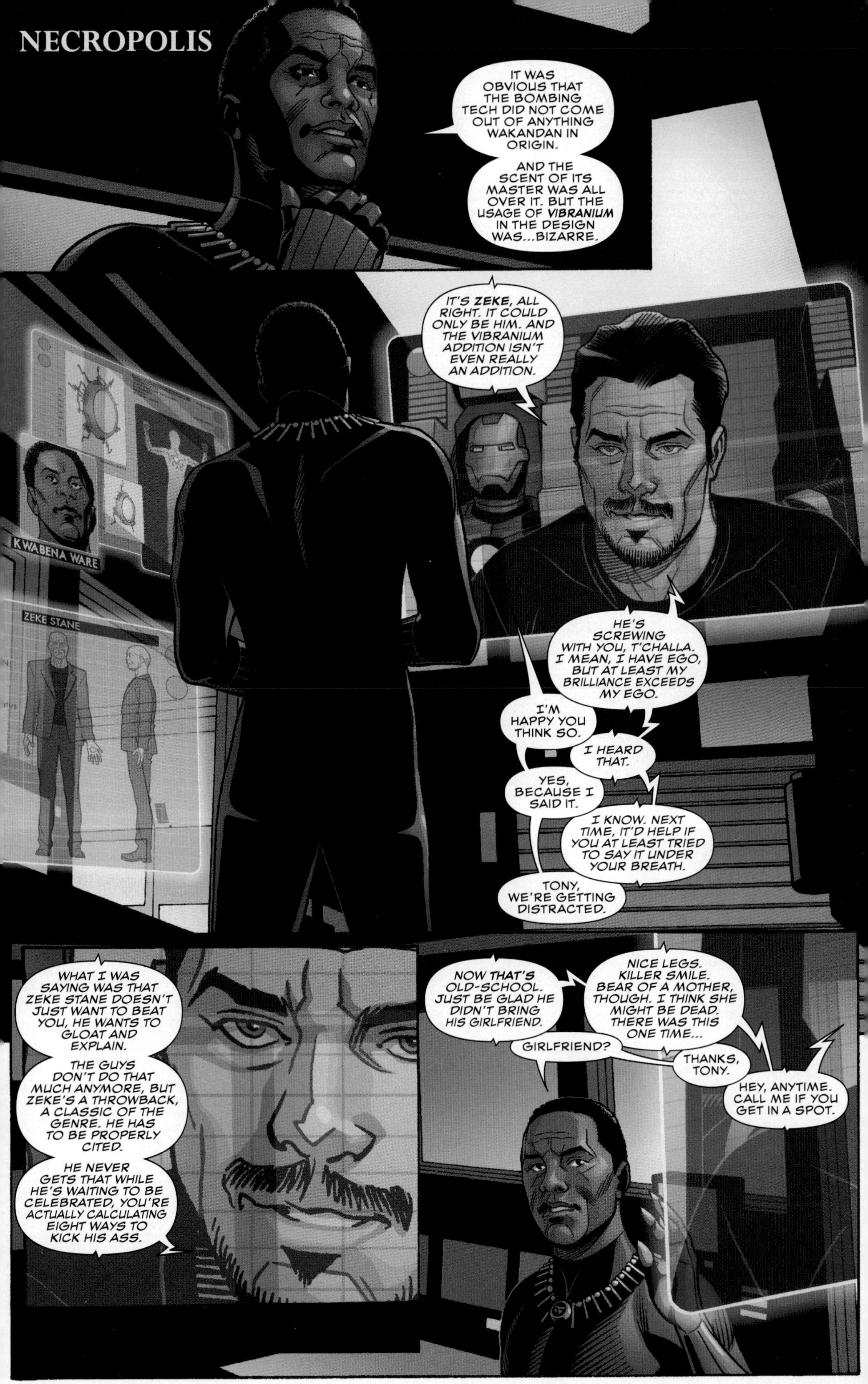
IT WAS OBVIOUS THAT THE BOMBING TECH DID NOT COME OUT OF ANYTHING WAKANDAN IN ORIGIN.
AND THE SCENT OF ITS MASTER WAS ALL OVER IT. BUT THE USAGE OF VIBRANIUM IN THE DESIGN WAS...BIZARRE.
KWABENA WARE
ZEKE STANE
IT'S ZEKE, ALL RIGHT. IT COULD ONLY BE HIM. AND THE VIBRANIUM ADDITION ISN'T EVEN REALLY AN ADDITION.
HE'S SCREWING WITH YOU, T'CHALLA. I MEAN, I HAVE EGO, BUT AT LEAST MY BRILLIANCE EXCEEDS MY EGO.
I'M HAPPY YOU THINK SO.
I HEARD THAT.
YES, BECAUSE I SAID IT.
I KNOW. NEXT TIME, IT'D HELP IF YOU AT LEAST TRIED TO SAY IT UNDER YOUR BREATH.
TONY, WE'RE GETTING DISTRACTED.
WHAT I WAS SAYING WAS THAT ZEKE STANE DOESN'T JUST WANT TO BEAT YOU, HE WANTS TO GLOAT AND EXPLAIN.
THE GUYS DON'T DO THAT MUCH ANYMORE, BUT ZEKE'S A THROWBACK, A CLASSIC OF THE GENRE. HE HAS TO BE PROPERLY CITED.
HE NEVER GETS THAT WHILE HE'S WAITING TO BE CELEBRATED, YOU'RE ACTUALLY CALCULATING EIGHT WAYS TO KICK HIS ASS.
NOW THAT'S OLD-SCHOOL. JUST BE GLAD HE DIDN'T BRING HIS GIRLFRIEND.
GIRLFRIEND?
NICE LEGS. KILLER SMILE. BEAR OF A MOTHER, THOUGH. I THINK SHE MIGHT BE DEAD. THERE WAS THIS ONE TIME...
THANKS, TONY.
HEY, ANYTIME. CALL ME IF YOU GET IN A SPOT.

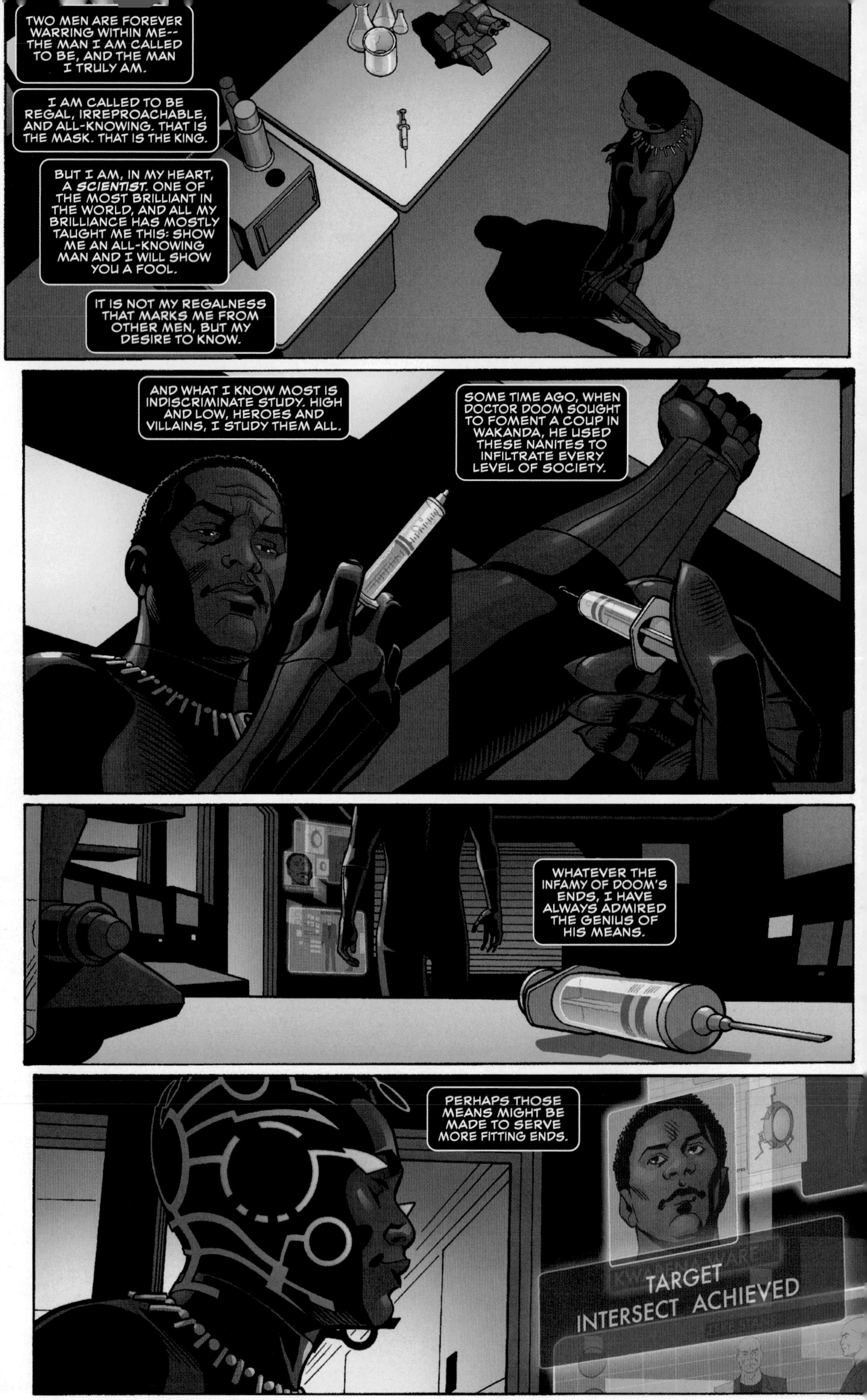
TWO MEN ARE FOREVER WARRING WITHIN ME-- THE MAN I AM CALLED TO BE, AND THE MAN I TRULY AM.
I AM CALLED TO BE REGAL, IRREPROACHABLE, AND ALL-KNOWING. THAT IS THE MASK. THAT IS THE KING.
BUT I AM, IN MY HEART, A SCIENTIST. ONE OF THE MOST BRILLIANT IN THE WORLD, AND ALL MY BRILLIANCE HAS MOSTLY TAUGHT ME THIS: SHOW ME AN ALL-KNOWING MAN AND I WILL SHOW YOU A FOOL.
IT IS NOT MY REGALNESS THAT MARKS ME FROM OTHER MEN, BUT MY DESIRE TO KNOW.
AND WHAT I KNOW MOST IS INDISCRIMINATE STUDY. HIGH AND LOW, HEROES AND VILLAINS, I STUDY THEM ALL.
SOME TIME AGO, WHEN DOCTOR DOOM SOUGHT TO FOMENT A COUP IN WAKANDA, HE USED THESE NANITES TO INFILTRATE EVERY LEVEL OF SOCIETY.
WHATEVER THE INFAMY OF DOOM'S ENDS, I HAVE ALWAYS ADMIRED THE GENIUS OF HIS MEANS.
PERHAPS THOSE MEANS MIGHT BE MADE TO SERVE MORE FITTING ENDS.
TARGET
INTERSECT ACHIEVED

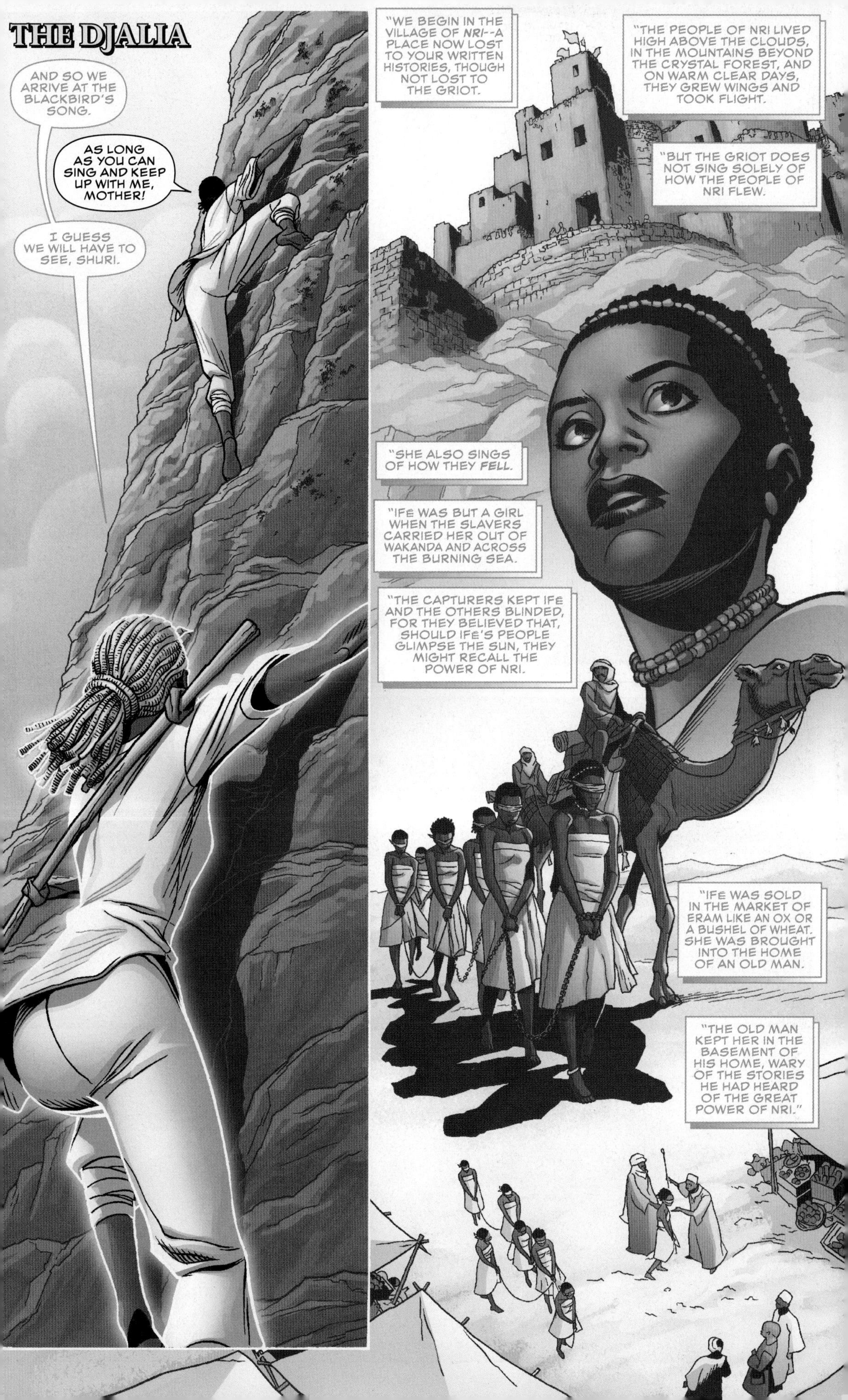
THE DJALIA
AND SO WE ARRIVE AT THE BLACKBIRD'S SONG.
AS LONG AS YOU CAN SING AND KEEP UP WITH ME, MOTHER!
I GUESS WE WILL HAVE TO SEE, SHURI.
"WE BEGIN IN THE VILLAGE OF NRI--A PLACE NOW LOST TO YOUR WRITTEN HISTORIES, THOUGH NOT LOST TO THE GRIOT.
"THE PEOPLE OF NRI LIVED HIGH ABOVE THE CLOUDS, IN THE MOUNTAINS BEYOND THE CRYSTAL FOREST, AND ON WARM CLEAR DAYS, THEY GREW WINGS AND TOOK FLIGHT.
"BUT THE GRIOT DOES NOT SING SOLELY OF HOW THE PEOPLE OF NRI FLEW.
"SHE ALSO SINGS OF HOW THEY FELL.
"IFE WAS BUT A GIRL WHEN THE SLAVERS CARRIED HER OUT OF WAKANDA AND ACROSS THE BURNING SEA.
"THE CAPTURERS KEPT IFE AND THE OTHERS BLINDED, FOR THEY BELIEVED THAT, SHOULD IFE'S PEOPLE GLIMPSE THE SUN, THEY MIGHT RECALL THE POWER OF NRI.
"IFE WAS SOLD IN THE MARKET OF ERAM LIKE AN OX OR A BUSHEL OF WHEAT. SHE WAS BROUGHT INTO THE HOME OF AN OLD MAN.
"THE OLD MAN KEPT HER IN THE BASEMENT OF HIS HOME, WARY OF THE STORIES HE HAD HEARD OF THE GREAT POWER OF NRI."

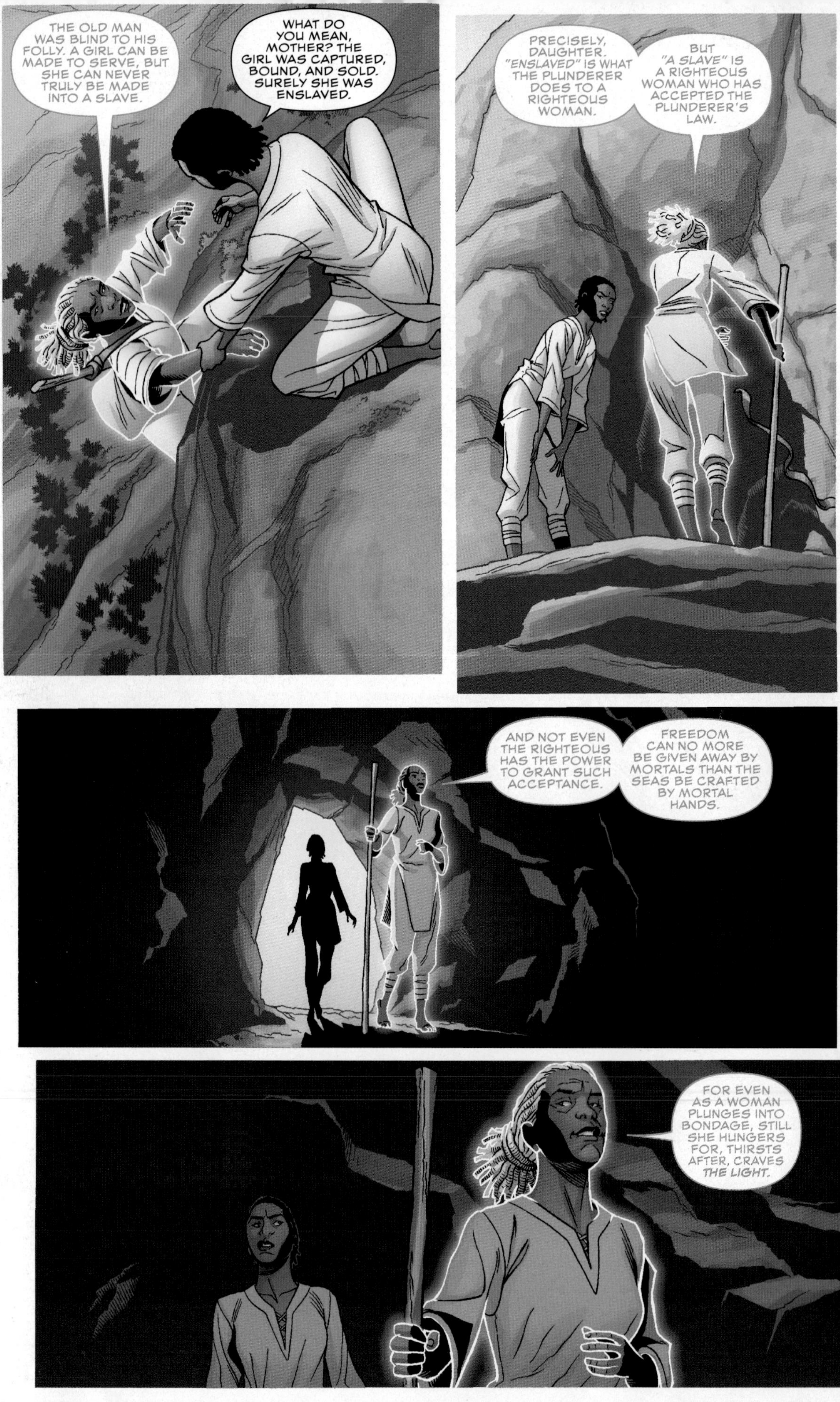
THE OLD MAN WAS BLIND TO HIS FOLLY. A GIRL CAN BE MADE TO SERVE, BUT SHE CAN NEVER TRULY BE MADE INTO A SLAVE.
WHAT DO YOU MEAN, MOTHER? THE GIRL WAS CAPTURED, BOUND, AND SOLD. SURELY SHE WAS ENSLAVED.
PRECISELY, DAUGHTER. "ENSLAVED" IS WHAT THE PLUNDERER DOES TO A RIGHTEOUS WOMAN.
BUT "A SLAVE" IS A RIGHTEOUS WOMAN WHO HAS ACCEPTED THE PLUNDERER'S LAW.
AND NOT EVEN THE RIGHTEOUS HAS THE POWER TO GRANT SUCH ACCEPTANCE.
FREEDOM CAN NO MORE BE GIVEN AWAY BY MORTALS THAN THE SEAS BE CRAFTED BY MORTAL HANDS.
FOR EVEN AS A WOMAN PLUNGES INTO BONDAGE, STILL SHE HUNGERS FOR, THIRSTS AFTER, CRAVES THE LIGHT.

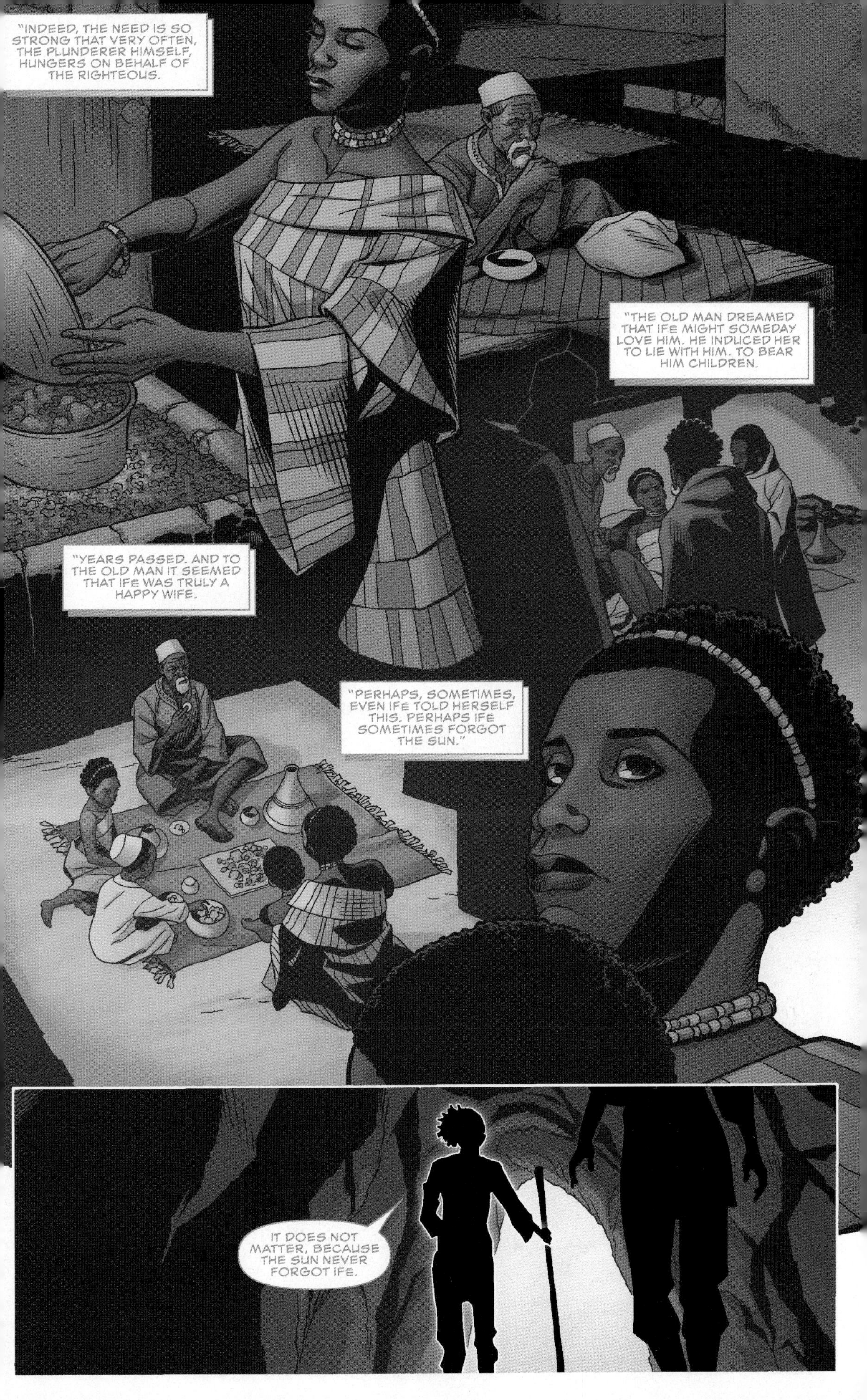
"INDEED, THE NEED IS SO STRONG THAT VERY OFTEN, THE PLUNDERER HIMSELF, HUNGERS ON BEHALF OF THE RIGHTEOUS.
"THE OLD MAN DREAMED THAT IFE MIGHT SOMEDAY LOVE HIM. HE INDUCED HER TO LIE WITH HIM. TO BEAR HIM CHILDREN.
"YEARS PASSED. AND TO THE OLD MAN IT SEEMED THAT IFE WAS TRULY A HAPPY WIFE.
"PERHAPS, SOMETIMES, EVEN IFE TOLD HERSELF THIS. PERHAPS IFE SOMETIMES FORGOT THE SUN."
IT DOES NOT MATTER, BECAUSE THE SUN NEVER FORGOT IFE.

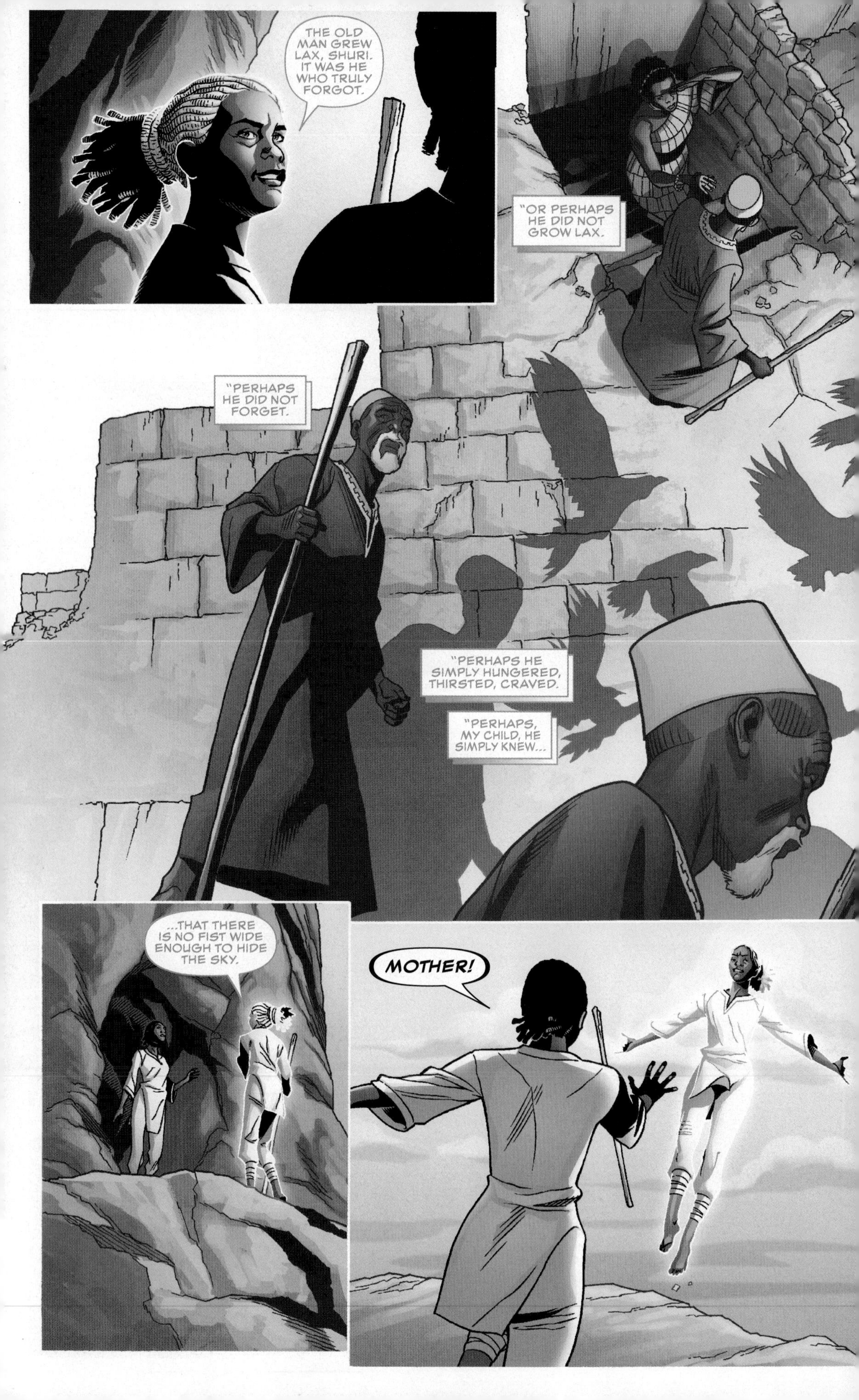
THE OLD MAN GREW LAX, SHURI. IT WAS HE WHO TRULY FORGOT.
"OR PERHAPS HE DID NOT GROW LAX.
"PERHAPS HE DID NOT FORGET.
"PERHAPS HE SIMPLY HUNGERED, THIRSTED, CRAVED.
"PERHAPS, MY CHILD, HE SIMPLY KNEW...
...THAT THERE IS NO FIST WIDE ENOUGH TO HIDE THE SKY.
MOTHER!

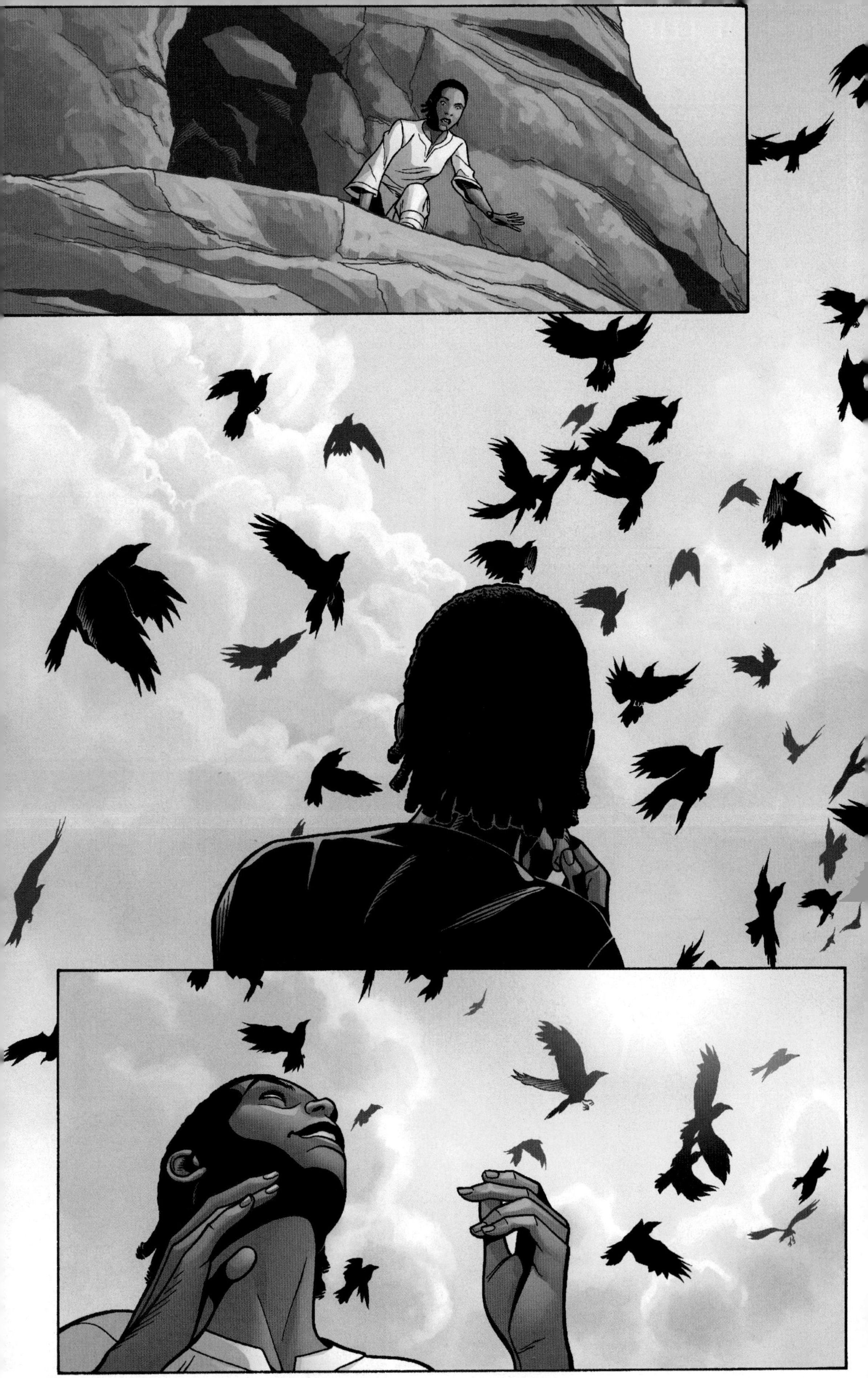

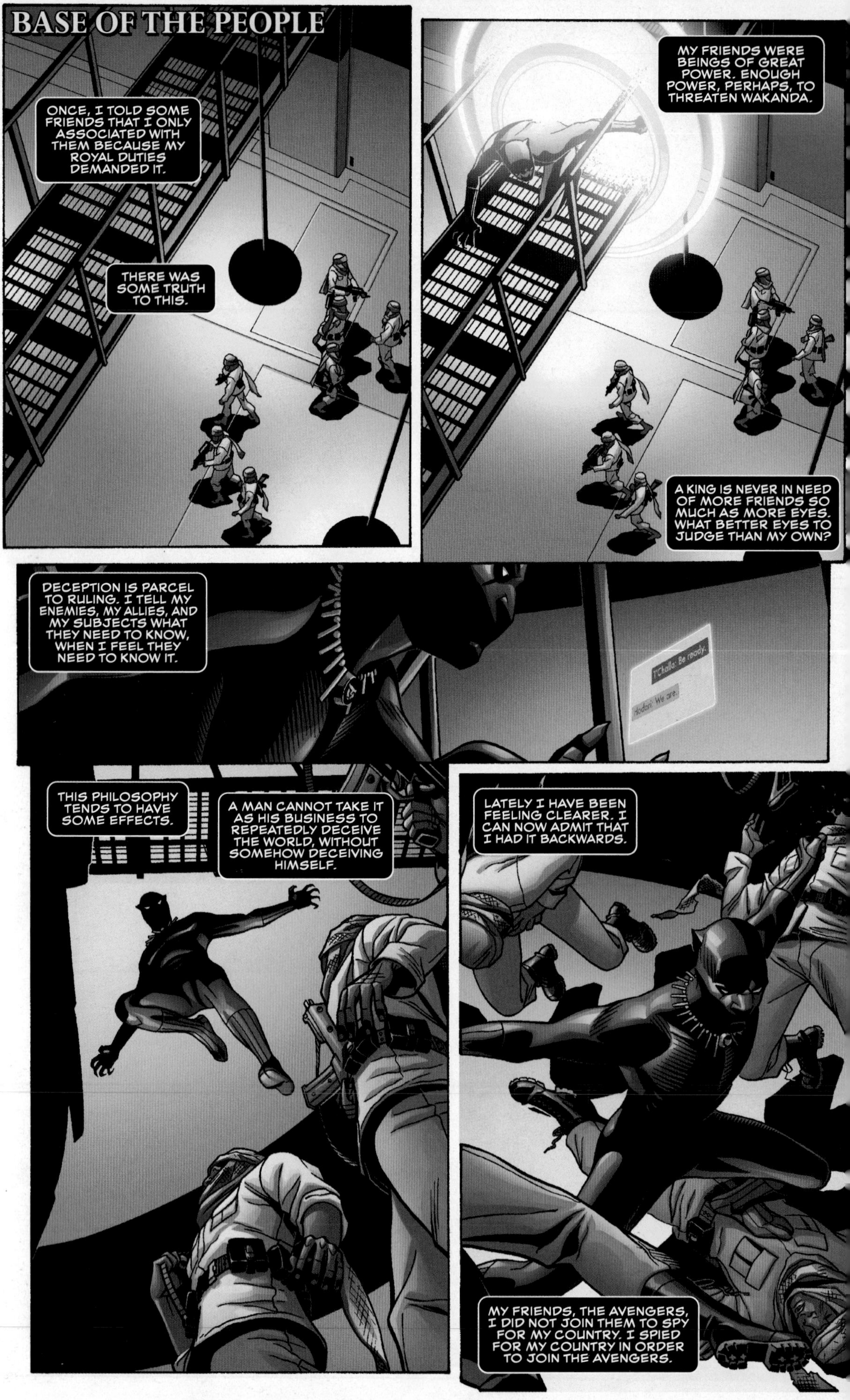
BASE OF THE PEOPLE
ONCE, I TOLD SOME FRIENDS THAT I ONLY ASSOCIATED WITH THEM BECAUSE MY ROYAL DUTIES DEMANDED IT.
THERE WAS SOME TRUTH TO THIS.
MY FRIENDS WERE BEINGS OF GREAT POWER. ENOUGH POWER, PERHAPS, TO THREATEN WAKANDA.
A KING IS NEVER IN NEED OF MORE FRIENDS SO MUCH AS MORE EYES. WHAT BETTER EYES TO JUDGE THAN MY OWN?
DECEPTION IS PARCEL TO RULING. I TELL MY ENEMIES, MY ALLIES, AND MY SUBJECTS WHAT THEY NEED TO KNOW, WHEN I FEEL THEY NEED TO KNOW IT.
T'Challa: Be ready.
Hodari: We are.
THIS PHILOSOPHY TENDS TO HAVE SOME EFFECTS.
A MAN CANNOT TAKE IT AS HIS BUSINESS TO REPEATEDLY DECEIVE THE WORLD, WITHOUT SOMEHOW DECEIVING HIMSELF.
LATELY I HAVE BEEN FEELING CLEARER. I CAN NOW ADMIT THAT I HAD IT BACKWARDS.
MY FRIENDS, THE AVENGERS, I DID NOT JOIN THEM TO SPY FOR MY COUNTRY. I SPIED FOR MY COUNTRY IN ORDER TO JOIN THE AVENGERS.

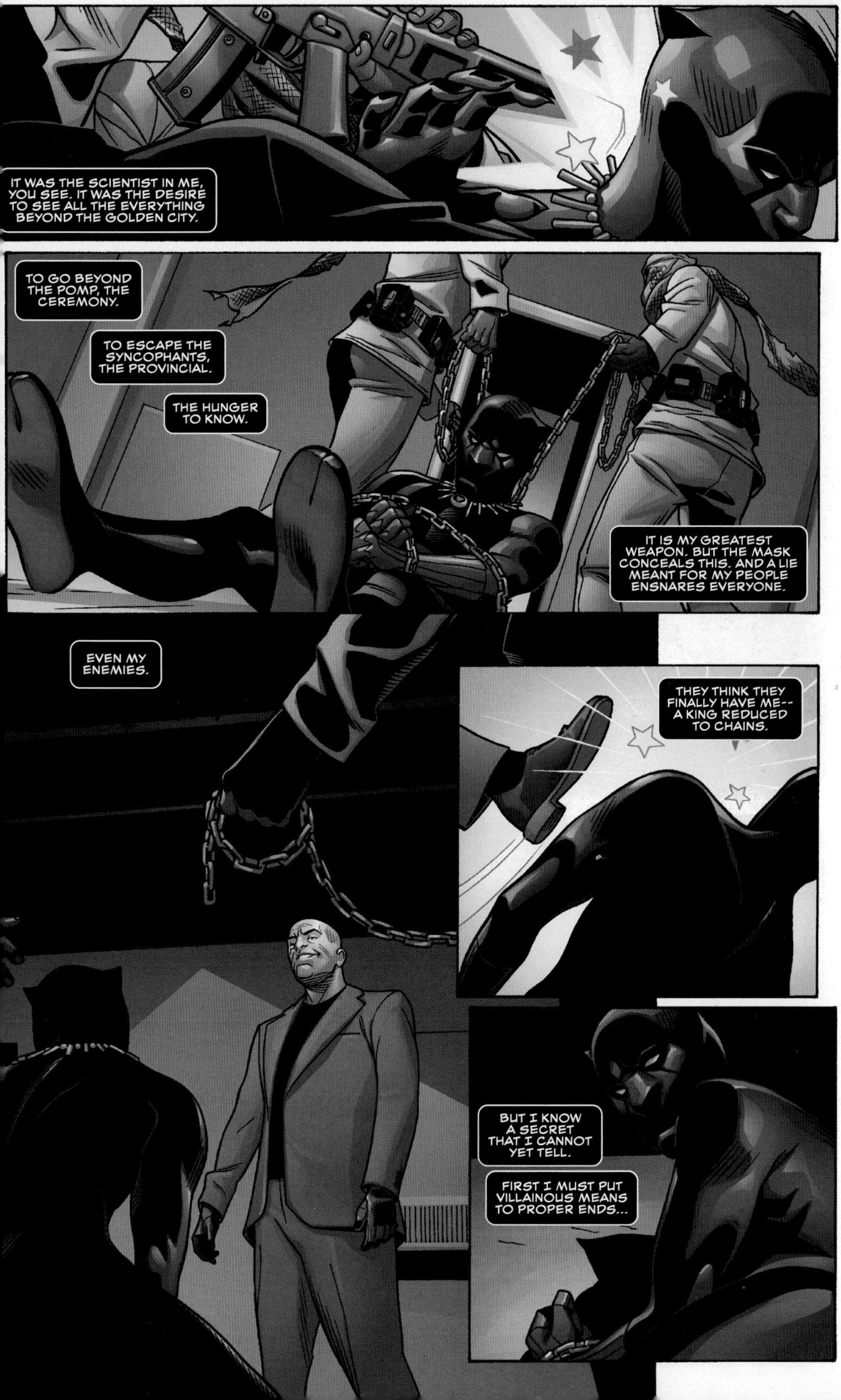
IT WAS THE SCIENTIST IN ME, YOU SEE. IT WAS THE DESIRE TO SEE ALL THE EVERYTHING BEYOND THE GOLDEN CITY.
TO GO BEYOND THE POMP, THE CEREMONY.
TO ESCAPE THE SYNCOPHANTS, THE PROVINCIAL.
THE HUNGER TO KNOW.
IT IS MY GREATEST WEAPON. BUT THE MASK CONCEALS THIS. AND A LIE MEANT FOR MY PEOPLE ENSNARES EVERYONE.
EVEN MY ENEMIES.
THEY THINK THEY FINALLY HAVE ME-- A KING REDUCED TO CHAINS.
BUT I KNOW A SECRET THAT I CANNOT YET TELL.
FIRST I MUST PUT VILLAINOUS MEANS TO PROPER ENDS...

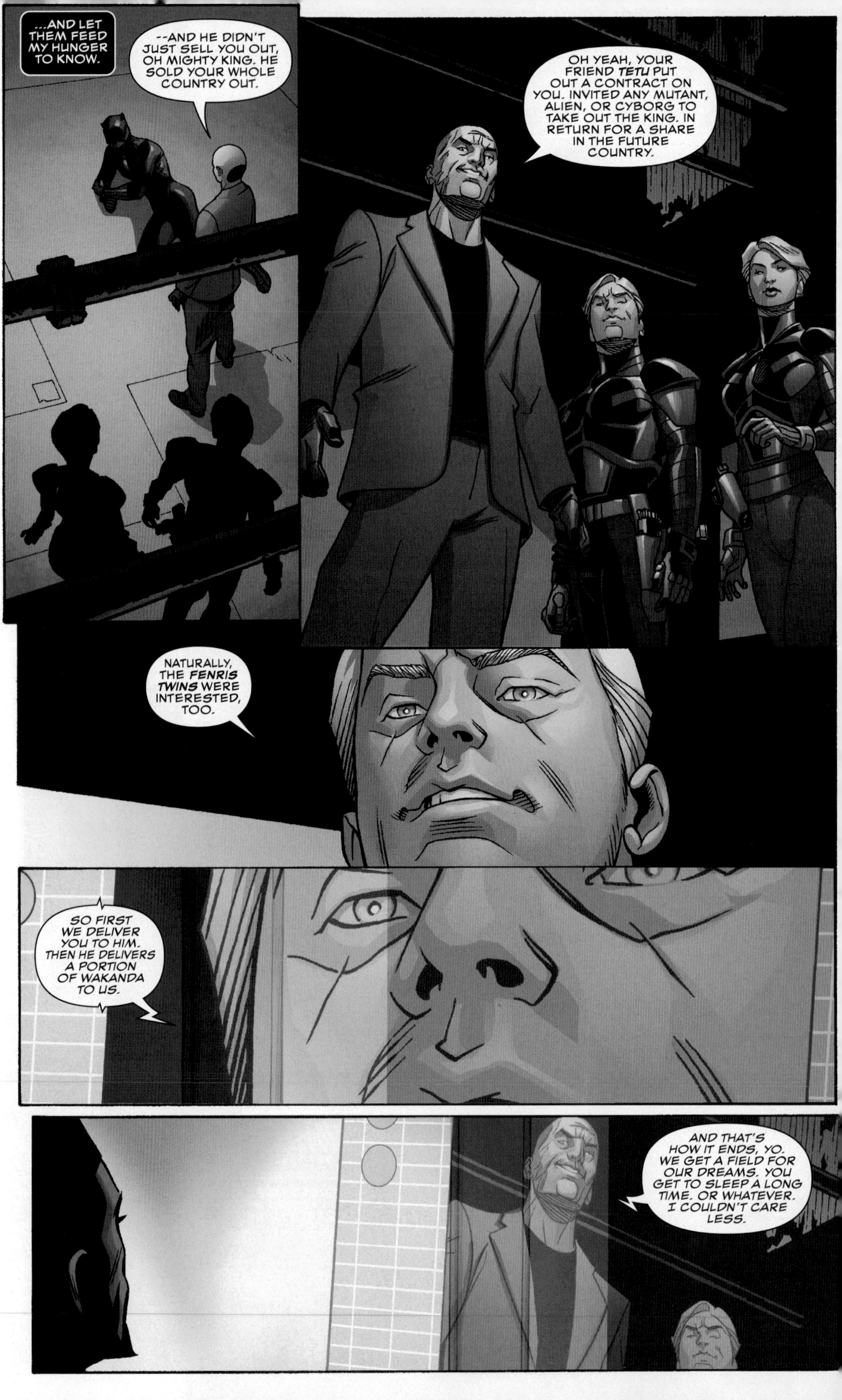
...AND LET THEM FEED MY HUNGER TO KNOW.
--AND HE DIDN'T JUST SELL YOU OUT, OH MIGHTY KING. HE SOLD YOUR WHOLE COUNTRY OUT.
OH YEAH, YOUR FRIEND TETU PUT OUT A CONTRACT ON YOU. INVITED ANY MUTANT, ALIEN, OR CYBORG TO TAKE OUT THE KING. IN RETURN FOR A SHARE IN THE FUTURE COUNTRY.
NATURALLY, THE FENRIS TWINS WERE INTERESTED, TOO.
SO FIRST WE DELIVER YOU TO HIM. THEN HE DELIVERS A PORTION OF WAKANDA TO US.
AND THAT'S HOW IT ENDS, YO. WE GET A FIELD FOR OUR DREAMS. YOU GET TO SLEEP A LONG TIME. OR WHATEVER. I COULDN'T CARE LESS.

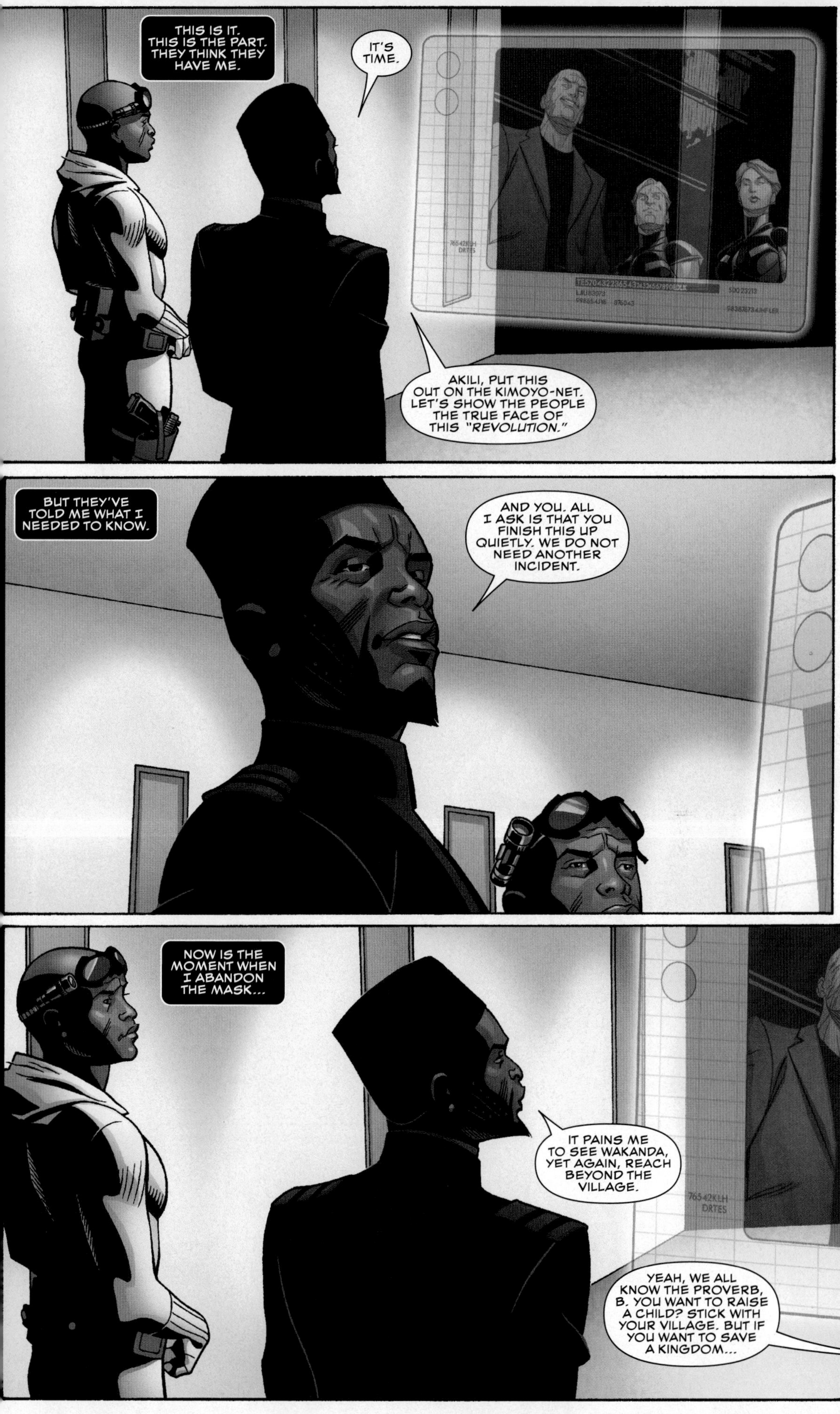
THIS IS IT. THIS IS THE PART. THEY THINK THEY HAVE ME.
IT'S TIME.
AKILI, PUT THIS OUT ON THE KIMOYO-NET. LET'S SHOW THE PEOPLE THE TRUE FACE OF THIS "REVOLUTION."
BUT THEY'VE TOLD ME WHAT I NEEDED TO KNOW.
AND YOU. ALL I ASK IS THAT YOU FINISH THIS UP QUIETLY. WE DO NOT NEED ANOTHER INCIDENT.
NOW IS THE MOMENT WHEN I ABANDON THE MASK...
IT PAINS ME TO SEE WAKANDA, YET AGAIN, REACH BEYOND THE VILLAGE.
YEAH, WE ALL KNOW THE PROVERB, B. YOU WANT TO RAISE A CHILD? STICK WITH YOUR VILLAGE. BUT IF YOU WANT TO SAVE A KINGDOM...

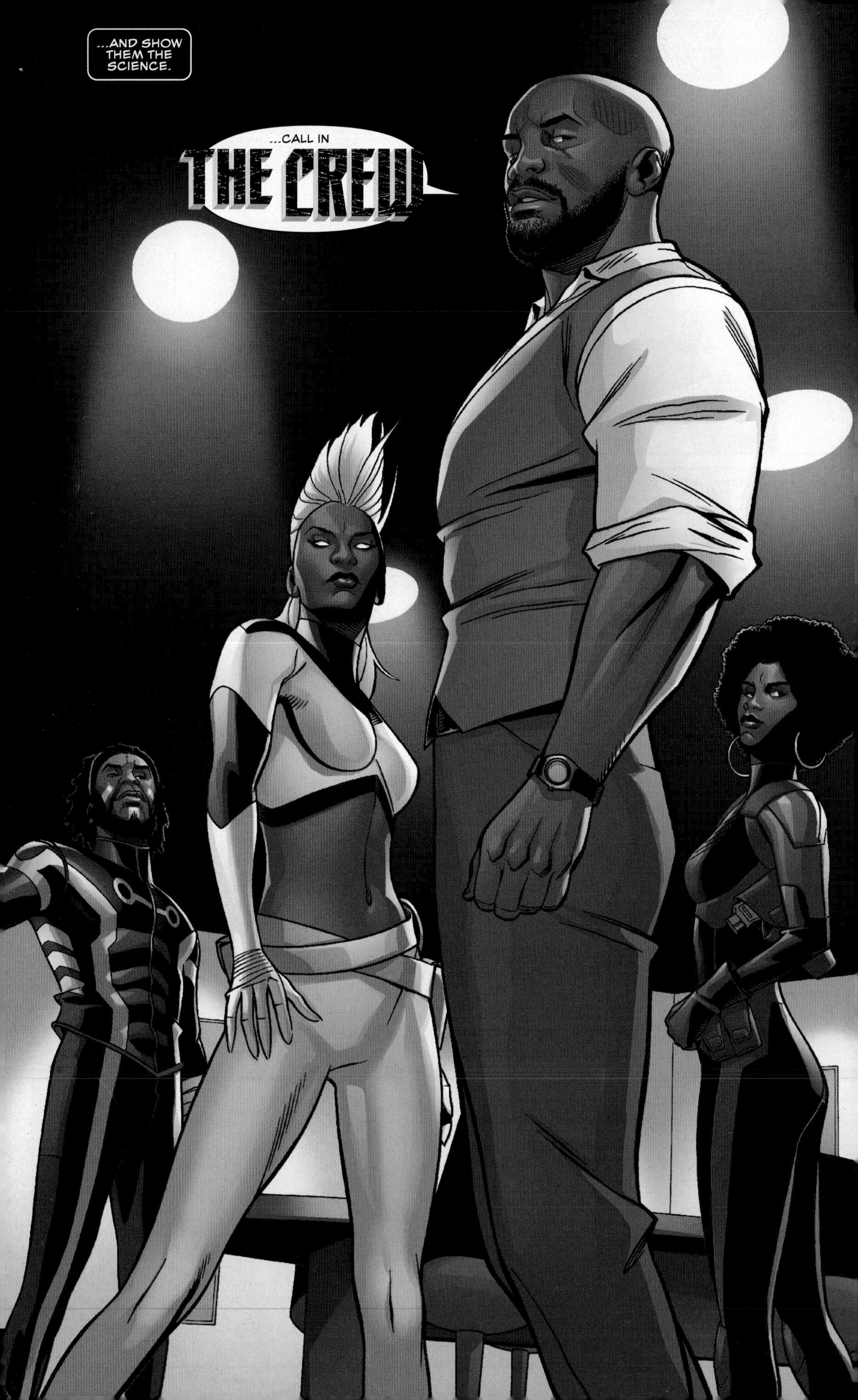
...AND SHOW THEM THE SCIENCE.
...CALL IN THE CREW

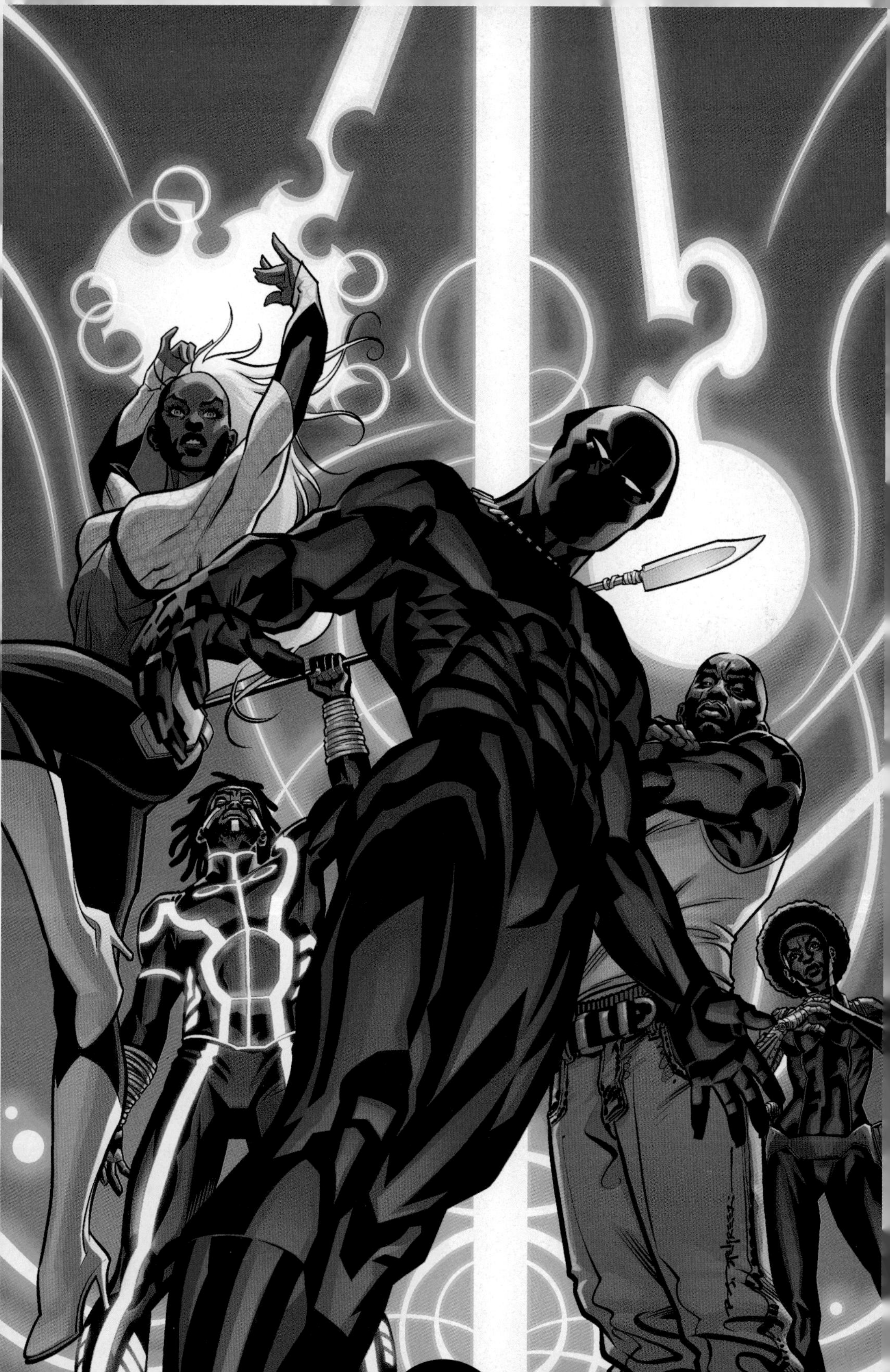

7

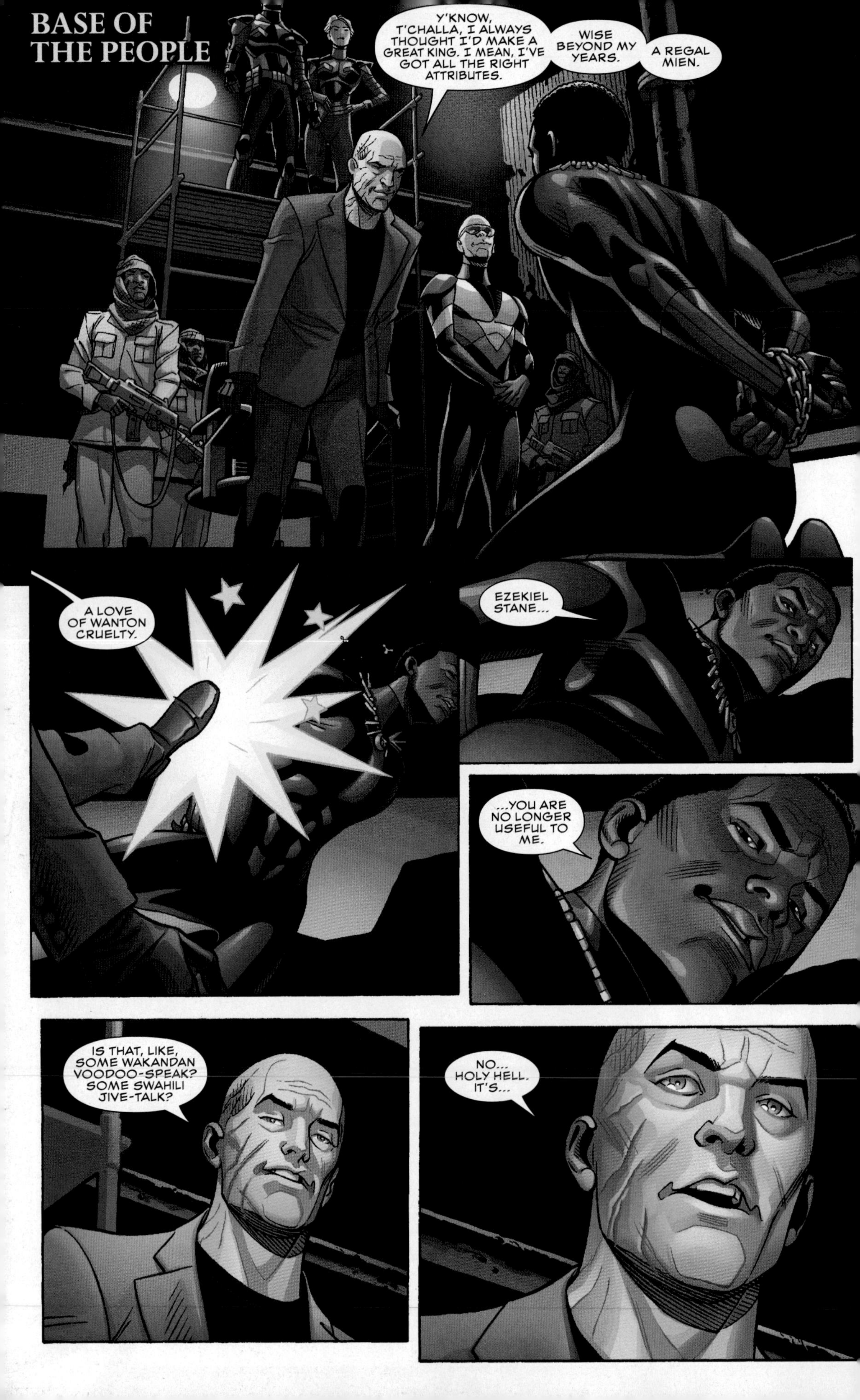
BASE OF THE PEOPLE
Y'KNOW, T'CHALLA, I ALWAYS THOUGHT I'D MAKE A GREAT KING. I MEAN, I'VE GOT ALL THE RIGHT ATTRIBUTES.
WISE BEYOND MY YEARS.
A REGAL MIEN.
A LOVE OF WANTON CRUELTY.
EZEKIEL STANE...
...YOU ARE NO LONGER USEFUL TO ME.
IS THAT, LIKE, SOME WAKANDAN VOODOO-SPEAK? SOME SWAHILI JIVE-TALK?
NO... HOLY HELL. IT'S...

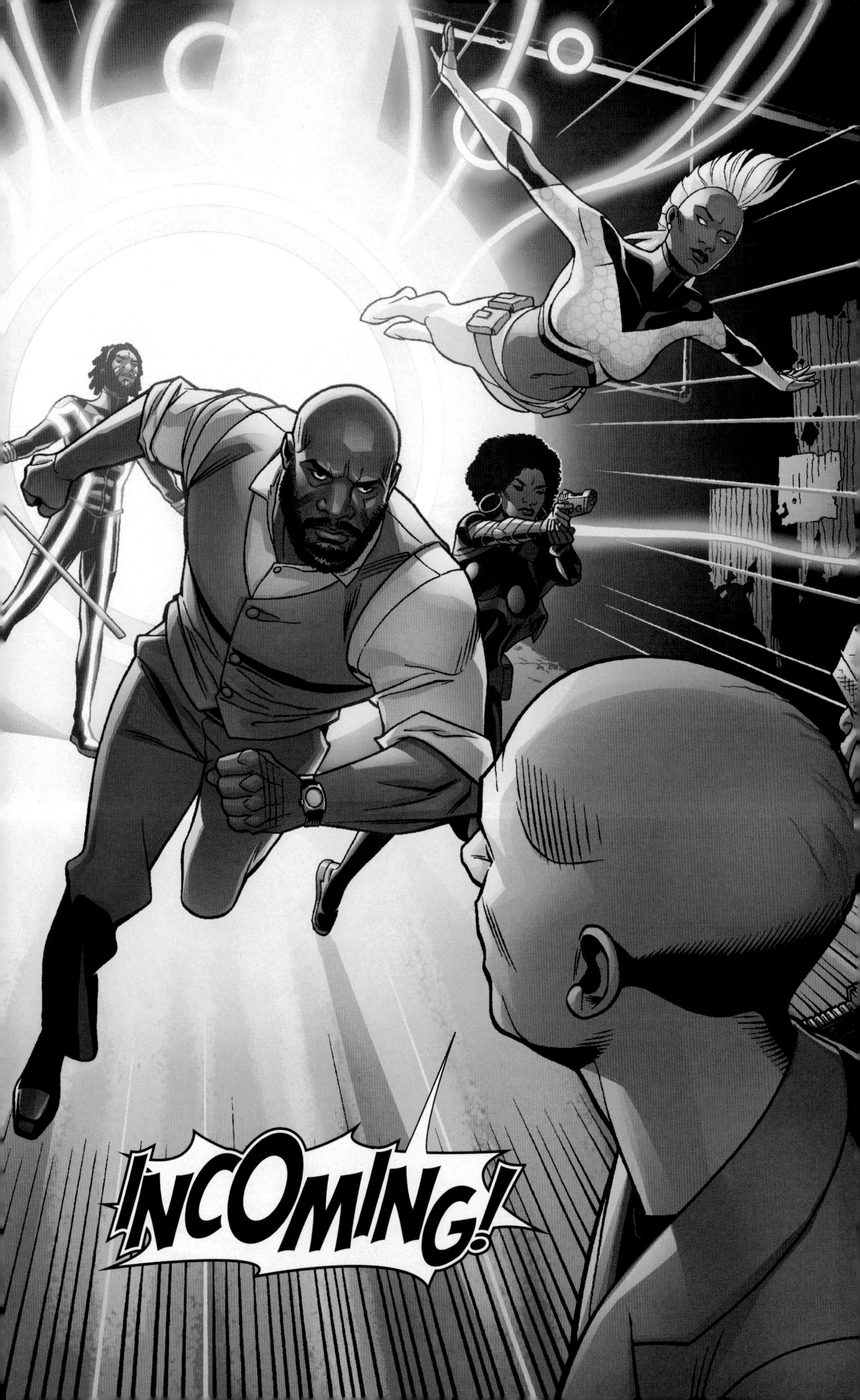
INCOMING!

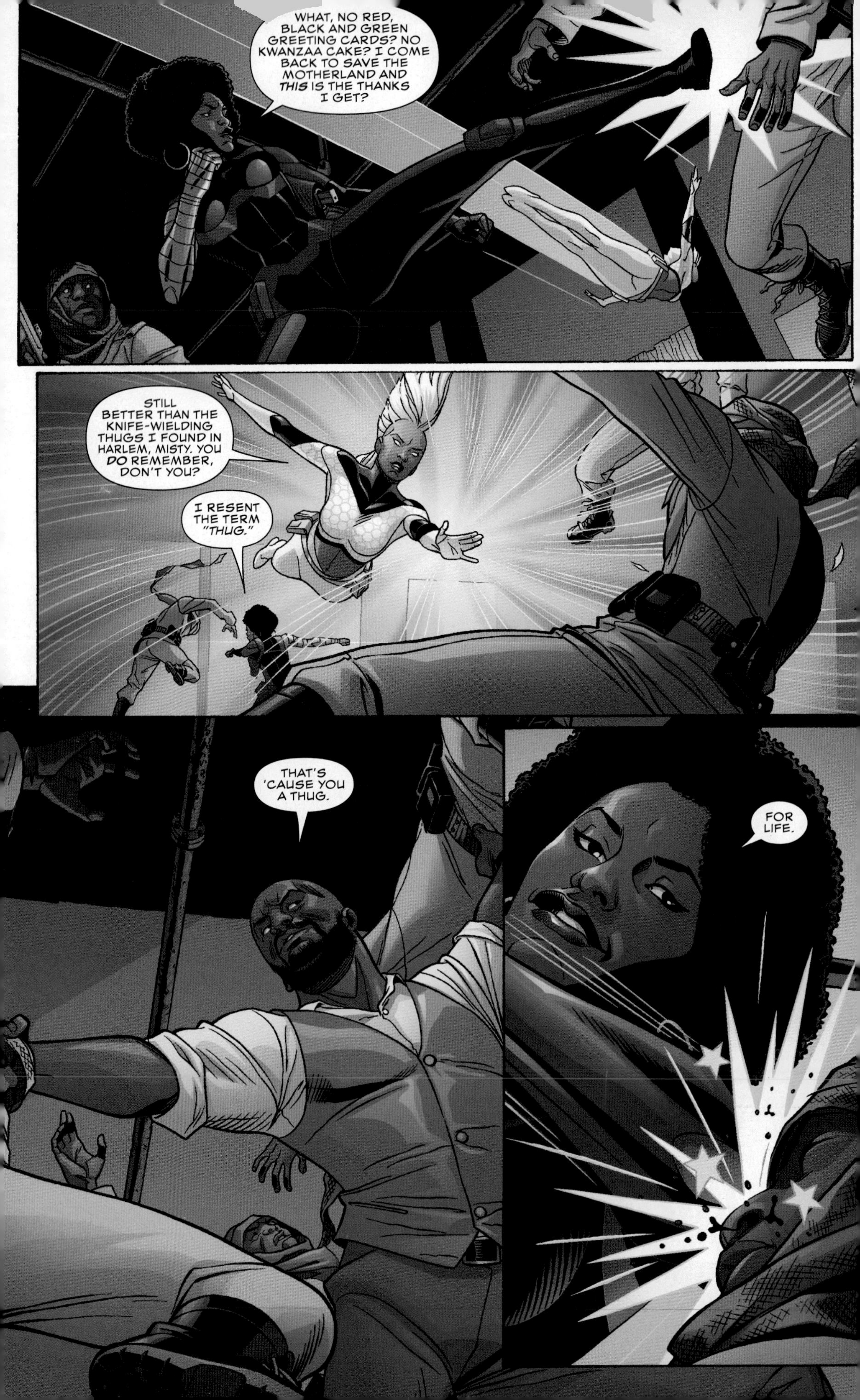
WHAT, NO RED, BLACK AND GREEN GREETING CARDS? NO KWANZAA CAKE? I COME BACK TO SAVE THE MOTHERLAND AND *THIS* IS THE THANKS I GET?
STILL BETTER THAN THE KNIFE-WIELDING THUGS I FOUND IN HARLEM, MISTY. YOU *DO* REMEMBER, DON'T YOU?
I RESENT THE TERM *"THUG."*
THAT'S 'CAUSE YOU A THUG.
FOR LIFE.

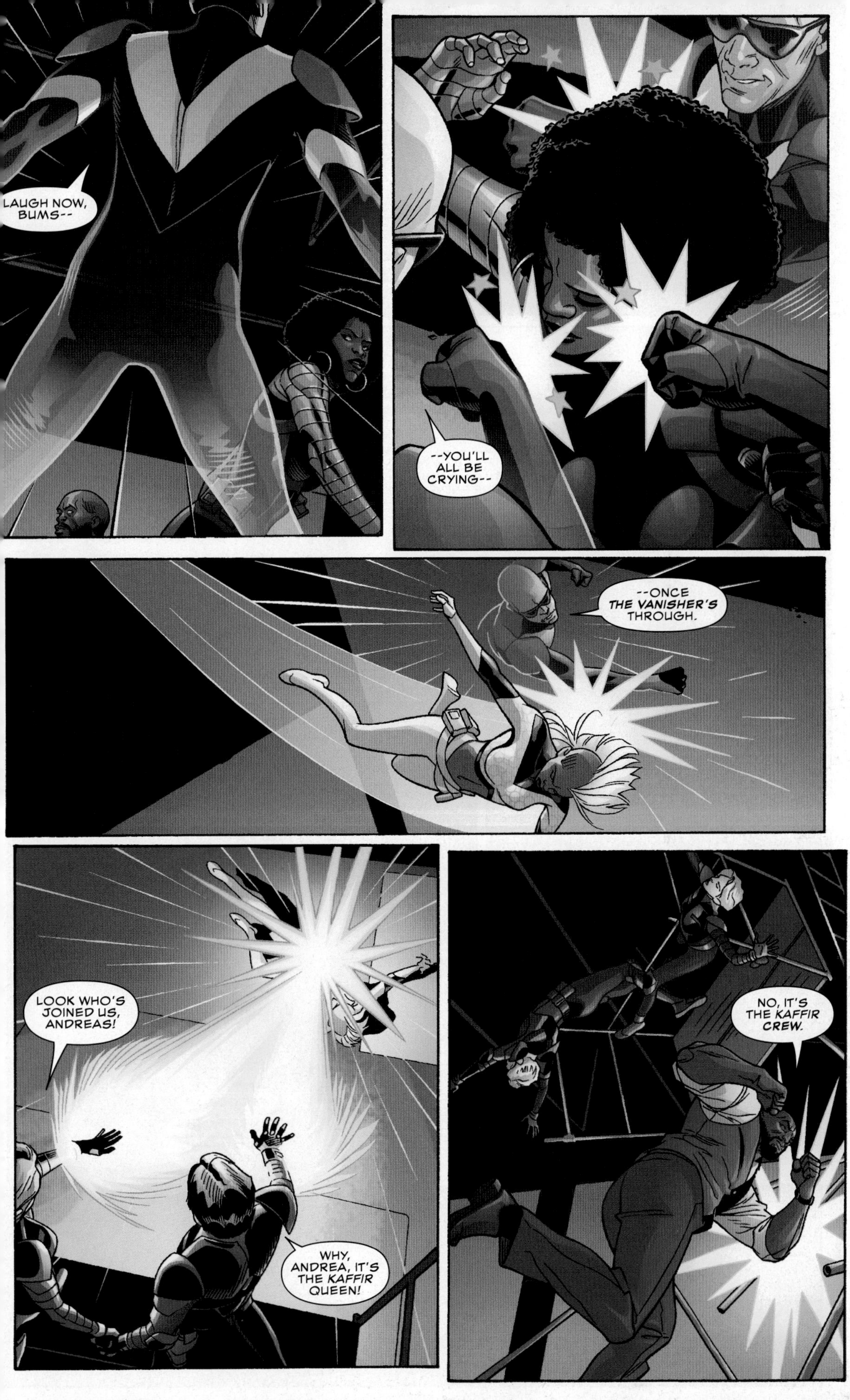
LAUGH NOW, BUMS--
--YOU'LL ALL BE CRYING--
--ONCE *THE VANISHER'S* THROUGH.
LOOK WHO'S JOINED US, ANDREAS!
WHY, ANDREA, IT'S THE *KAFFIR* QUEEN!
NO, IT'S THE *KAFFIR CREW.*

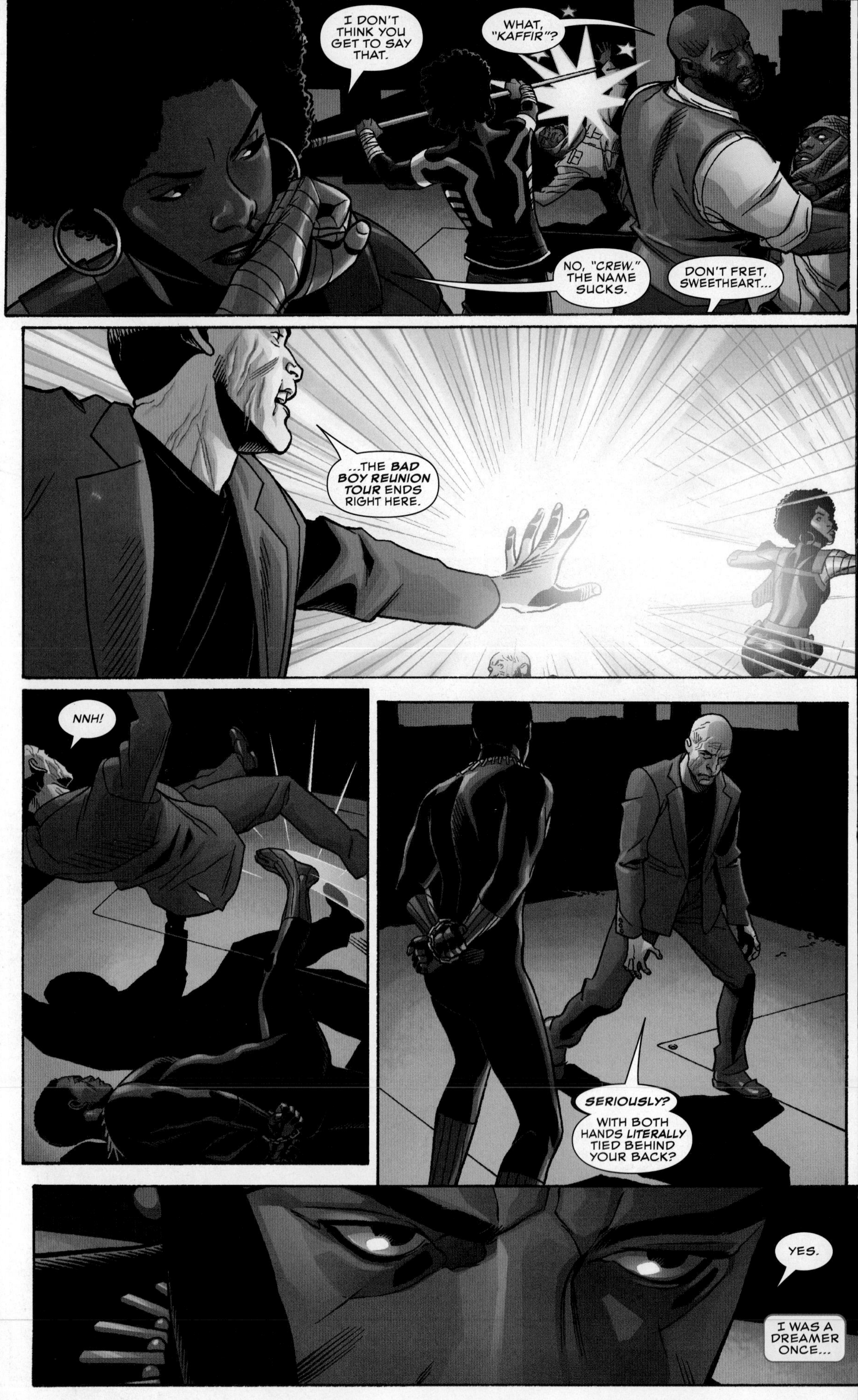
I DON'T THINK YOU GET TO SAY THAT.
WHAT, "KAFFIR"?
NO, "CREW." THE NAME SUCKS.
DON'T FRET, SWEETHEART...
...THE BAD BOY REUNION TOUR ENDS RIGHT HERE.
NNH!
SERIOUSLY? WITH BOTH HANDS LITERALLY TIED BEHIND YOUR BACK?
YES.
I WAS A DREAMER ONCE...

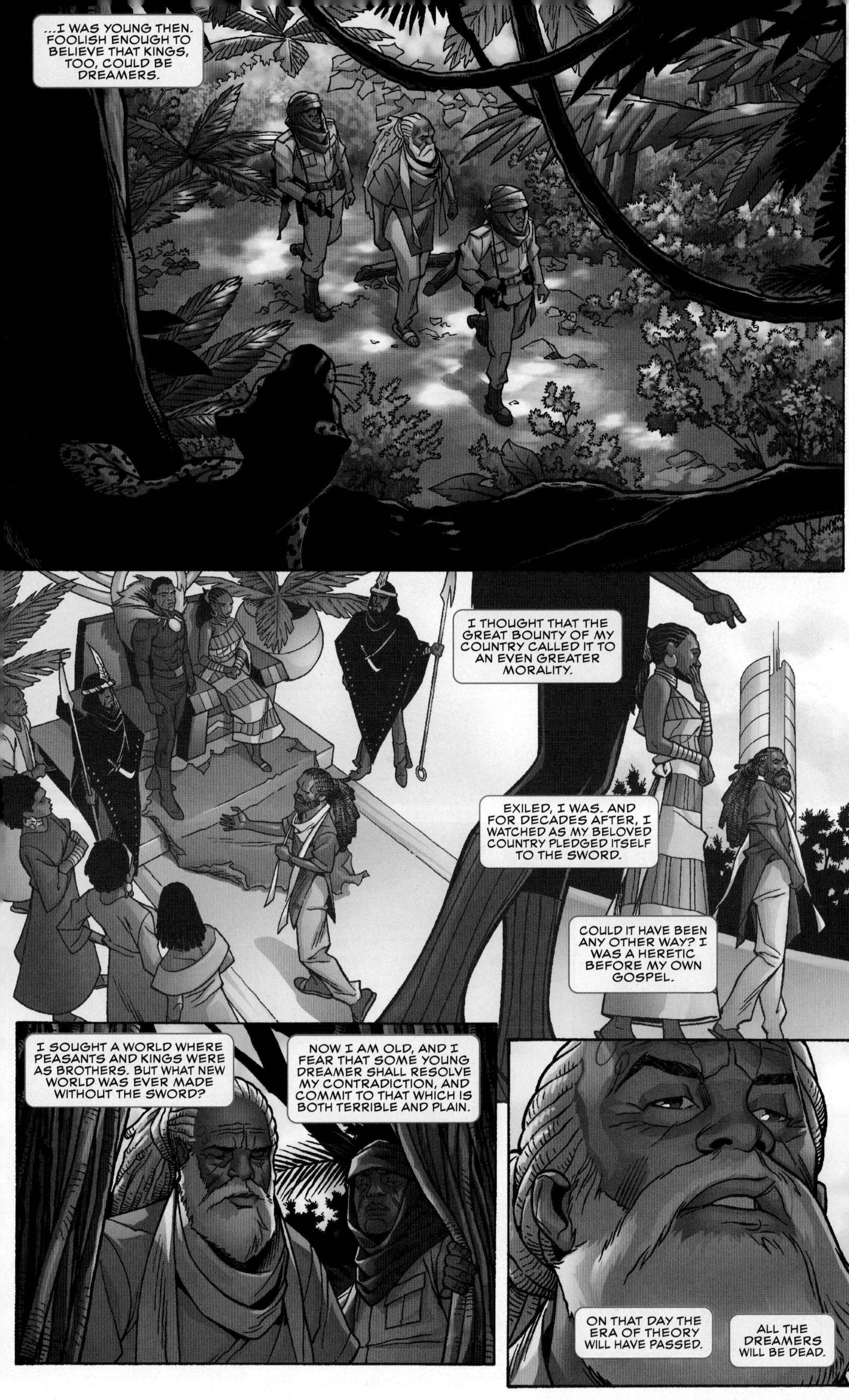
...I WAS YOUNG THEN. FOOLISH ENOUGH TO BELIEVE THAT KINGS, TOO, COULD BE DREAMERS.
I THOUGHT THAT THE GREAT BOUNTY OF MY COUNTRY CALLED IT TO AN EVEN GREATER MORALITY.
EXILED, I WAS. AND FOR DECADES AFTER, I WATCHED AS MY BELOVED COUNTRY PLEDGED ITSELF TO THE SWORD.
COULD IT HAVE BEEN ANY OTHER WAY? I WAS A HERETIC BEFORE MY OWN GOSPEL.
I SOUGHT A WORLD WHERE PEASANTS AND KINGS WERE AS BROTHERS. BUT WHAT NEW WORLD WAS EVER MADE WITHOUT THE SWORD?
NOW I AM OLD, AND I FEAR THAT SOME YOUNG DREAMER SHALL RESOLVE MY CONTRADICTION, AND COMMIT TO THAT WHICH IS BOTH TERRIBLE AND PLAIN.
ON THAT DAY THE ERA OF THEORY WILL HAVE PASSED.
ALL THE DREAMERS WILL BE DEAD.

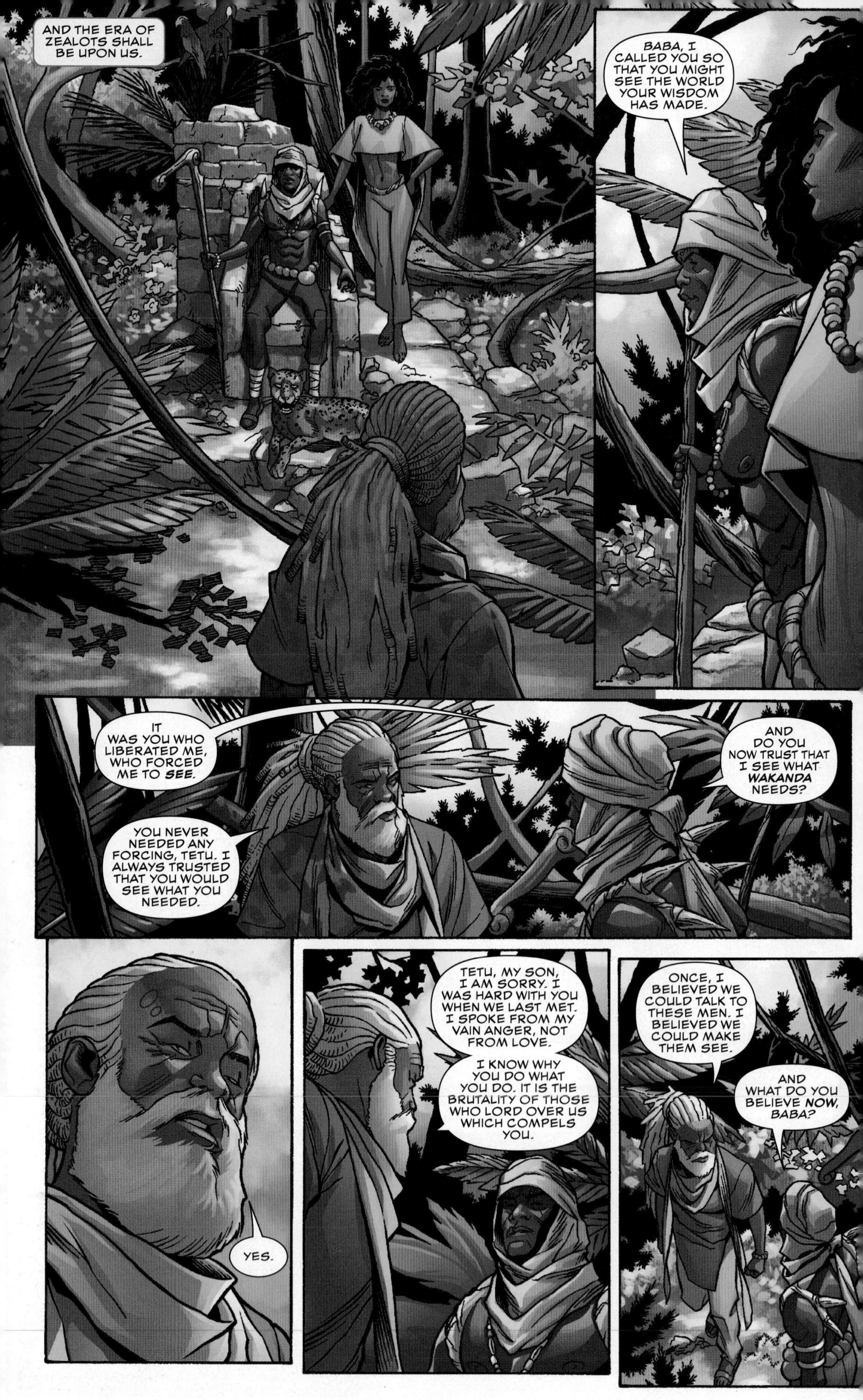
AND THE ERA OF ZEALOTS SHALL BE UPON US.
BABA, I CALLED YOU SO THAT YOU MIGHT SEE THE WORLD YOUR WISDOM HAS MADE.
IT WAS YOU WHO LIBERATED ME, WHO FORCED ME TO SEE.
AND DO YOU NOW TRUST THAT I SEE WHAT WAKANDA NEEDS?
YOU NEVER NEEDED ANY FORCING, TETU. I ALWAYS TRUSTED THAT YOU WOULD SEE WHAT YOU NEEDED.
YES.
TETU, MY SON, I AM SORRY. I WAS HARD WITH YOU WHEN WE LAST MET. I SPOKE FROM MY VAIN ANGER, NOT FROM LOVE.
I KNOW WHY YOU DO WHAT YOU DO. IT IS THE BRUTALITY OF THOSE WHO LORD OVER US WHICH COMPELS YOU.
ONCE, I BELIEVED WE COULD TALK TO THESE MEN. I BELIEVED WE COULD MAKE THEM SEE.
AND WHAT DO YOU BELIEVE NOW, BABA?

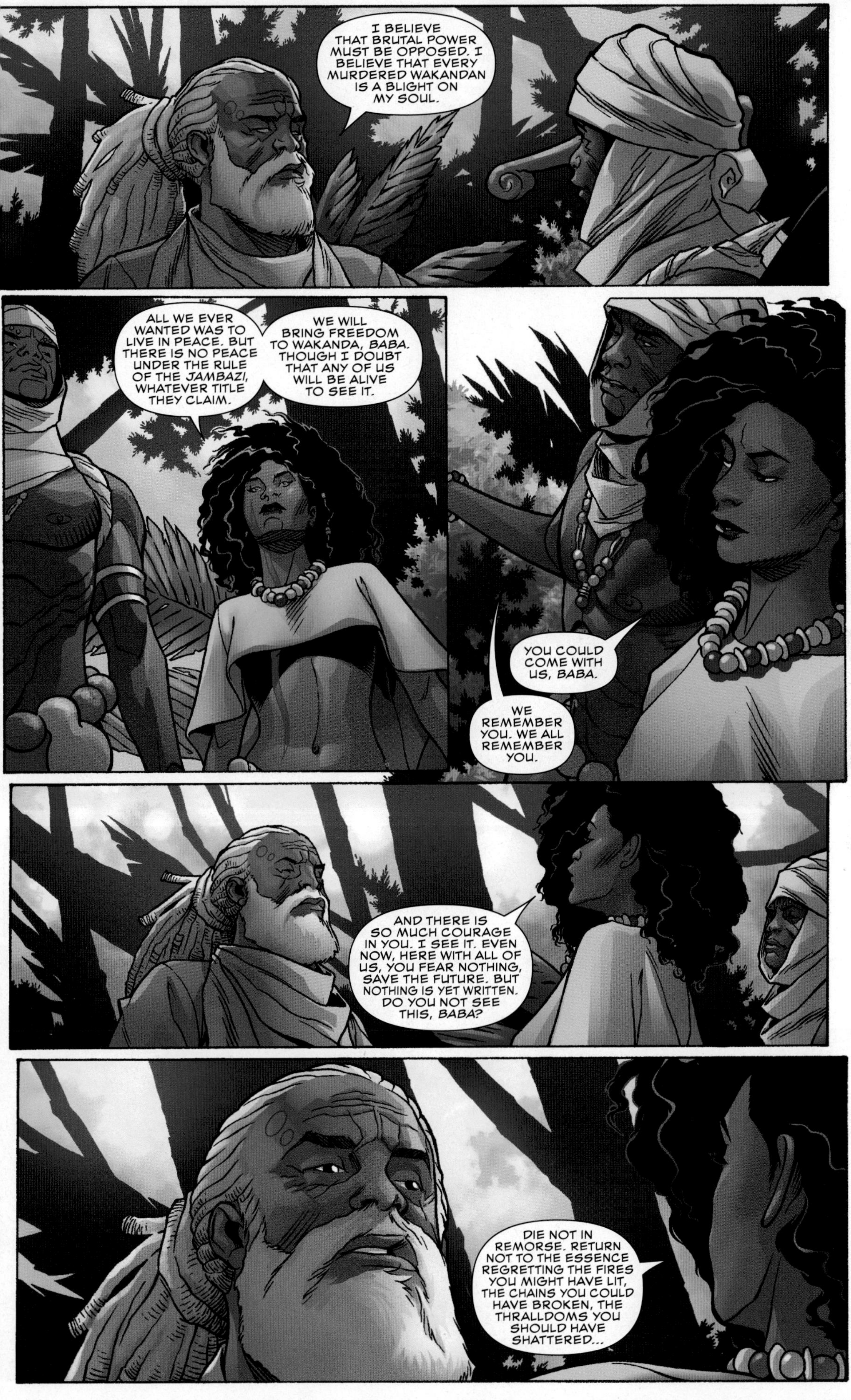
I BELIEVE THAT BRUTAL POWER MUST BE OPPOSED. I BELIEVE THAT EVERY MURDERED WAKANDAN IS A BLIGHT ON MY SOUL.
ALL WE EVER WANTED WAS TO LIVE IN PEACE. BUT THERE IS NO PEACE UNDER THE RULE OF THE *JAMBAZI*, WHATEVER TITLE THEY CLAIM.
WE WILL BRING FREEDOM TO WAKANDA, *BABA*. THOUGH I DOUBT THAT ANY OF US WILL BE ALIVE TO SEE IT.
YOU COULD COME WITH US, *BABA*.
WE REMEMBER YOU. WE ALL REMEMBER YOU.
AND THERE IS SO MUCH COURAGE IN YOU. I SEE IT. EVEN NOW, HERE WITH ALL OF US, YOU FEAR NOTHING, SAVE THE FUTURE. BUT NOTHING IS YET WRITTEN. DO YOU NOT SEE THIS, *BABA*?
DIE NOT IN REMORSE. RETURN NOT TO THE ESSENCE REGRETTING THE FIRES YOU MIGHT HAVE LIT, THE CHAINS YOU COULD HAVE BROKEN, THE THRALLDOMS YOU SHOULD HAVE SHATTERED...

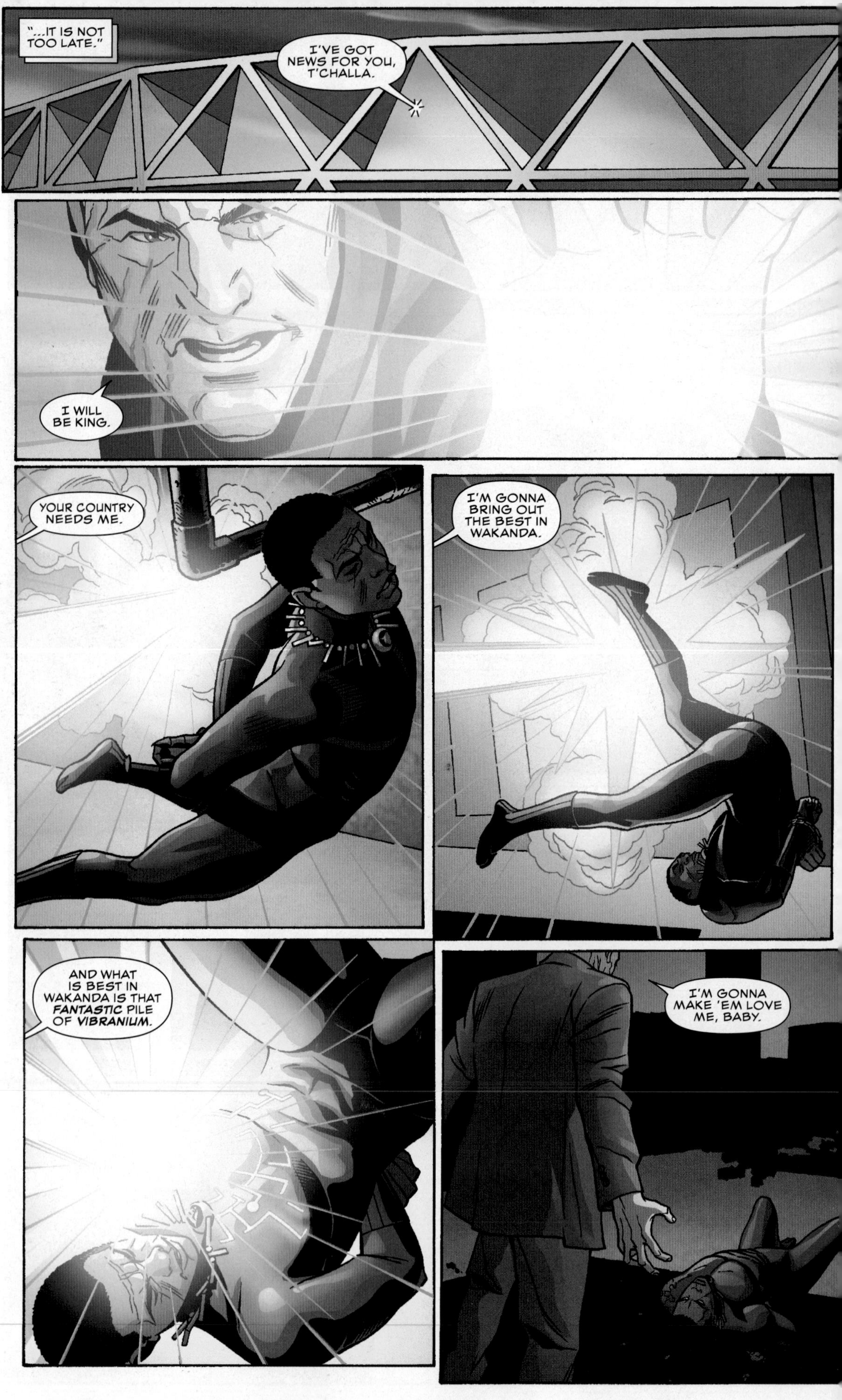
"...IT IS NOT TOO LATE."
I'VE GOT NEWS FOR YOU, T'CHALLA.
I WILL BE KING.
YOUR COUNTRY NEEDS ME.
I'M GONNA BRING OUT THE BEST IN WAKANDA.
AND WHAT IS BEST IN WAKANDA IS THAT *FANTASTIC* PILE OF **VIBRANIUM**.
I'M GONNA MAKE 'EM LOVE ME, BABY.

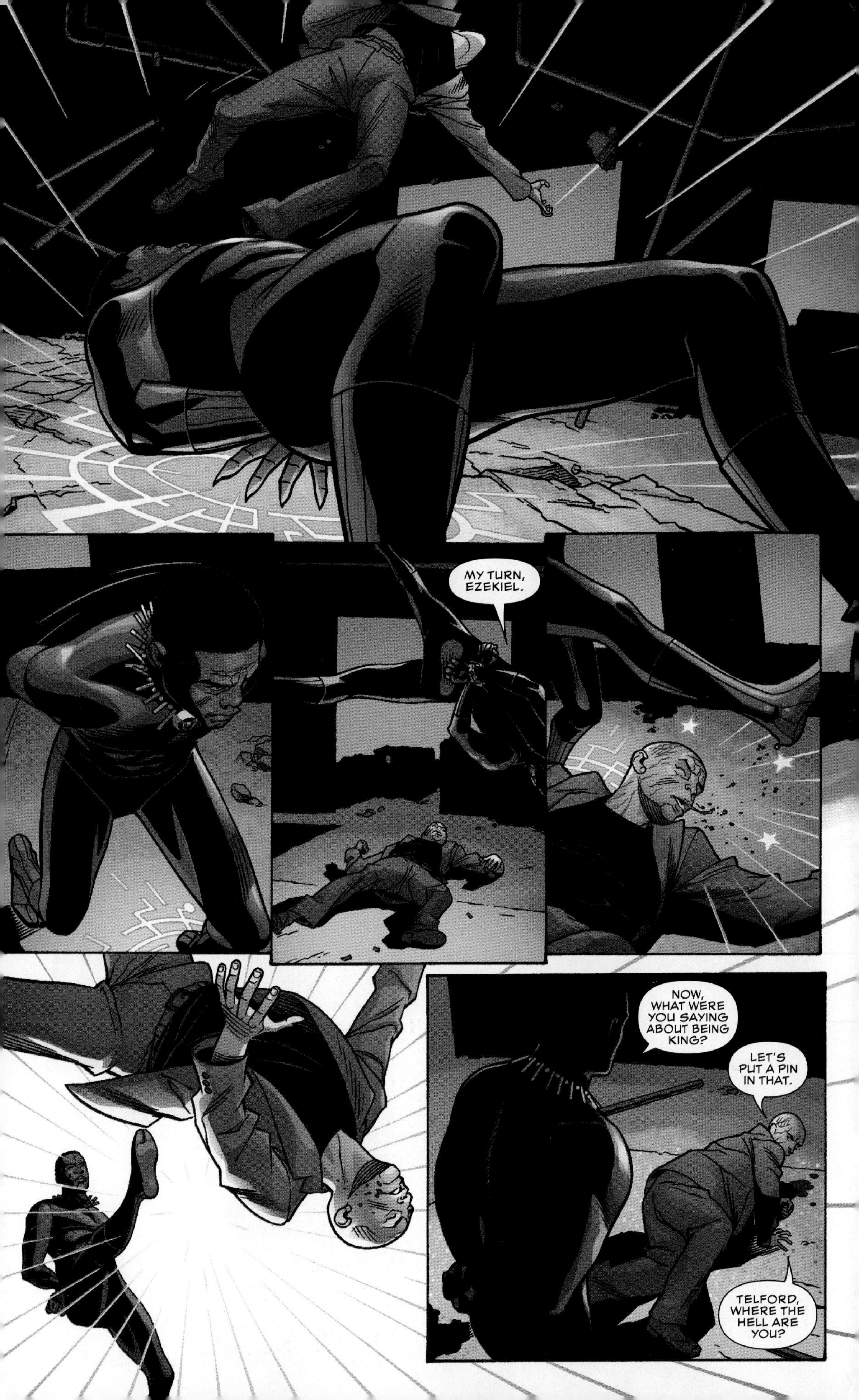
MY TURN, EZEKIEL.
NOW, WHAT WERE YOU SAYING ABOUT BEING KING?
LET'S PUT A PIN IN THAT.
TELFORD, WHERE THE HELL ARE YOU?

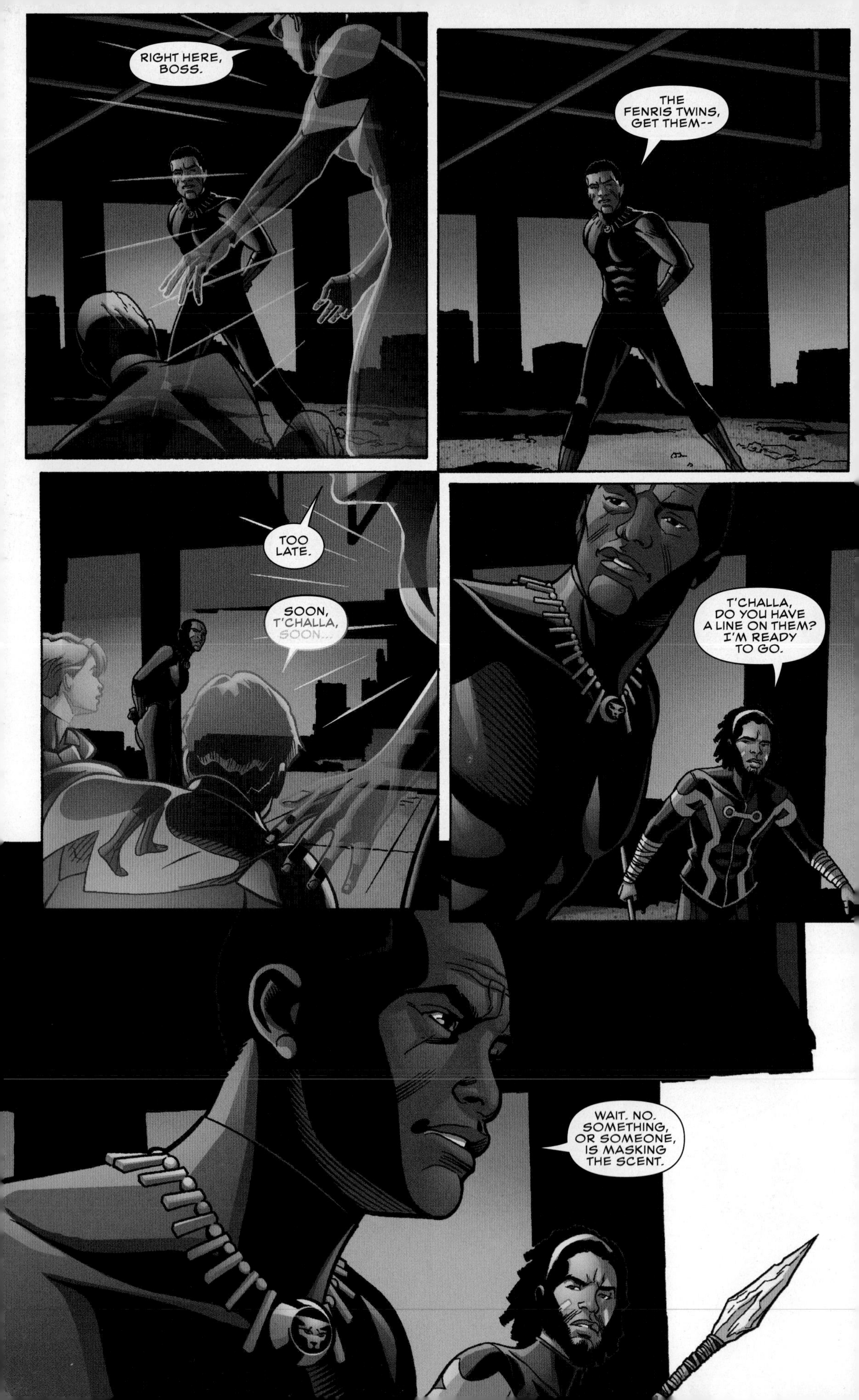
RIGHT HERE, BOSS.
THE FENRIS TWINS, GET THEM--
TOO LATE.
SOON, T'CHALLA, SOON...
T'CHALLA, DO YOU HAVE A LINE ON THEM? I'M READY TO GO.
WAIT. NO. SOMETHING, OR SOMEONE, IS MASKING THE SCENT.

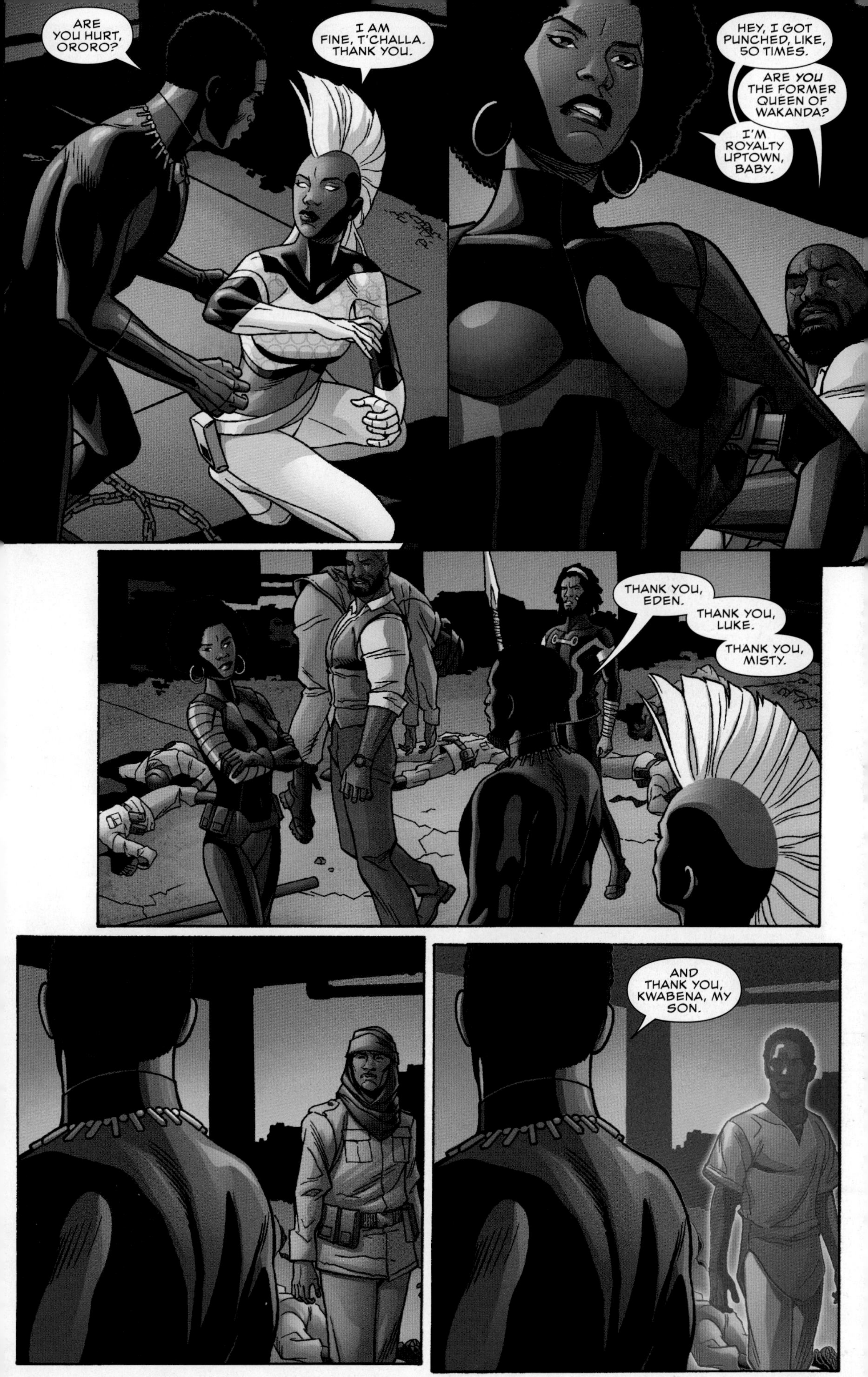
ARE YOU HURT, ORORO?
I AM FINE, T'CHALLA. THANK YOU.
HEY, I GOT PUNCHED, LIKE, 50 TIMES.
ARE YOU THE FORMER QUEEN OF WAKANDA?
I'M ROYALTY UPTOWN, BABY.
THANK YOU, EDEN.
THANK YOU, LUKE.
THANK YOU, MISTY.
AND THANK YOU, KWABENA, MY SON.

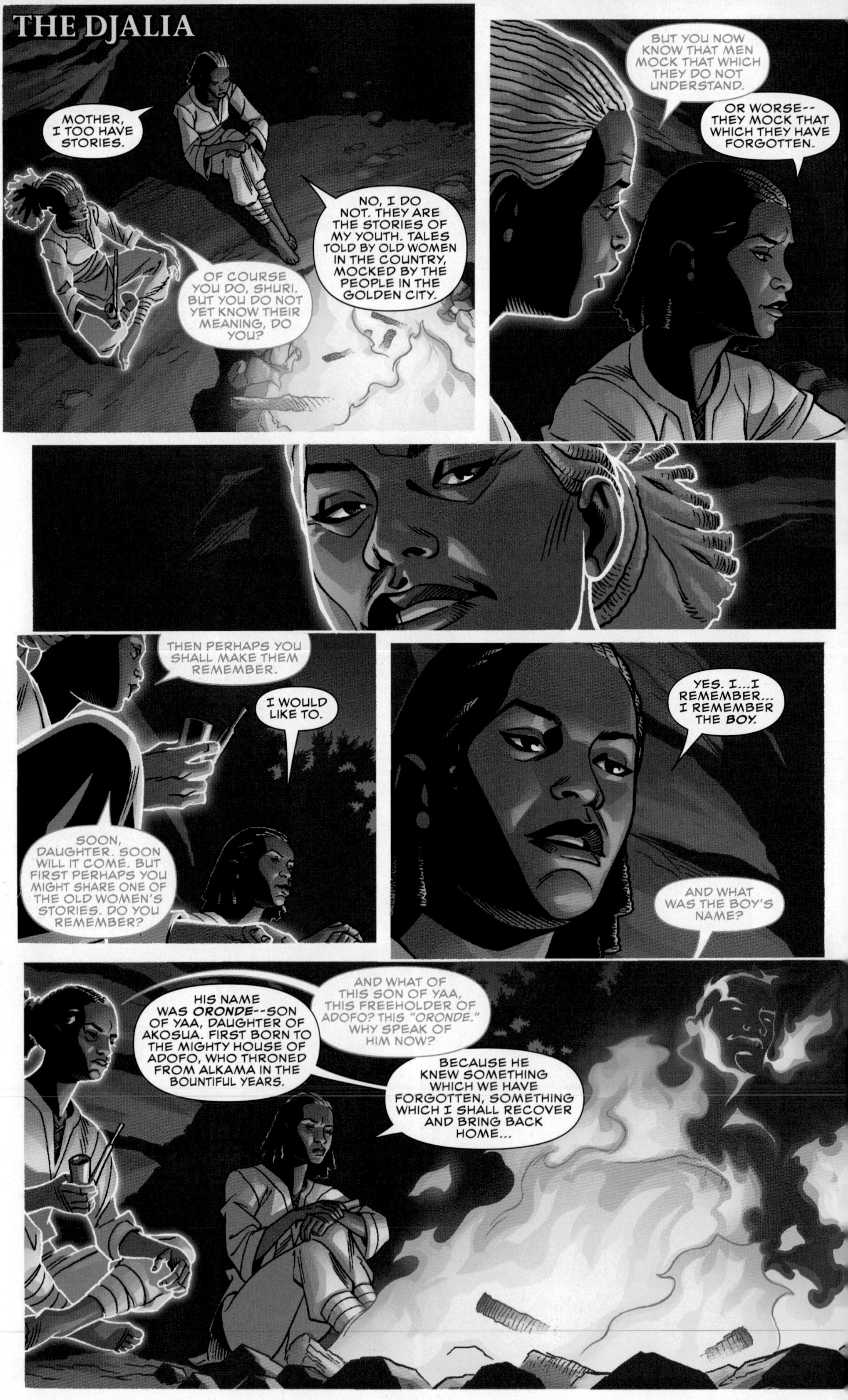
THE DJALIA
MOTHER, I TOO HAVE STORIES.
OF COURSE YOU DO, SHURI. BUT YOU DO NOT YET KNOW THEIR MEANING, DO YOU?
NO, I DO NOT. THEY ARE THE STORIES OF MY YOUTH. TALES TOLD BY OLD WOMEN IN THE COUNTRY, MOCKED BY THE PEOPLE IN THE GOLDEN CITY.
BUT YOU NOW KNOW THAT MEN MOCK THAT WHICH THEY DO NOT UNDERSTAND.
OR WORSE--THEY MOCK THAT WHICH THEY HAVE FORGOTTEN.
THEN PERHAPS YOU SHALL MAKE THEM REMEMBER.
I WOULD LIKE TO.
SOON, DAUGHTER. SOON WILL IT COME. BUT FIRST PERHAPS YOU MIGHT SHARE ONE OF THE OLD WOMEN'S STORIES. DO YOU REMEMBER?
YES. I...I REMEMBER... I REMEMBER THE BOY.
AND WHAT WAS THE BOY'S NAME?
HIS NAME WAS ORONDE--SON OF YAA, DAUGHTER OF AKOSUA. FIRST BORN TO THE MIGHTY HOUSE OF ADOFO, WHO THRONED FROM ALKAMA IN THE BOUNTIFUL YEARS.
AND WHAT OF THIS SON OF YAA, THIS FREEHOLDER OF ADOFO? THIS "ORONDE." WHY SPEAK OF HIM NOW?
BECAUSE HE KNEW SOMETHING WHICH WE HAVE FORGOTTEN, SOMETHING WHICH I SHALL RECOVER AND BRING BACK HOME...

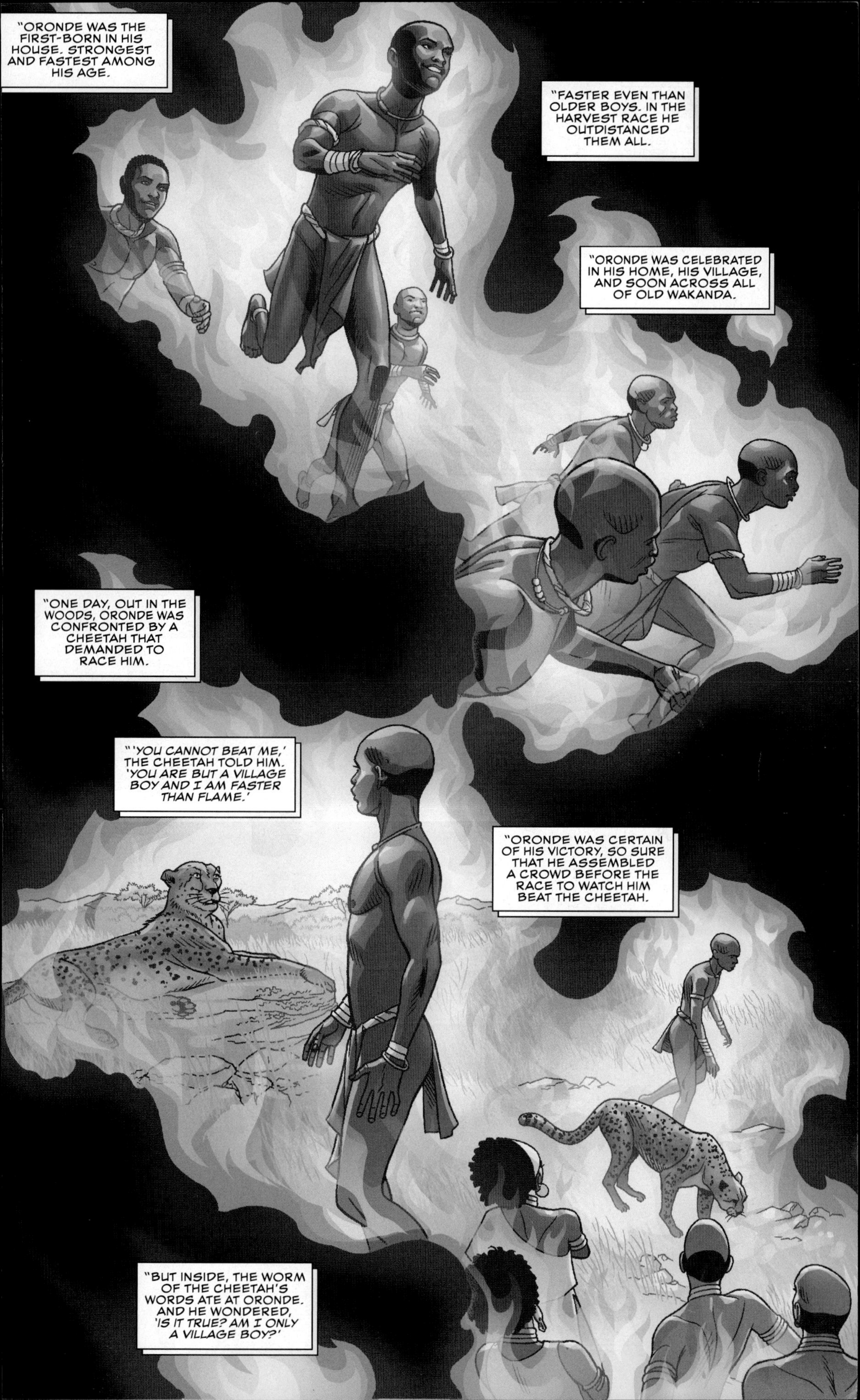
"ORONDE WAS THE FIRST-BORN IN HIS HOUSE. STRONGEST AND FASTEST AMONG HIS AGE.
"FASTER EVEN THAN OLDER BOYS. IN THE HARVEST RACE HE OUTDISTANCED THEM ALL.
"ORONDE WAS CELEBRATED IN HIS HOME, HIS VILLAGE, AND SOON ACROSS ALL OF OLD WAKANDA.
"ONE DAY, OUT IN THE WOODS, ORONDE WAS CONFRONTED BY A CHEETAH THAT DEMANDED TO RACE HIM.
"'YOU CANNOT BEAT ME,' THE CHEETAH TOLD HIM. 'YOU ARE BUT A VILLAGE BOY AND I AM FASTER THAN FLAME.'
"ORONDE WAS CERTAIN OF HIS VICTORY, SO SURE THAT HE ASSEMBLED A CROWD BEFORE THE RACE TO WATCH HIM BEAT THE CHEETAH.
"BUT INSIDE, THE WORM OF THE CHEETAH'S WORDS ATE AT ORONDE. AND HE WONDERED, 'IS IT TRUE? AM I ONLY A VILLAGE BOY?'

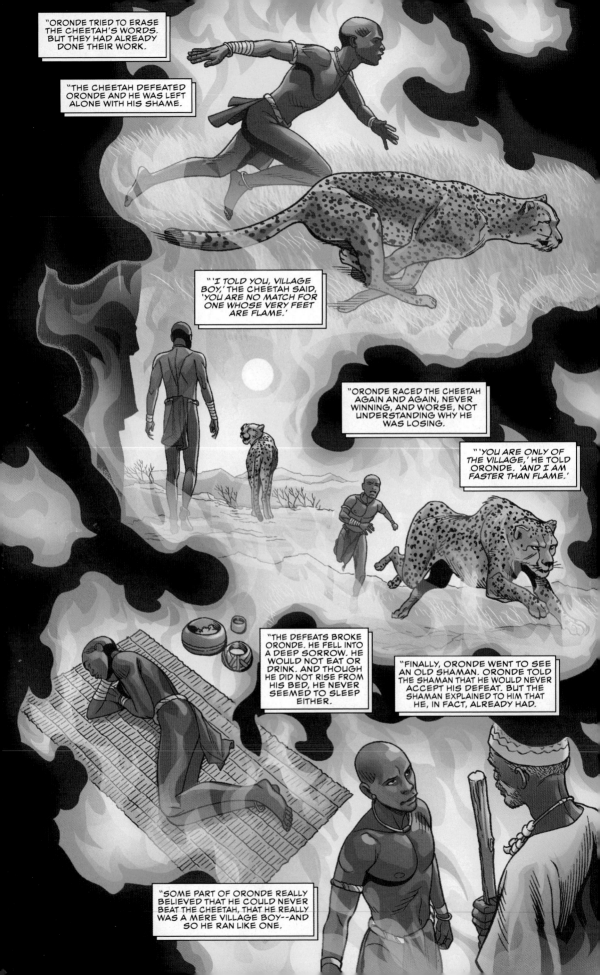

"ORONDE TRIED TO ERASE THE CHEETAH'S WORDS. BUT THEY HAD ALREADY DONE THEIR WORK.

"THE CHEETAH DEFEATED ORONDE AND HE WAS LEFT ALONE WITH HIS SHAME.

"'I TOLD YOU, VILLAGE BOY,' THE CHEETAH SAID, 'YOU ARE NO MATCH FOR ONE WHOSE VERY FEET ARE FLAME.'

"ORONDE RACED THE CHEETAH AGAIN AND AGAIN, NEVER WINNING, AND WORSE, NOT UNDERSTANDING WHY HE WAS LOSING.

"'YOU ARE ONLY OF THE VILLAGE,' HE TOLD ORONDE. 'AND I AM FASTER THAN FLAME.'

"THE DEFEATS BROKE ORONDE. HE FELL INTO A DEEP SORROW. HE WOULD NOT EAT OR DRINK. AND THOUGH HE DID NOT RISE FROM HIS BED, HE NEVER SEEMED TO SLEEP EITHER.

"FINALLY, ORONDE WENT TO SEE AN OLD SHAMAN. ORONDE TOLD THE SHAMAN THAT HE WOULD NEVER ACCEPT HIS DEFEAT. BUT THE SHAMAN EXPLAINED TO HIM THAT HE, IN FACT, ALREADY HAD.

"SOME PART OF ORONDE REALLY BELIEVED THAT HE COULD NEVER BEAT THE CHEETAH, THAT HE REALLY WAS A MERE VILLAGE BOY--AND SO HE RAN LIKE ONE.

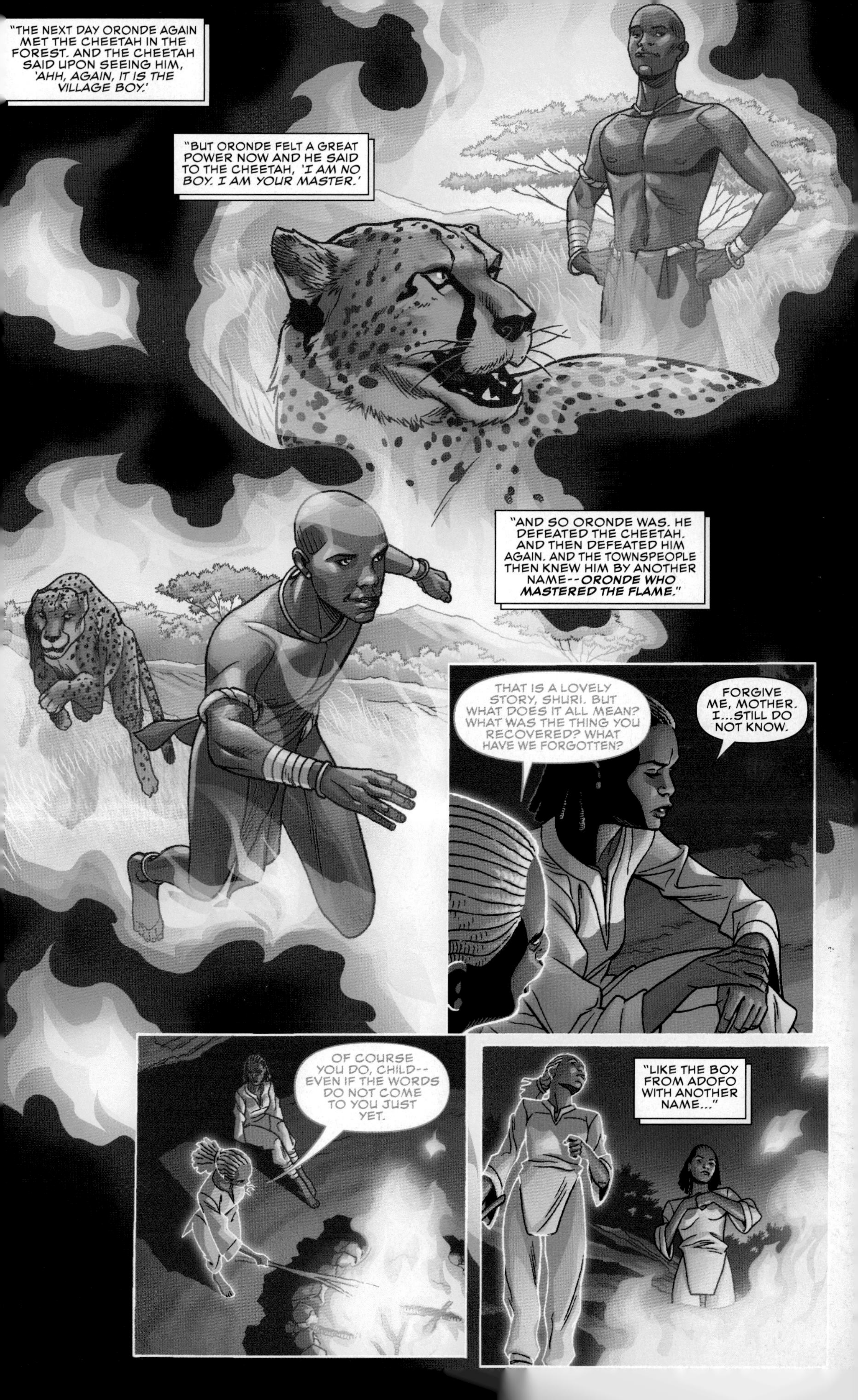
"THE NEXT DAY ORONDE AGAIN MET THE CHEETAH IN THE FOREST. AND THE CHEETAH SAID UPON SEEING HIM, 'AHH, AGAIN, IT IS THE VILLAGE BOY.'
"BUT ORONDE FELT A GREAT POWER NOW AND HE SAID TO THE CHEETAH, 'I AM NO BOY. I AM YOUR MASTER.'
"AND SO ORONDE WAS. HE DEFEATED THE CHEETAH. AND THEN DEFEATED HIM AGAIN. AND THE TOWNSPEOPLE THEN KNEW HIM BY ANOTHER NAME--ORONDE WHO MASTERED THE FLAME."
THAT IS A LOVELY STORY, SHURI. BUT WHAT DOES IT ALL MEAN? WHAT WAS THE THING YOU RECOVERED? WHAT HAVE WE FORGOTTEN?
FORGIVE ME, MOTHER. I...STILL DO NOT KNOW.
OF COURSE YOU DO, CHILD-- EVEN IF THE WORDS DO NOT COME TO YOU JUST YET.
"LIKE THE BOY FROM ADOFO WITH ANOTHER NAME..."

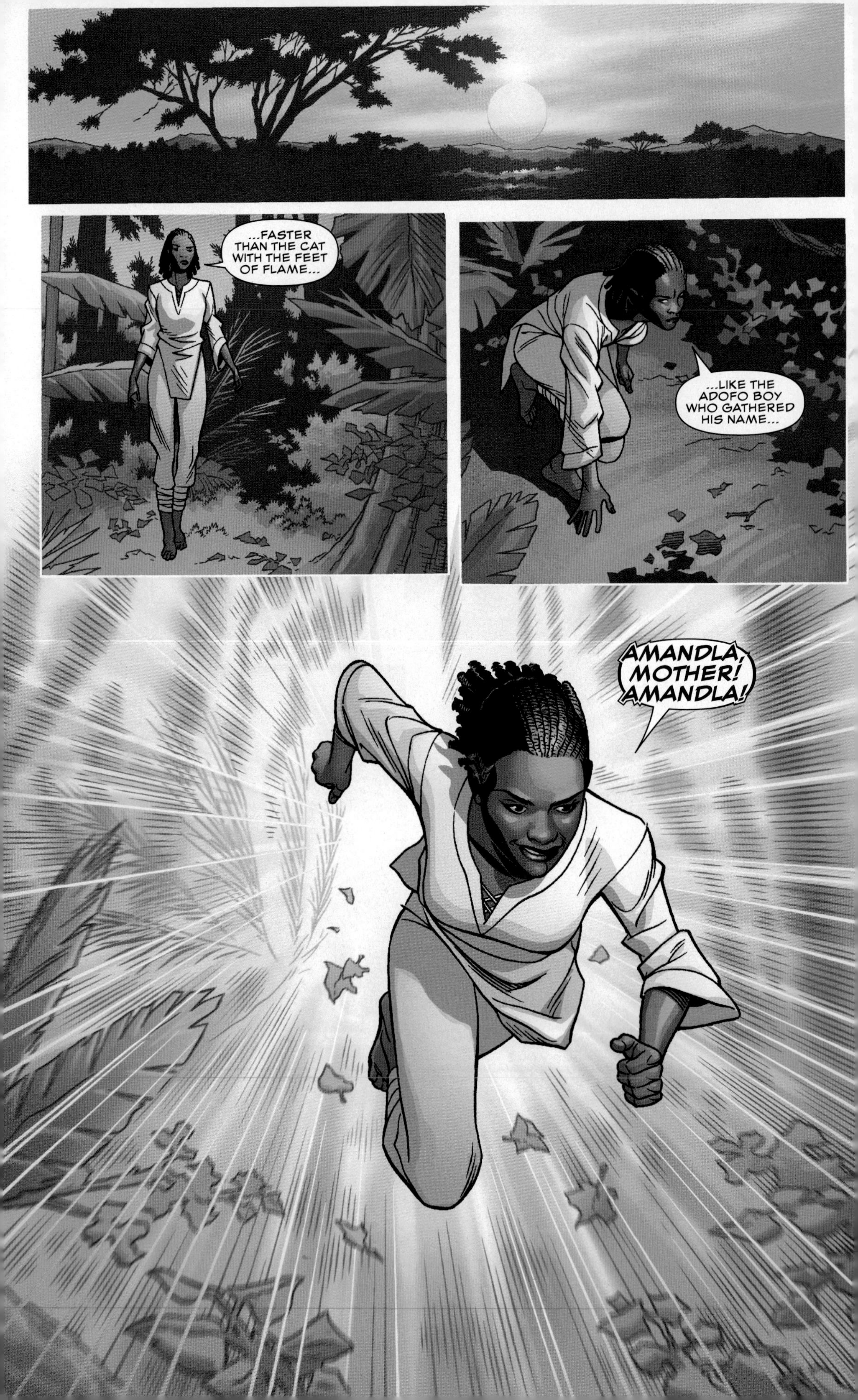
...FASTER THAN THE CAT WITH THE FEET OF FLAME...
...LIKE THE ADOFO BOY WHO GATHERED HIS NAME...
AMANDLA, MOTHER! AMANDLA!

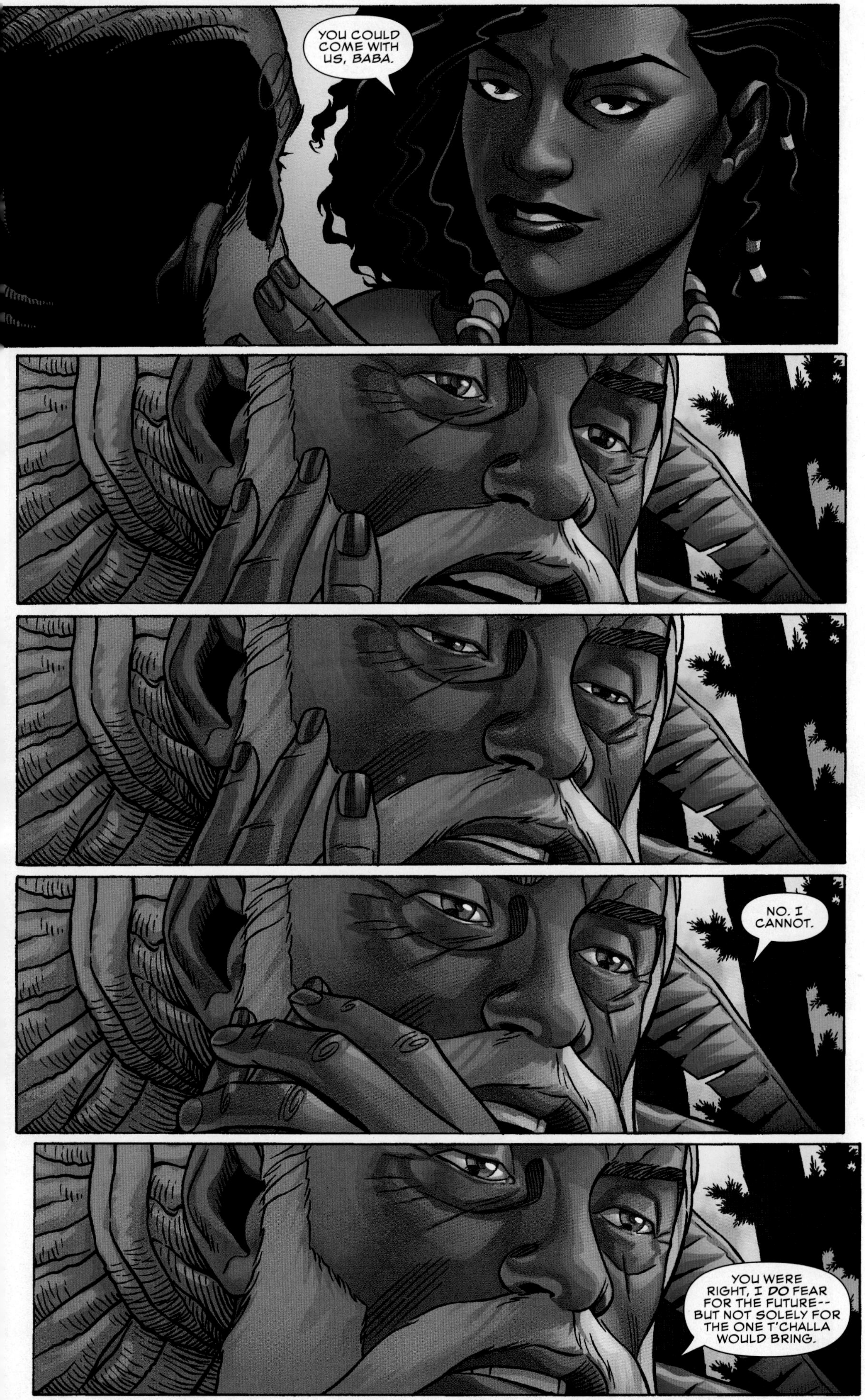
YOU COULD COME WITH US, BABA.
NO. I CANNOT.
YOU WERE RIGHT, I *DO* FEAR FOR THE FUTURE-- BUT NOT SOLELY FOR THE ONE T'CHALLA WOULD BRING.

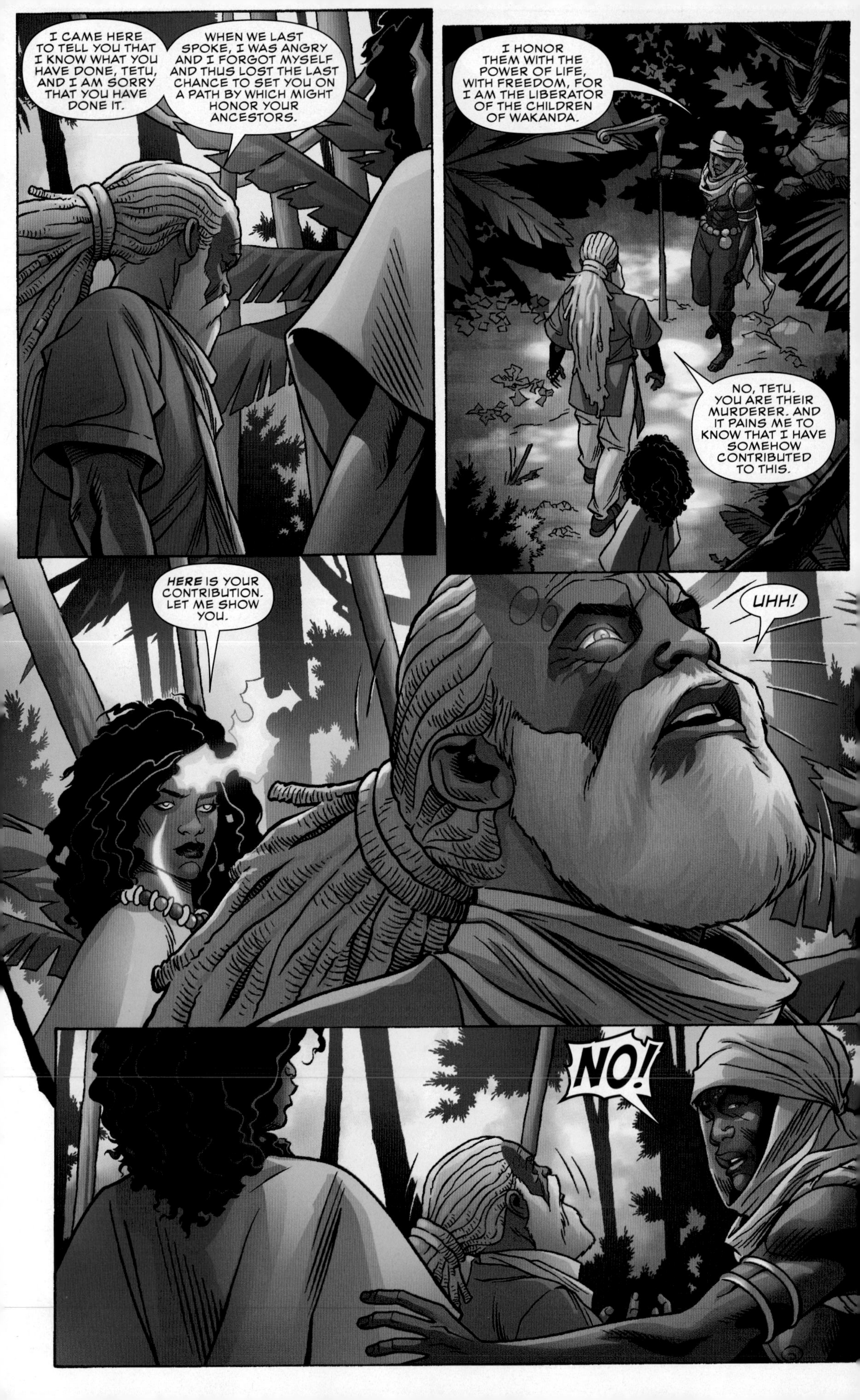

I CAME HERE TO TELL YOU THAT I KNOW WHAT YOU HAVE DONE, TETU, AND I AM SORRY THAT YOU HAVE DONE IT.
WHEN WE LAST SPOKE, I WAS ANGRY AND I FORGOT MYSELF AND THUS LOST THE LAST CHANCE TO SET YOU ON A PATH BY WHICH MIGHT HONOR YOUR ANCESTORS.
I HONOR THEM WITH THE POWER OF LIFE, WITH FREEDOM, FOR I AM THE LIBERATOR OF THE CHILDREN OF WAKANDA.
NO, TETU. YOU ARE THEIR MURDERER. AND IT PAINS ME TO KNOW THAT I HAVE SOMEHOW CONTRIBUTED TO THIS.
HERE IS YOUR CONTRIBUTION. LET ME SHOW YOU.
UHH!
NO!

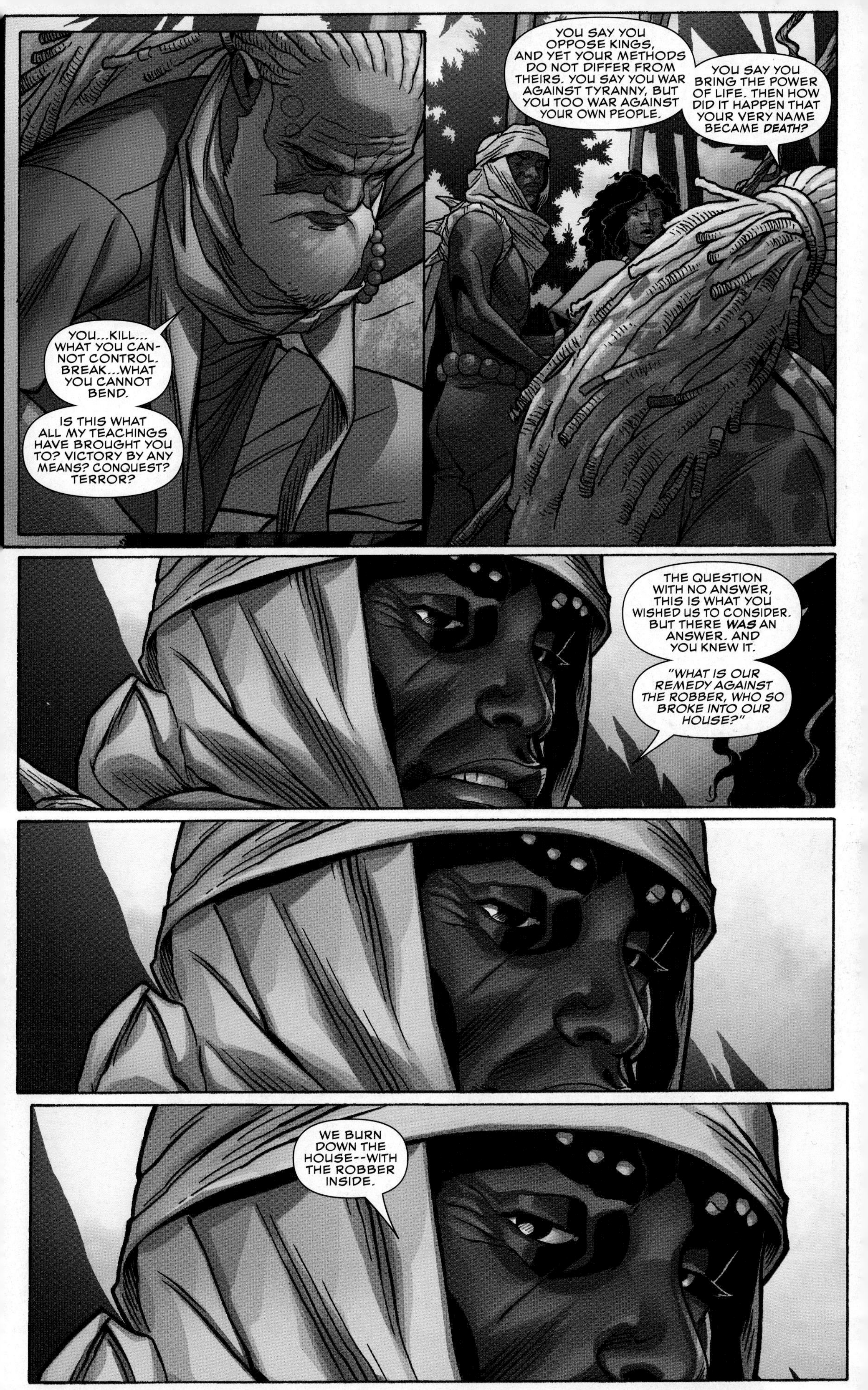
YOU...KILL... WHAT YOU CAN-NOT CONTROL. BREAK...WHAT YOU CANNOT BEND.
IS THIS WHAT ALL MY TEACHINGS HAVE BROUGHT YOU TO? VICTORY BY ANY MEANS? CONQUEST? TERROR?
YOU SAY YOU OPPOSE KINGS, AND YET YOUR METHODS DO NOT DIFFER FROM THEIRS. YOU SAY YOU WAR AGAINST TYRANNY, BUT YOU TOO WAR AGAINST YOUR OWN PEOPLE.
YOU SAY YOU BRING THE POWER OF LIFE. THEN HOW DID IT HAPPEN THAT YOUR VERY NAME BECAME *DEATH?*
THE QUESTION WITH NO ANSWER, THIS IS WHAT YOU WISHED US TO CONSIDER. BUT THERE **WAS** AN ANSWER. AND YOU KNEW IT.
"WHAT IS OUR REMEDY AGAINST THE ROBBER, WHO SO BROKE INTO OUR HOUSE?"
WE BURN DOWN THE HOUSE--WITH THE ROBBER INSIDE.

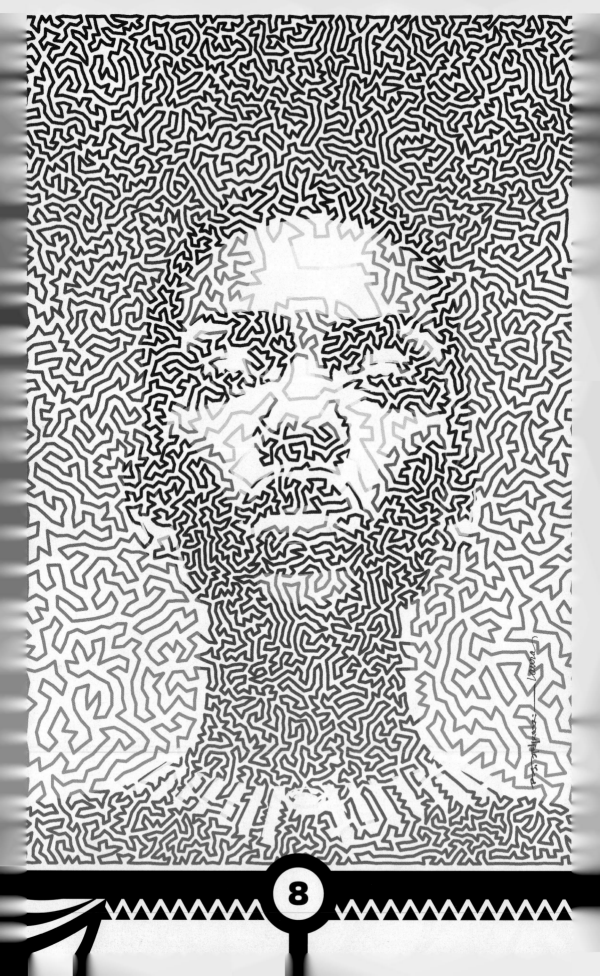

8

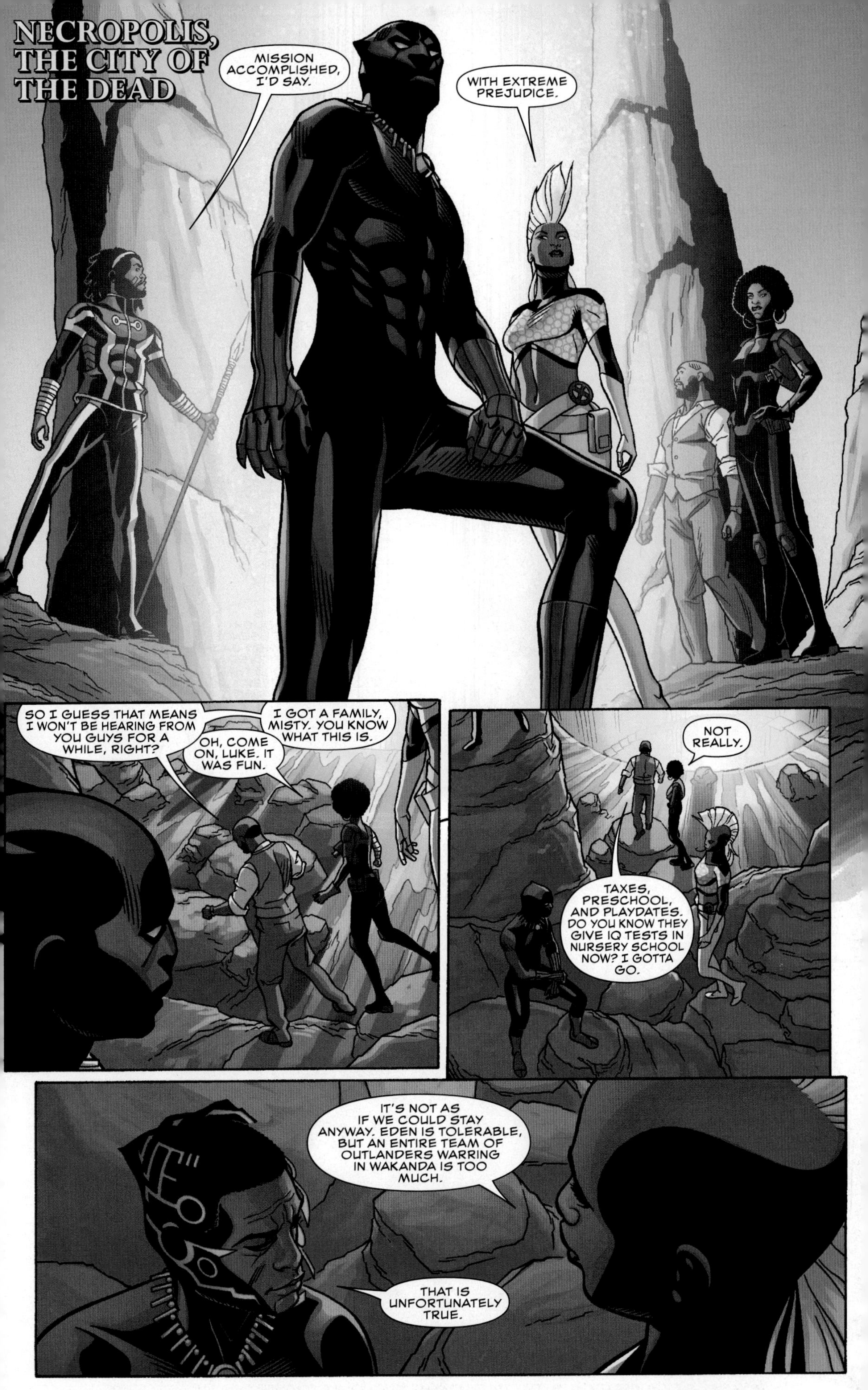
NECROPOLIS, THE CITY OF THE DEAD
MISSION ACCOMPLISHED, I'D SAY.
WITH EXTREME PREJUDICE.
SO I GUESS THAT MEANS I WON'T BE HEARING FROM YOU GUYS FOR A WHILE, RIGHT?
OH, COME ON, LUKE. IT WAS FUN.
I GOT A FAMILY, MISTY. YOU KNOW WHAT THIS IS.
NOT REALLY.
TAXES, PRESCHOOL, AND PLAYDATES. DO YOU KNOW THEY GIVE IQ TESTS IN NURSERY SCHOOL NOW? I GOTTA GO.
IT'S NOT AS IF WE COULD STAY ANYWAY. EDEN IS TOLERABLE, BUT AN ENTIRE TEAM OF OUTLANDERS WARRING IN WAKANDA IS TOO MUCH.
THAT IS UNFORTUNATELY TRUE.

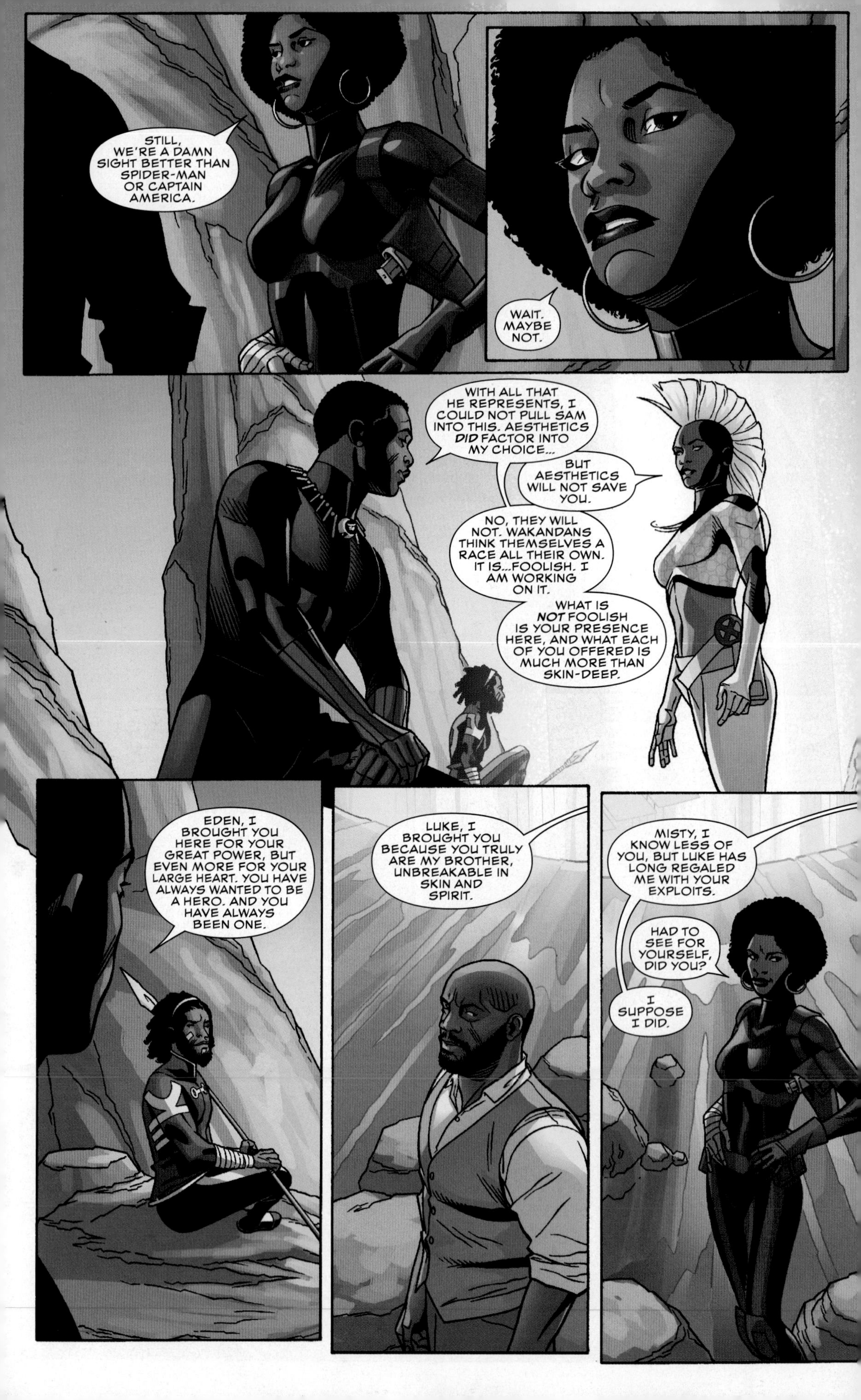
STILL, WE'RE A DAMN SIGHT BETTER THAN SPIDER-MAN OR CAPTAIN AMERICA.
WAIT. MAYBE NOT.
WITH ALL THAT HE REPRESENTS, I COULD NOT PULL SAM INTO THIS. AESTHETICS *DID* FACTOR INTO MY CHOICE...
BUT AESTHETICS WILL NOT SAVE YOU.
NO, THEY WILL NOT. WAKANDANS THINK THEMSELVES A RACE ALL THEIR OWN. IT IS...FOOLISH. I AM WORKING ON IT.
WHAT IS *NOT* FOOLISH IS YOUR PRESENCE HERE, AND WHAT EACH OF YOU OFFERED IS MUCH MORE THAN SKIN-DEEP.
EDEN, I BROUGHT YOU HERE FOR YOUR GREAT POWER, BUT EVEN MORE FOR YOUR LARGE HEART. YOU HAVE ALWAYS WANTED TO BE A HERO. AND YOU HAVE ALWAYS BEEN ONE.
LUKE, I BROUGHT YOU BECAUSE YOU TRULY ARE MY BROTHER, UNBREAKABLE IN SKIN AND SPIRIT.
MISTY, I KNOW LESS OF YOU, BUT LUKE HAS LONG REGALED ME WITH YOUR EXPLOITS.
HAD TO SEE FOR YOURSELF, DID YOU?
I SUPPOSE I DID.

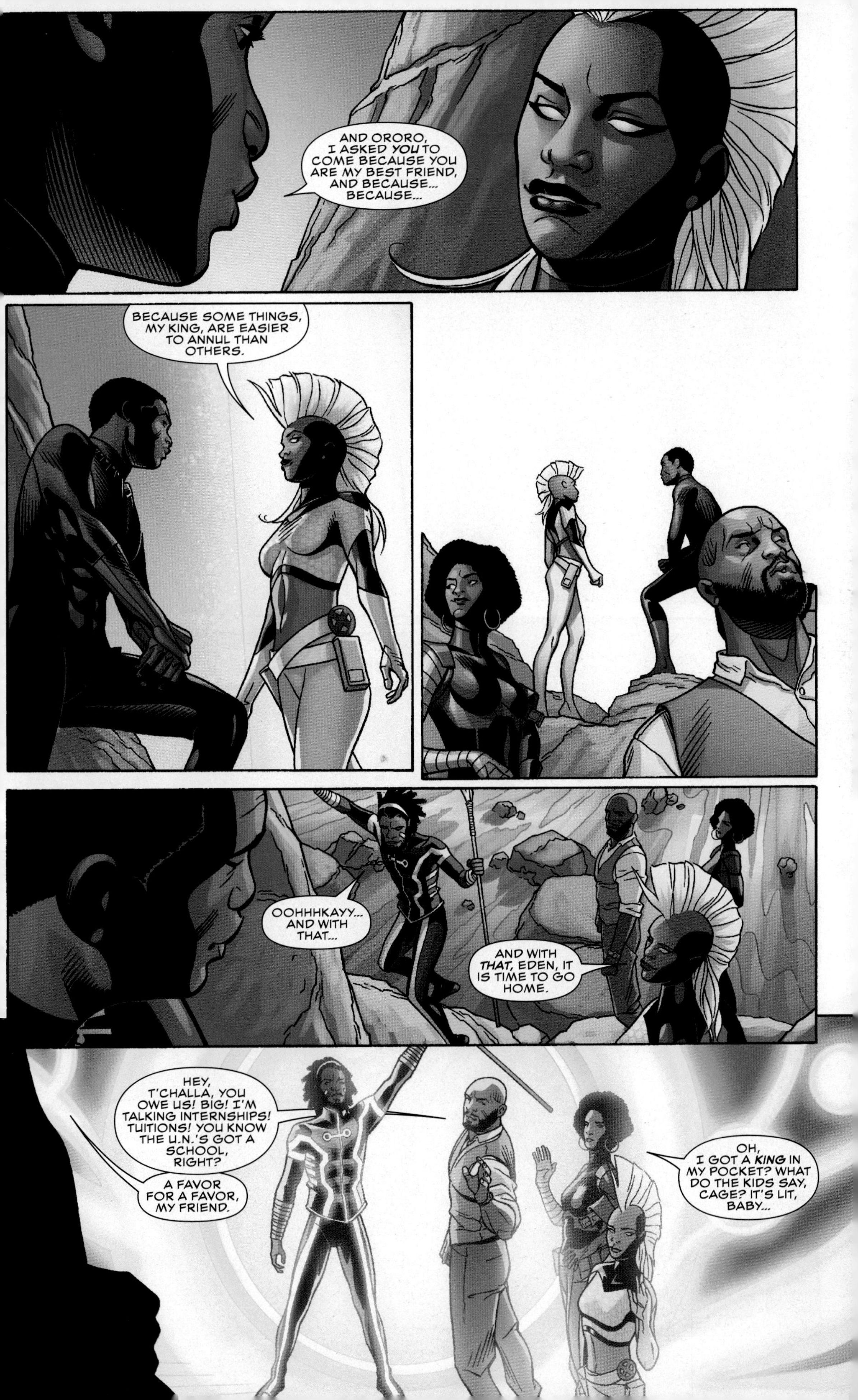
AND ORORO, I ASKED *YOU* TO COME BECAUSE YOU ARE MY BEST FRIEND, AND BECAUSE... BECAUSE...
BECAUSE SOME THINGS, MY KING, ARE EASIER TO ANNUL THAN OTHERS.
OOHHHKAYY... AND WITH THAT...
AND WITH *THAT*, EDEN, IT IS TIME TO GO HOME.
HEY, T'CHALLA, YOU OWE US! BIG! I'M TALKING INTERNSHIPS! TUITIONS! YOU KNOW THE U.N.'S GOT A SCHOOL, RIGHT?
A FAVOR FOR A FAVOR, MY FRIEND.
OH, I GOT A *KING* IN MY POCKET? WHAT DO THE KIDS SAY, CAGE? IT'S LIT, BABY...

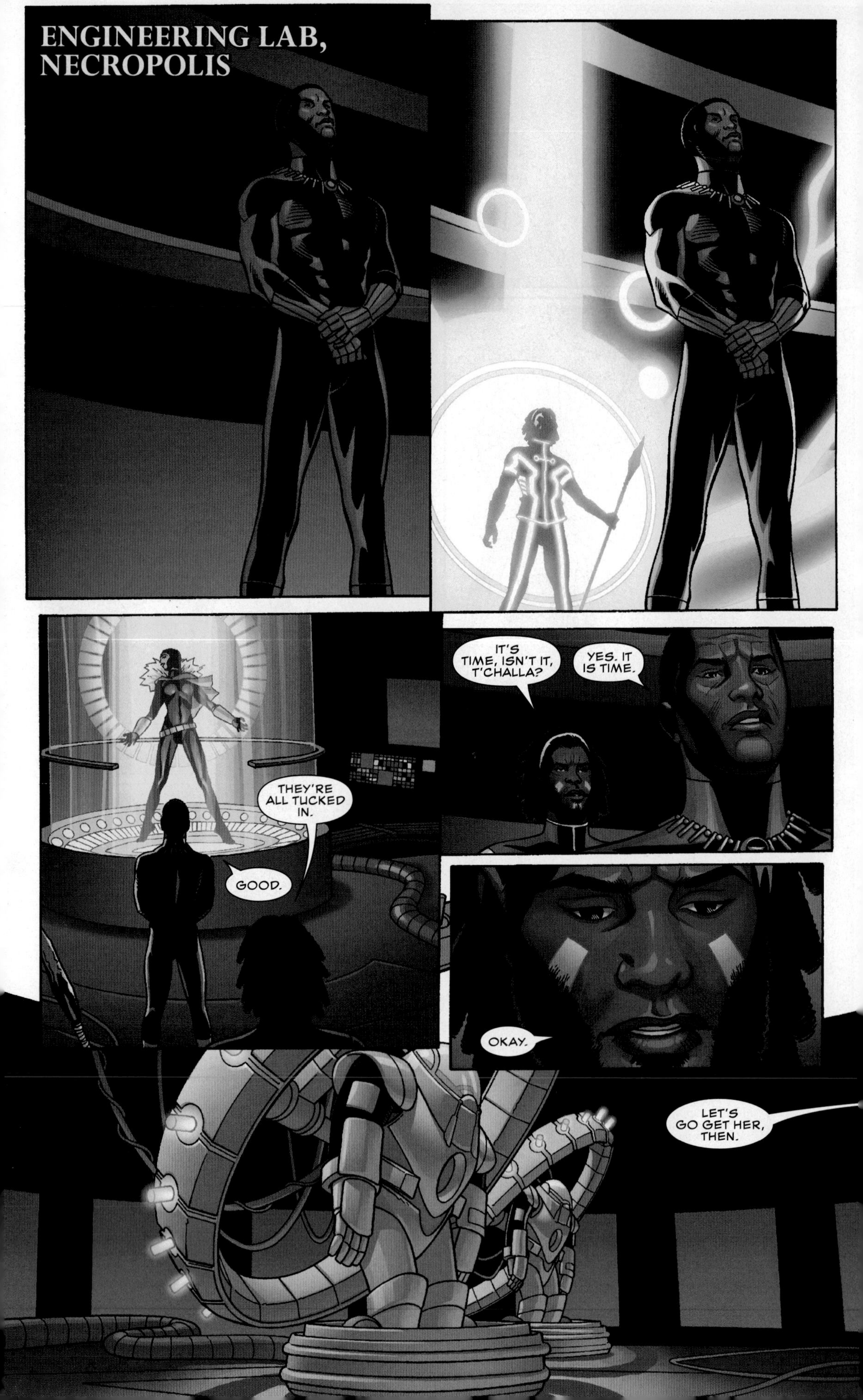

ENGINEERING LAB, NECROPOLIS
THEY'RE ALL TUCKED IN.
GOOD.
IT'S TIME, ISN'T IT, T'CHALLA?
YES. IT IS TIME.
OKAY.
LET'S GO GET HER, THEN.

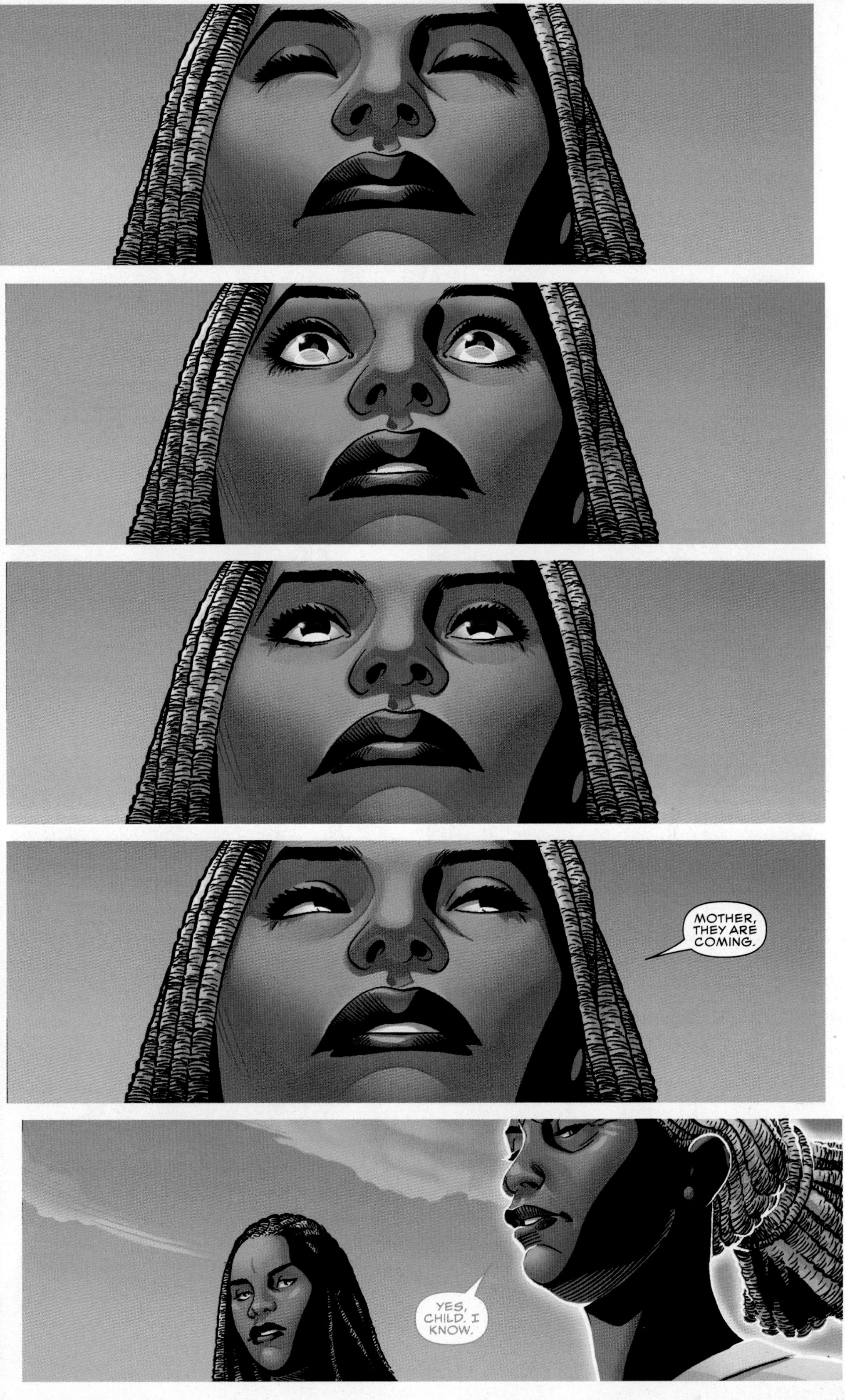
MOTHER, THEY ARE COMING.
YES, CHILD. I KNOW.

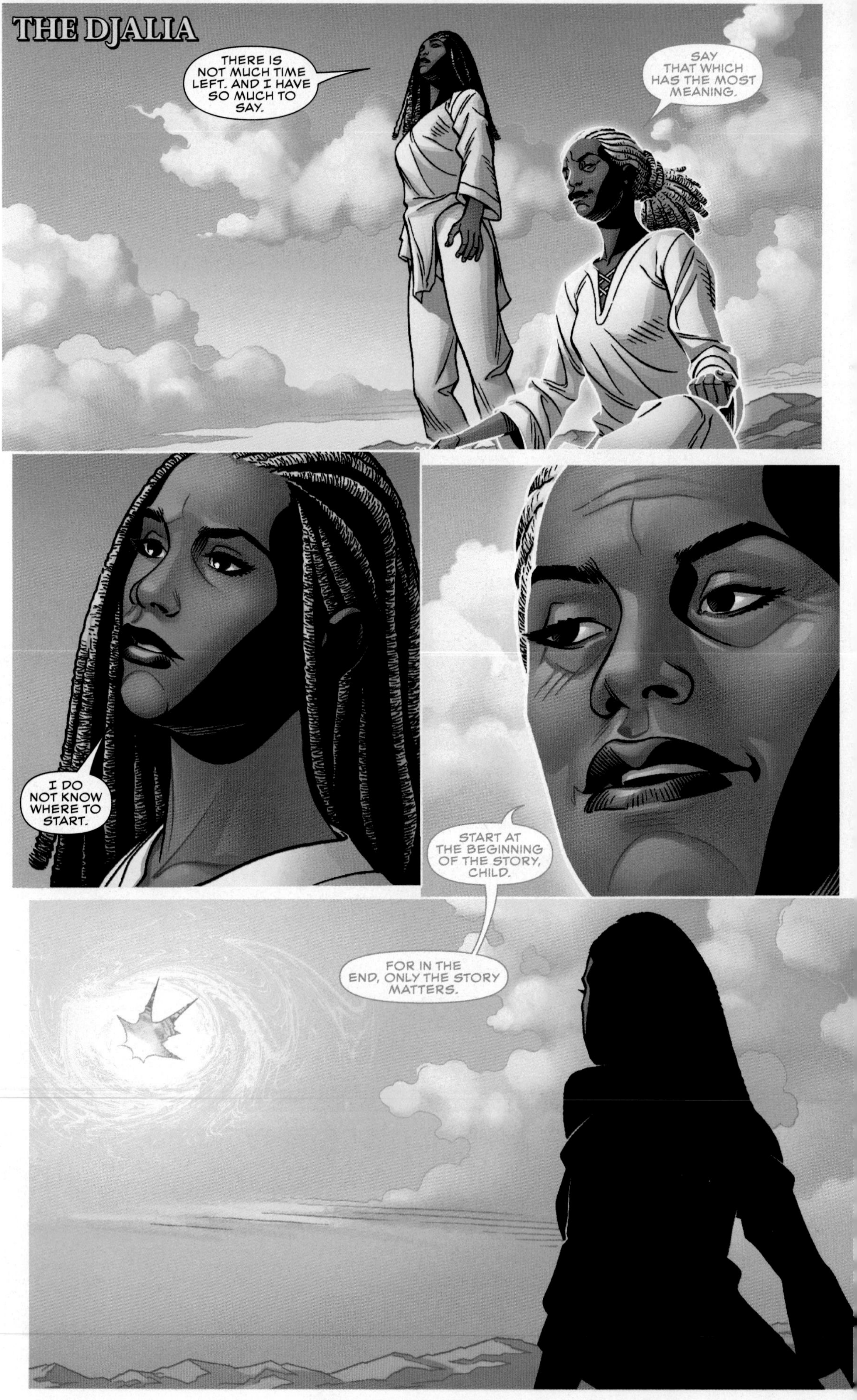
THE DJALIA
THERE IS NOT MUCH TIME LEFT. AND I HAVE SO MUCH TO SAY.
SAY THAT WHICH HAS THE MOST MEANING.
I DO NOT KNOW WHERE TO START.
START AT THE BEGINNING OF THE STORY, CHILD.
FOR IN THE END, ONLY THE STORY MATTERS.

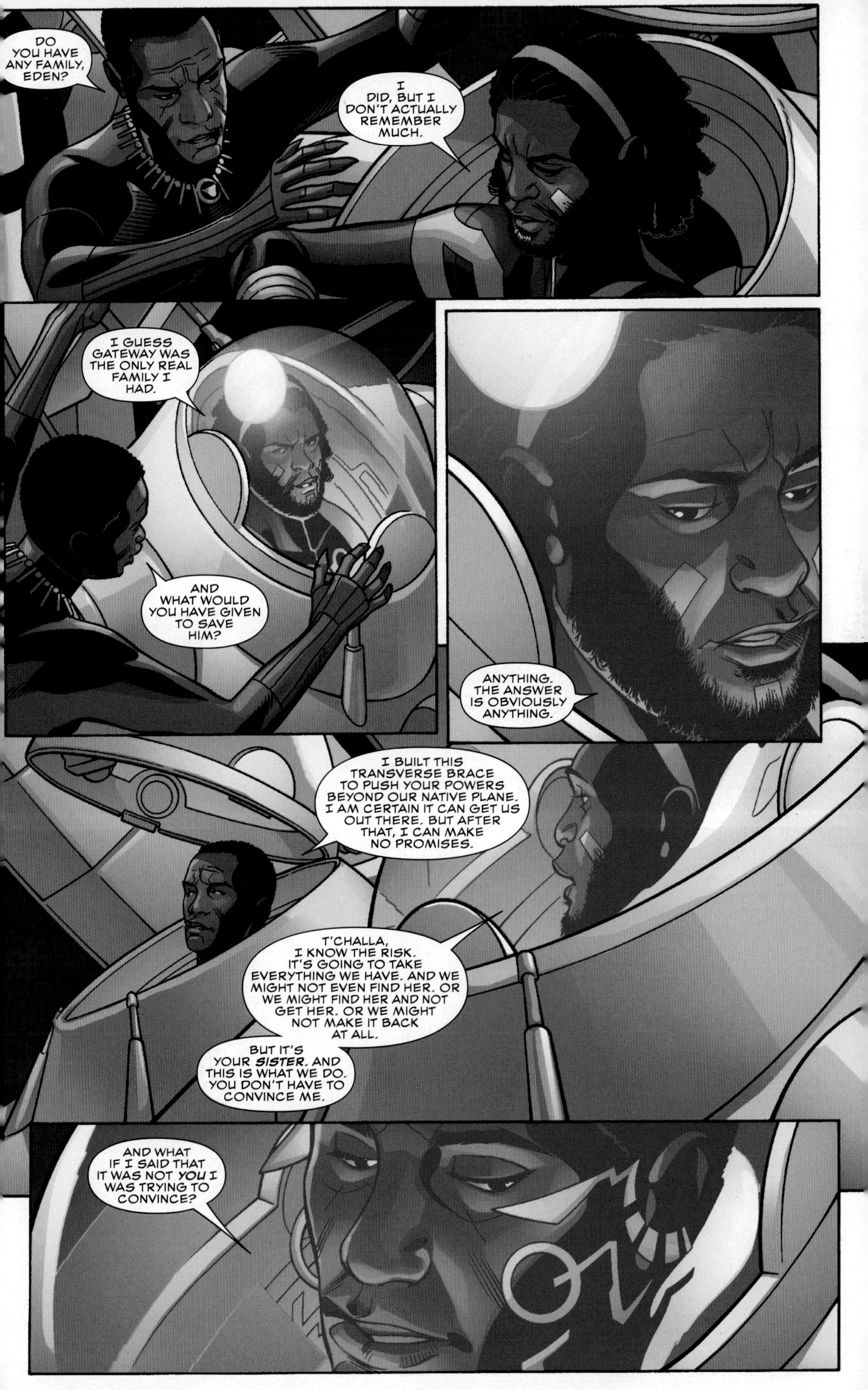
DO YOU HAVE ANY FAMILY, EDEN?
I DID, BUT I DON'T ACTUALLY REMEMBER MUCH.
I GUESS GATEWAY WAS THE ONLY REAL FAMILY I HAD.
AND WHAT WOULD YOU HAVE GIVEN TO SAVE HIM?
ANYTHING. THE ANSWER IS OBVIOUSLY ANYTHING.
I BUILT THIS TRANSVERSE BRACE TO PUSH YOUR POWERS BEYOND OUR NATIVE PLANE. I AM CERTAIN IT CAN GET US OUT THERE. BUT AFTER THAT, I CAN MAKE NO PROMISES.
T'CHALLA, I KNOW THE RISK. IT'S GOING TO TAKE EVERYTHING WE HAVE. AND WE MIGHT NOT EVEN FIND HER. OR WE MIGHT FIND HER AND NOT GET HER. OR WE MIGHT NOT MAKE IT BACK AT ALL.
BUT IT'S YOUR *SISTER*. AND THIS IS WHAT WE DO. YOU DON'T HAVE TO CONVINCE ME.
AND WHAT IF I SAID THAT IT WAS NOT *YOU* I WAS TRYING TO CONVINCE?

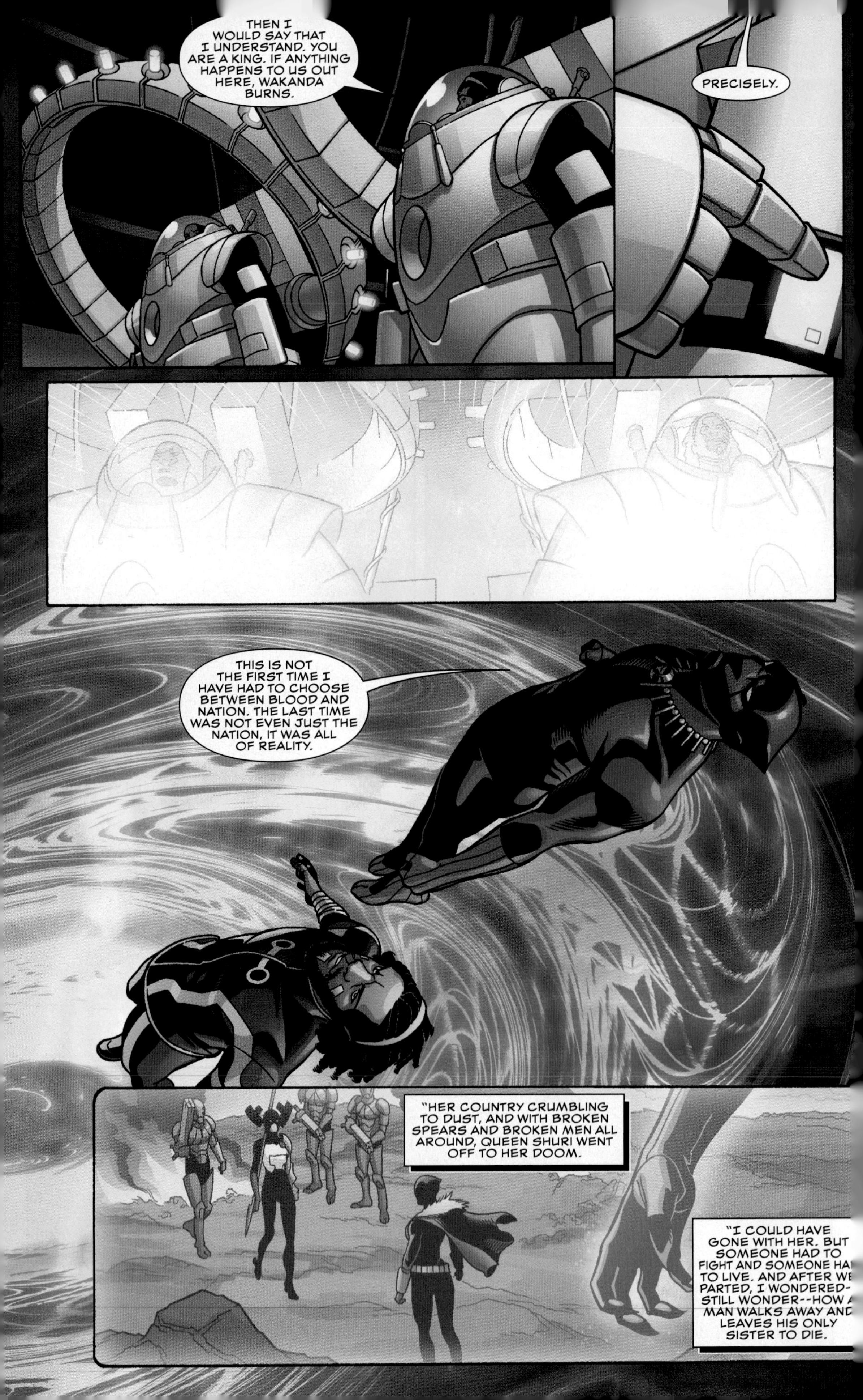
THEN I WOULD SAY THAT I UNDERSTAND. YOU ARE A KING. IF ANYTHING HAPPENS TO US OUT HERE, WAKANDA BURNS.
PRECISELY.
THIS IS NOT THE FIRST TIME I HAVE HAD TO CHOOSE BETWEEN BLOOD AND NATION. THE LAST TIME WAS NOT EVEN JUST THE NATION, IT WAS ALL OF REALITY.
"HER COUNTRY CRUMBLING TO DUST, AND WITH BROKEN SPEARS AND BROKEN MEN ALL AROUND, QUEEN SHURI WENT OFF TO HER DOOM.
"I COULD HAVE GONE WITH HER. BUT SOMEONE HAD TO FIGHT AND SOMEONE HA TO LIVE. AND AFTER WE PARTED, I WONDERED- STILL WONDER--HOW A MAN WALKS AWAY AND LEAVES HIS ONLY SISTER TO DIE.

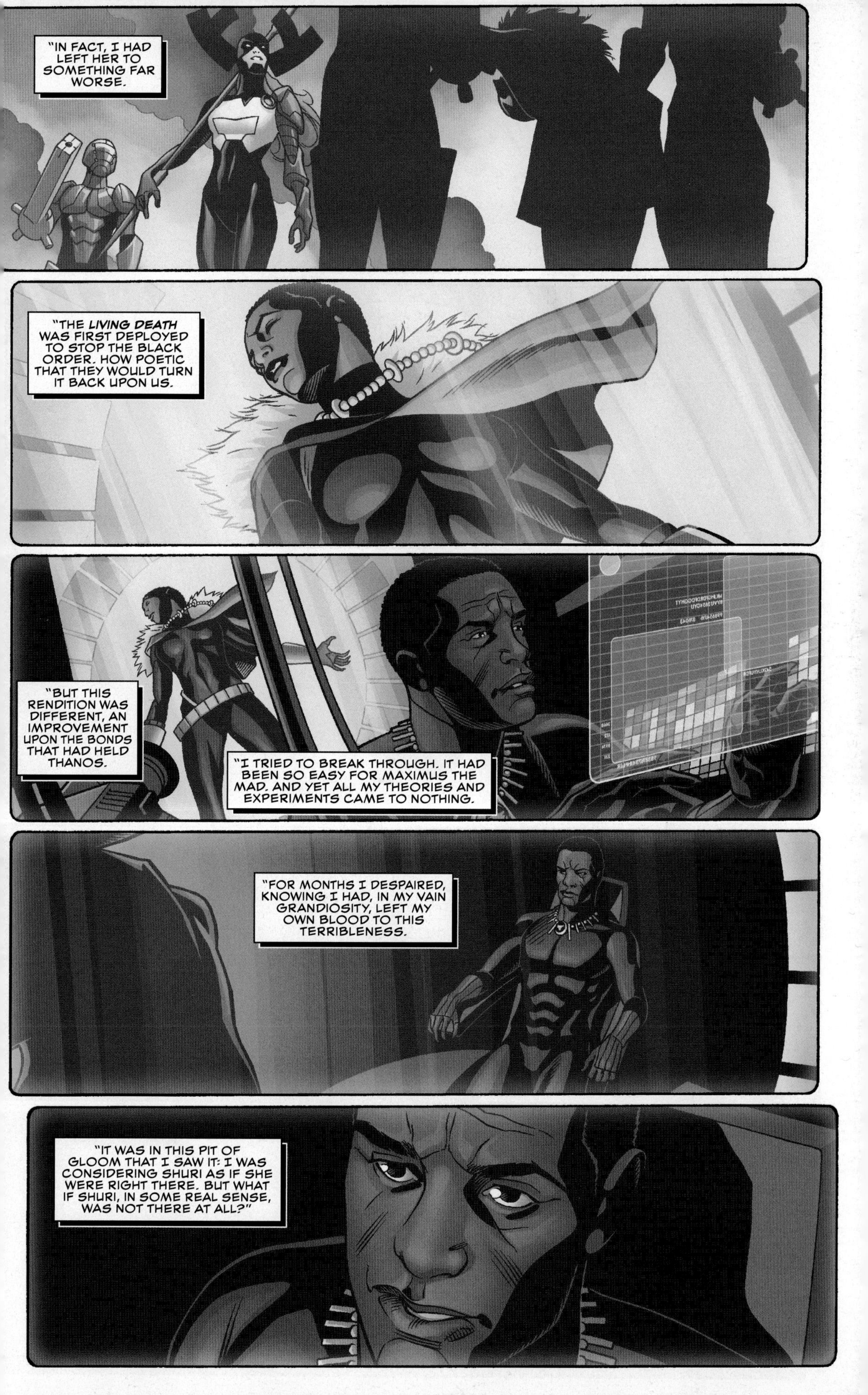
"IN FACT, I HAD LEFT HER TO SOMETHING FAR WORSE.
"THE *LIVING DEATH* WAS FIRST DEPLOYED TO STOP THE BLACK ORDER. HOW POETIC THAT THEY WOULD TURN IT BACK UPON US.
"BUT THIS RENDITION WAS DIFFERENT, AN IMPROVEMENT UPON THE BONDS THAT HAD HELD THANOS.
"I TRIED TO BREAK THROUGH. IT HAD BEEN SO EASY FOR MAXIMUS THE MAD. AND YET ALL MY THEORIES AND EXPERIMENTS CAME TO NOTHING.
"FOR MONTHS I DESPAIRED, KNOWING I HAD, IN MY VAIN GRANDIOSITY, LEFT MY OWN BLOOD TO THIS TERRIBLENESS.
"IT WAS IN THIS PIT OF GLOOM THAT I SAW IT: I WAS CONSIDERING SHURI AS IF SHE WERE RIGHT THERE. BUT WHAT IF SHURI, IN SOME REAL SENSE, WAS NOT THERE AT ALL?"

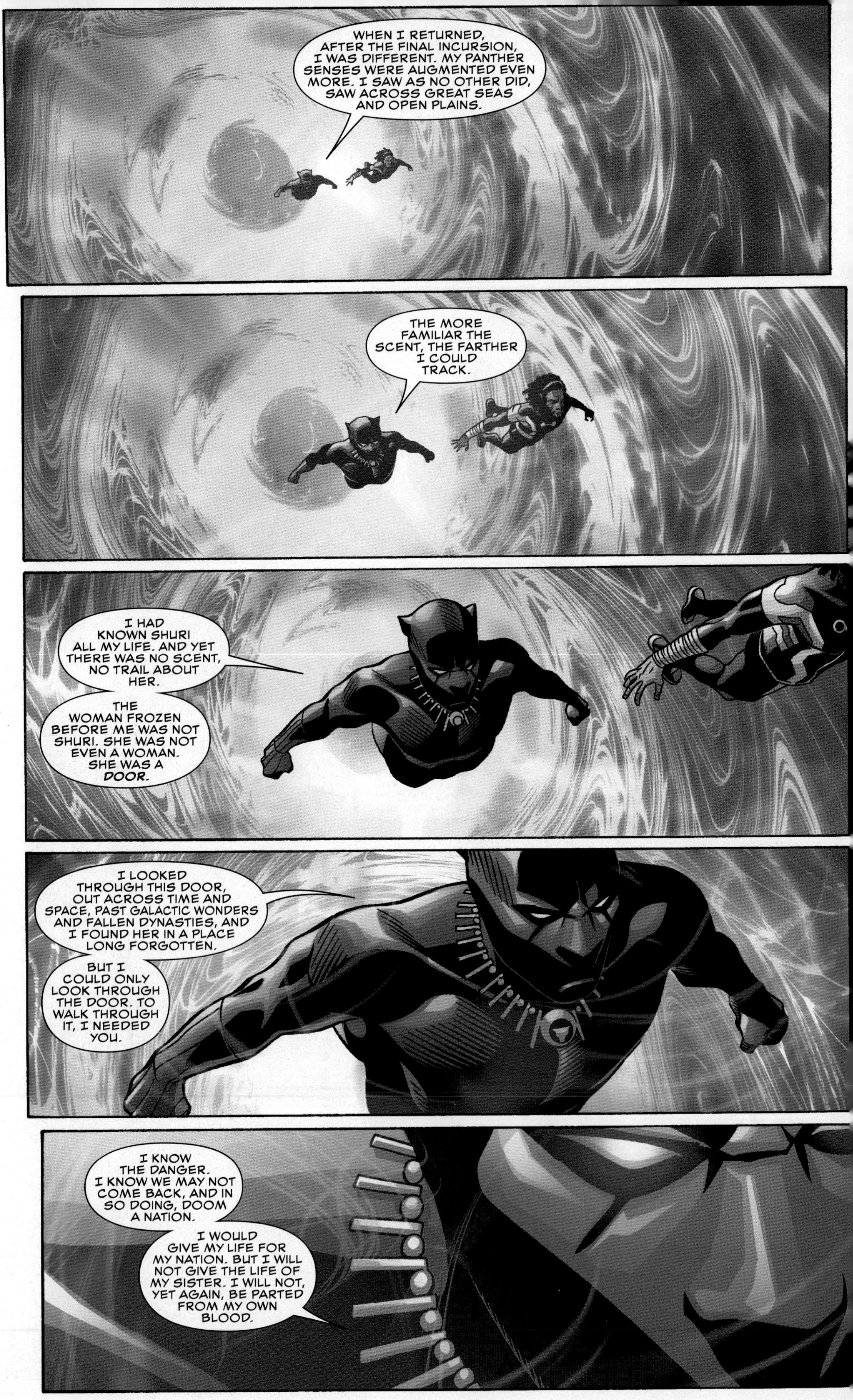
WHEN I RETURNED, AFTER THE FINAL INCURSION, I WAS DIFFERENT. MY PANTHER SENSES WERE AUGMENTED EVEN MORE. I SAW AS NO OTHER DID, SAW ACROSS GREAT SEAS AND OPEN PLAINS.
THE MORE FAMILIAR THE SCENT, THE FARTHER I COULD TRACK.
I HAD KNOWN SHURI ALL MY LIFE. AND YET THERE WAS NO SCENT, NO TRAIL ABOUT HER.
THE WOMAN FROZEN BEFORE ME WAS NOT SHURI. SHE WAS NOT EVEN A WOMAN. SHE WAS A *DOOR.*
I LOOKED THROUGH THIS DOOR, OUT ACROSS TIME AND SPACE, PAST GALACTIC WONDERS AND FALLEN DYNASTIES, AND I FOUND HER IN A PLACE LONG FORGOTTEN.
BUT I COULD ONLY LOOK THROUGH THE DOOR. TO WALK THROUGH IT, I NEEDED YOU.
I KNOW THE DANGER. I KNOW WE MAY NOT COME BACK, AND IN SO DOING, DOOM A NATION.
I WOULD GIVE MY LIFE FOR MY NATION. BUT I WILL NOT GIVE THE LIFE OF MY SISTER. I WILL NOT, YET AGAIN, BE PARTED FROM MY OWN BLOOD.

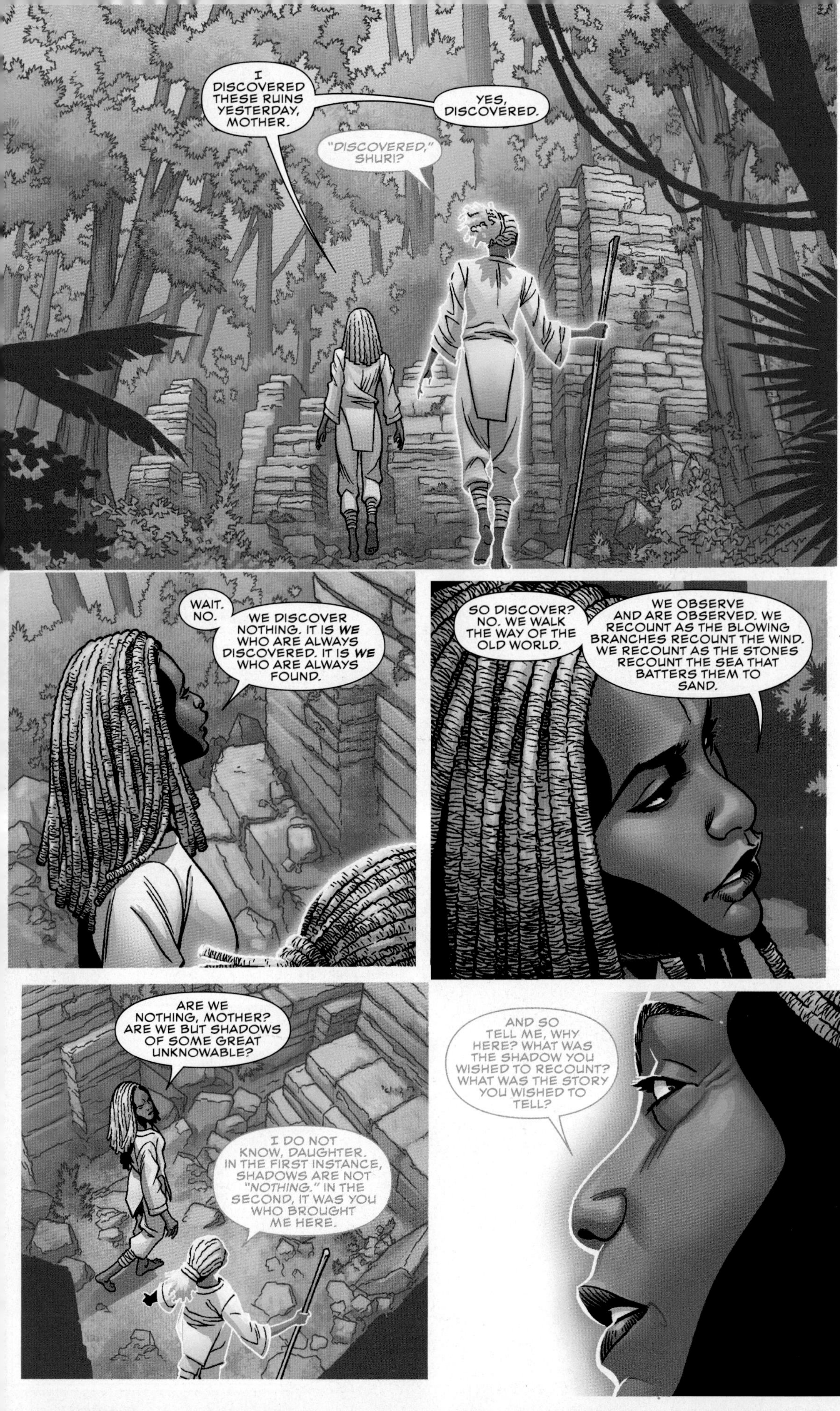

I DISCOVERED THESE RUINS YESTERDAY, MOTHER.
"DISCOVERED," SHURI?
YES, DISCOVERED.
WAIT. NO.
WE DISCOVER NOTHING. IT IS *WE* WHO ARE ALWAYS DISCOVERED. IT IS *WE* WHO ARE ALWAYS FOUND.
SO DISCOVER? NO. WE WALK THE WAY OF THE OLD WORLD.
WE OBSERVE AND ARE OBSERVED. WE RECOUNT AS THE BLOWING BRANCHES RECOUNT THE WIND. WE RECOUNT AS THE STONES RECOUNT THE SEA THAT BATTERS THEM TO SAND.
ARE WE NOTHING, MOTHER? ARE WE BUT SHADOWS OF SOME GREAT UNKNOWABLE?
I DO NOT KNOW, DAUGHTER. IN THE FIRST INSTANCE, SHADOWS ARE NOT "*NOTHING*." IN THE SECOND, IT WAS YOU WHO BROUGHT ME HERE.
AND SO TELL ME, WHY HERE? WHAT WAS THE SHADOW YOU WISHED TO RECOUNT? WHAT WAS THE STORY YOU WISHED TO TELL?

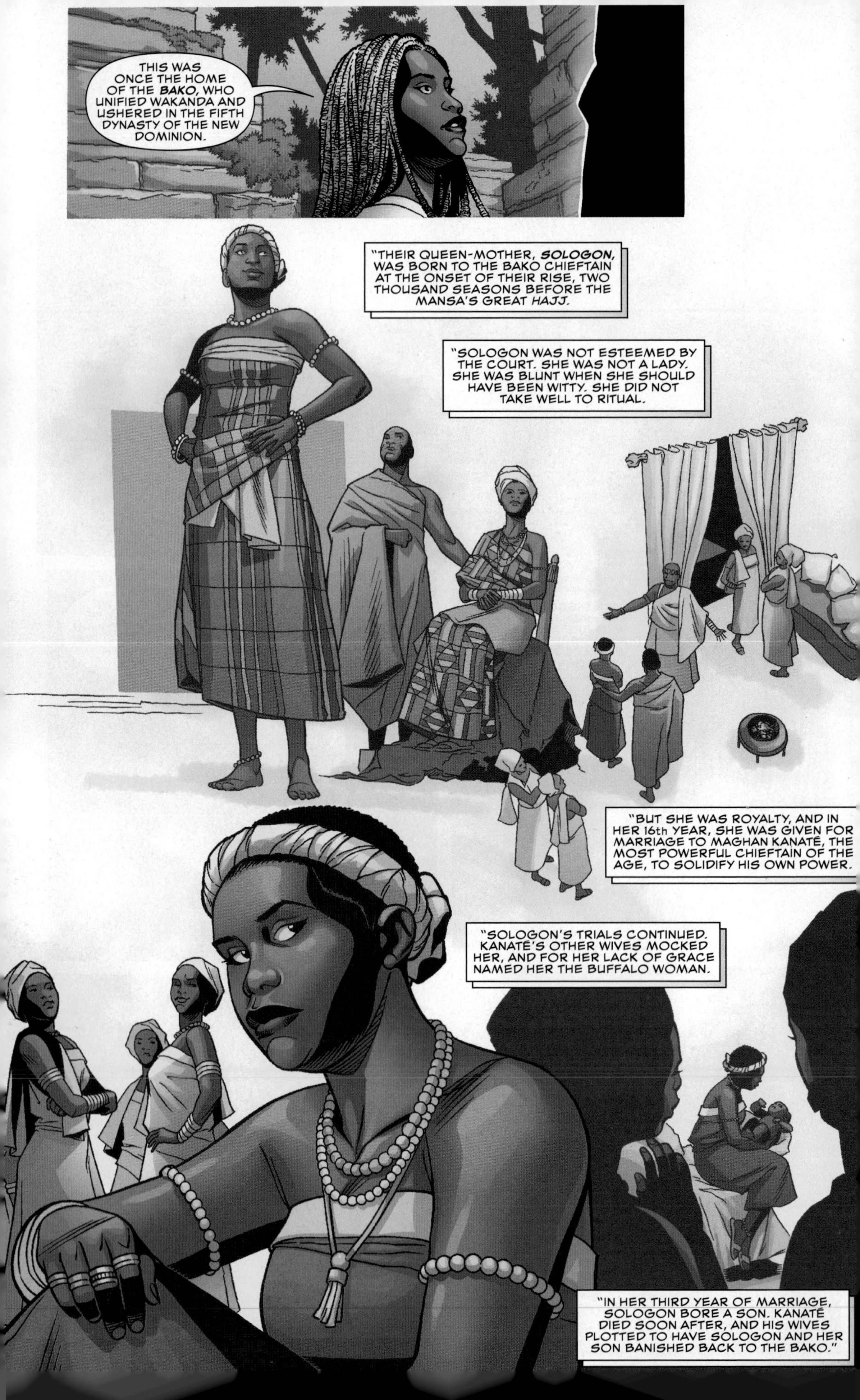
THIS WAS ONCE THE HOME OF THE BAKO, WHO UNIFIED WAKANDA AND USHERED IN THE FIFTH DYNASTY OF THE NEW DOMINION.
"THEIR QUEEN-MOTHER, SOLOGON, WAS BORN TO THE BAKO CHIEFTAIN AT THE ONSET OF THEIR RISE, TWO THOUSAND SEASONS BEFORE THE MANSA'S GREAT HAJJ.
"SOLOGON WAS NOT ESTEEMED BY THE COURT. SHE WAS NOT A LADY. SHE WAS BLUNT WHEN SHE SHOULD HAVE BEEN WITTY. SHE DID NOT TAKE WELL TO RITUAL.
"BUT SHE WAS ROYALTY, AND IN HER 16th YEAR, SHE WAS GIVEN FOR MARRIAGE TO MAGHAN KANATÉ, THE MOST POWERFUL CHIEFTAIN OF THE AGE, TO SOLIDIFY HIS OWN POWER.
"SOLOGON'S TRIALS CONTINUED. KANATÉ'S OTHER WIVES MOCKED HER, AND FOR HER LACK OF GRACE NAMED HER THE BUFFALO WOMAN.
"IN HER THIRD YEAR OF MARRIAGE, SOLOGON BORE A SON. KANATÉ DIED SOON AFTER, AND HIS WIVES PLOTTED TO HAVE SOLOGON AND HER SON BANISHED BACK TO THE BAKO."

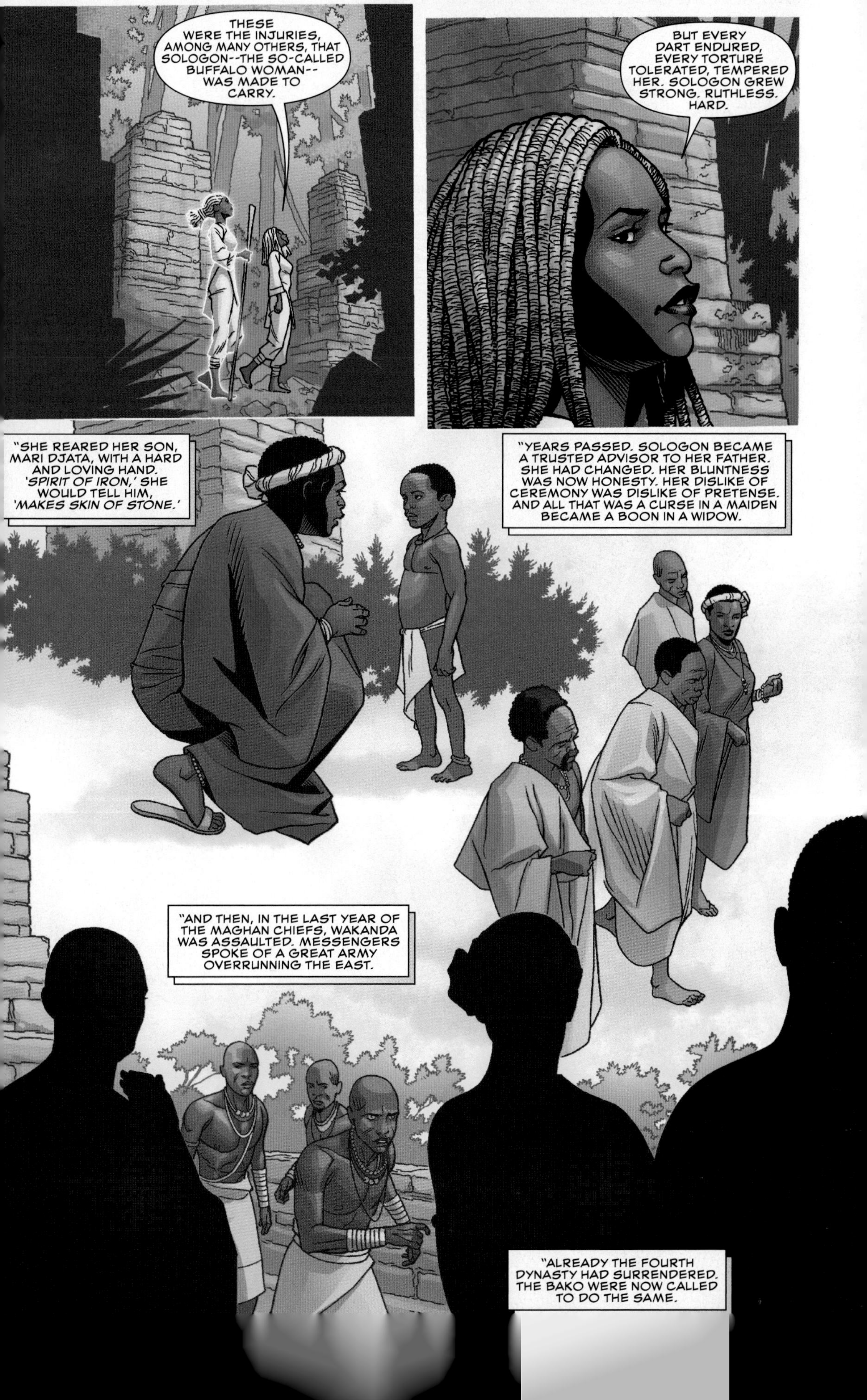
THESE WERE THE INJURIES, AMONG MANY OTHERS, THAT SOLOGON--THE SO-CALLED BUFFALO WOMAN--WAS MADE TO CARRY.
BUT EVERY DART ENDURED, EVERY TORTURE TOLERATED, TEMPERED HER. SOLOGON GREW STRONG. RUTHLESS. HARD.
"SHE REARED HER SON, MARI DJATA, WITH A HARD AND LOVING HAND. '*SPIRIT OF IRON*,' SHE WOULD TELL HIM, '*MAKES SKIN OF STONE*.'
"YEARS PASSED. SOLOGON BECAME A TRUSTED ADVISOR TO HER FATHER. SHE HAD CHANGED. HER BLUNTNESS WAS NOW HONESTY. HER DISLIKE OF CEREMONY WAS DISLIKE OF PRETENSE. AND ALL THAT WAS A CURSE IN A MAIDEN BECAME A BOON IN A WIDOW.
"AND THEN, IN THE LAST YEAR OF THE MAGHAN CHIEFS, WAKANDA WAS ASSAULTED. MESSENGERS SPOKE OF A GREAT ARMY OVERRUNNING THE EAST.
"ALREADY THE FOURTH DYNASTY HAD SURRENDERED. THE BAKO WERE NOW CALLED TO DO THE SAME.

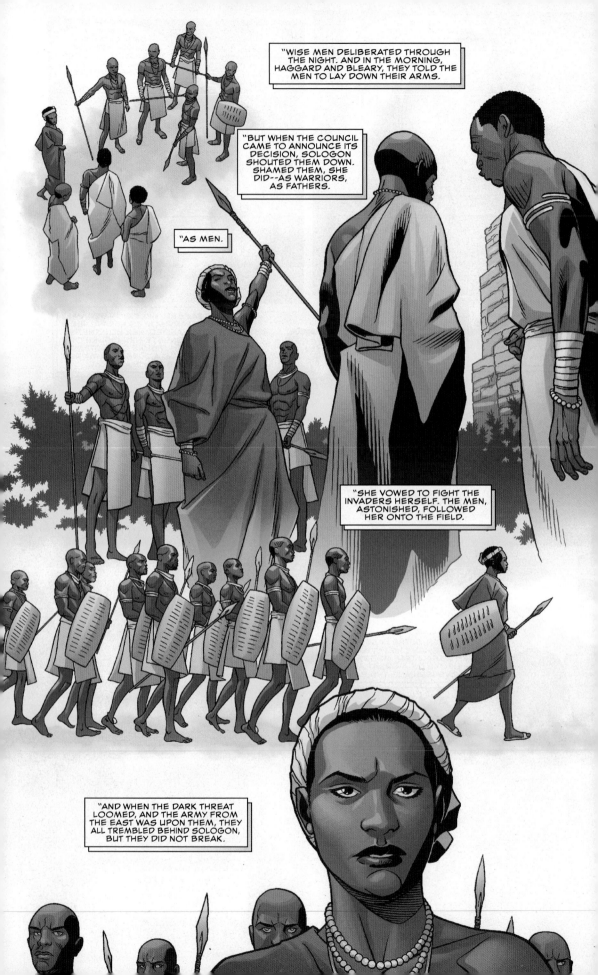

"WISE MEN DELIBERATED THROUGH THE NIGHT. AND IN THE MORNING, HAGGARD AND BLEARY, THEY TOLD THE MEN TO LAY DOWN THEIR ARMS.

"BUT WHEN THE COUNCIL CAME TO ANNOUNCE ITS DECISION, SOLOGON SHOUTED THEM DOWN. SHAMED THEM, SHE DID--AS WARRIORS, AS FATHERS.

"AS MEN.

"SHE VOWED TO FIGHT THE INVADERS HERSELF. THE MEN, ASTONISHED, FOLLOWED HER ONTO THE FIELD.

"AND WHEN THE DARK THREAT LOOMED, AND THE ARMY FROM THE EAST WAS UPON THEM, THEY ALL TREMBLED BEHIND SOLOGON, BUT THEY DID NOT BREAK.

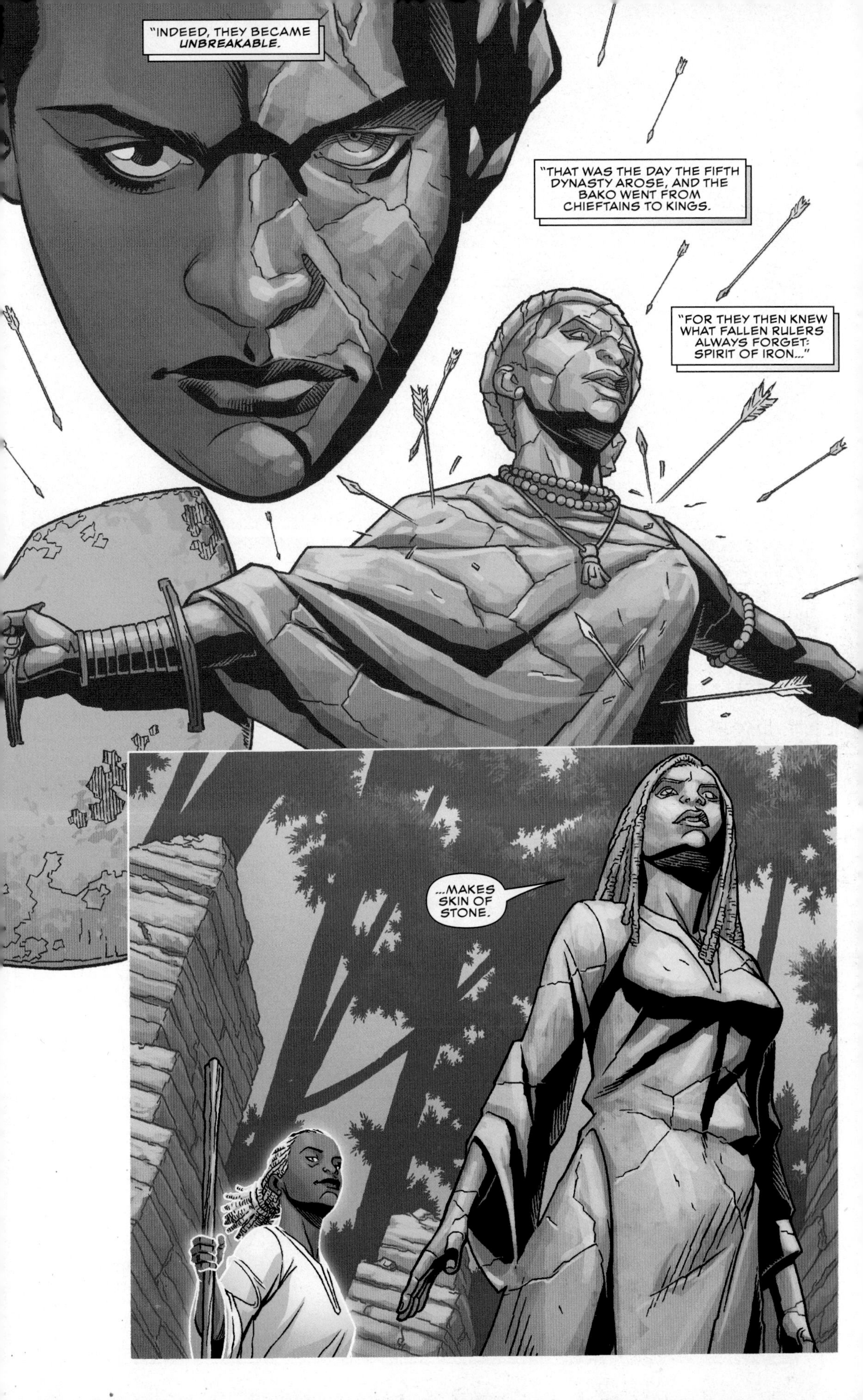
"INDEED, THEY BECAME UNBREAKABLE.
"THAT WAS THE DAY THE FIFTH DYNASTY AROSE, AND THE BAKO WENT FROM CHIEFTAINS TO KINGS.
"FOR THEY THEN KNEW WHAT FALLEN RULERS ALWAYS FORGET: SPIRIT OF IRON..."
...MAKES SKIN OF STONE.

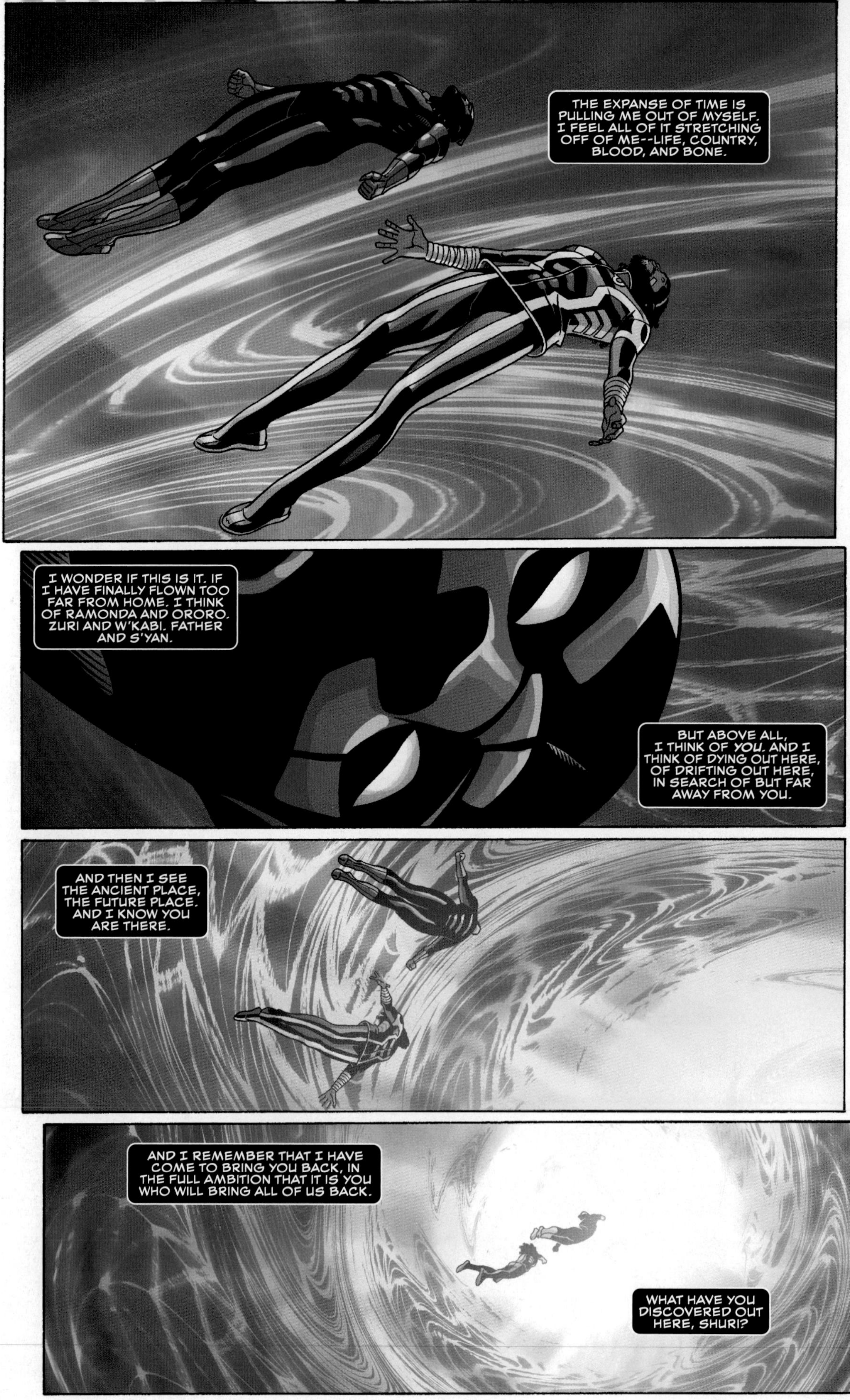
THE EXPANSE OF TIME IS PULLING ME OUT OF MYSELF. I FEEL ALL OF IT STRETCHING OFF OF ME--LIFE, COUNTRY, BLOOD, AND BONE.
I WONDER IF THIS IS IT. IF I HAVE FINALLY FLOWN TOO FAR FROM HOME. I THINK OF RAMONDA AND ORORO. ZURI AND W'KABI. FATHER AND S'YAN.
BUT ABOVE ALL, I THINK OF *YOU*. AND I THINK OF DYING OUT HERE, OF DRIFTING OUT HERE, IN SEARCH OF BUT FAR AWAY FROM YOU.
AND THEN I SEE THE ANCIENT PLACE, THE FUTURE PLACE. AND I KNOW YOU ARE THERE.
AND I REMEMBER THAT I HAVE COME TO BRING YOU BACK, IN THE FULL AMBITION THAT IT IS YOU WHO WILL BRING ALL OF US BACK.
WHAT HAVE YOU DISCOVERED OUT HERE, SHURI?

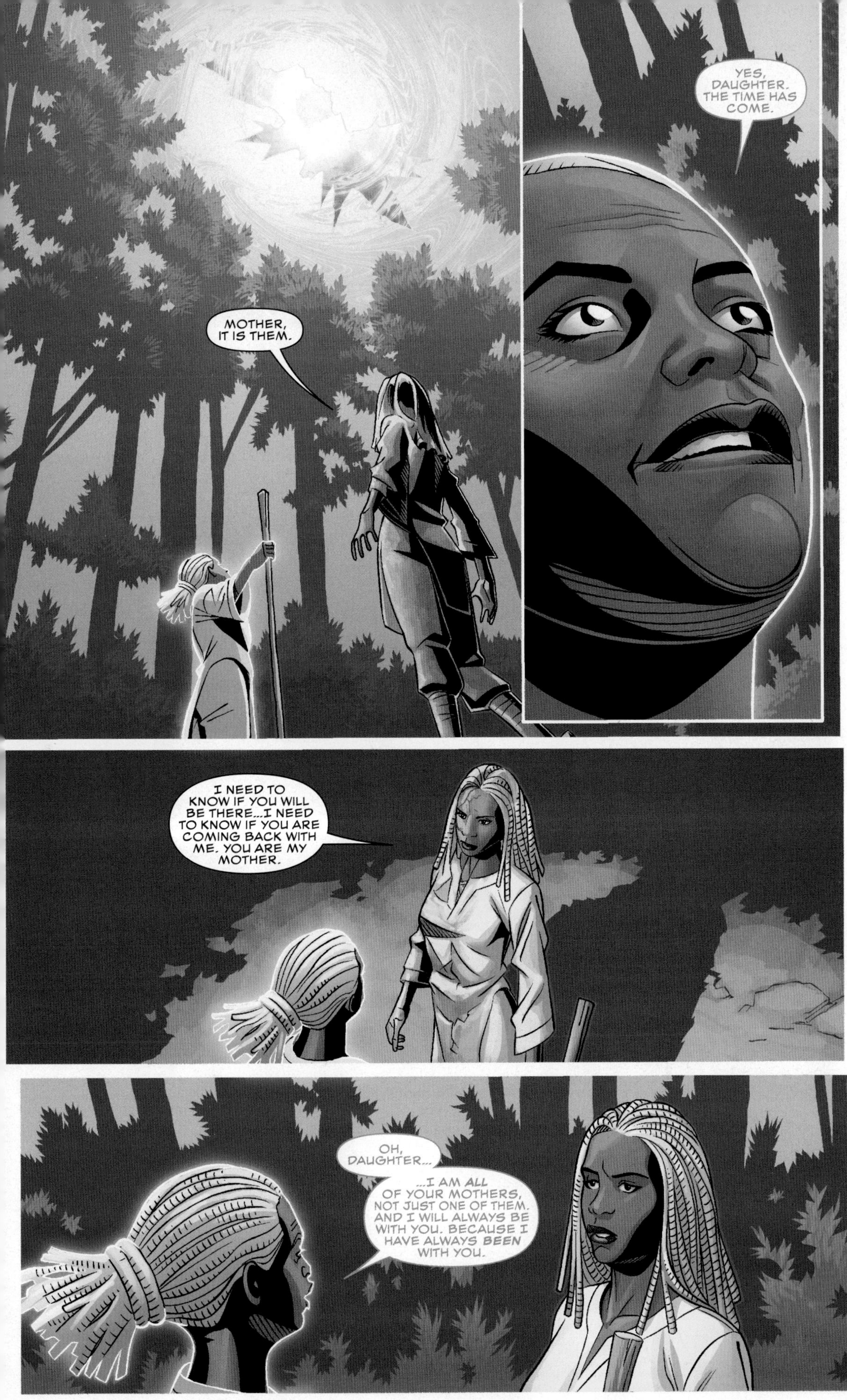

MOTHER, IT IS THEM.
YES, DAUGHTER. THE TIME HAS COME.
I NEED TO KNOW IF YOU WILL BE THERE...I NEED TO KNOW IF YOU ARE COMING BACK WITH ME. YOU ARE MY MOTHER.
OH, DAUGHTER...
...I AM ALL OF YOUR MOTHERS, NOT JUST ONE OF THEM. AND I WILL ALWAYS BE WITH YOU. BECAUSE I HAVE ALWAYS BEEN WITH YOU.

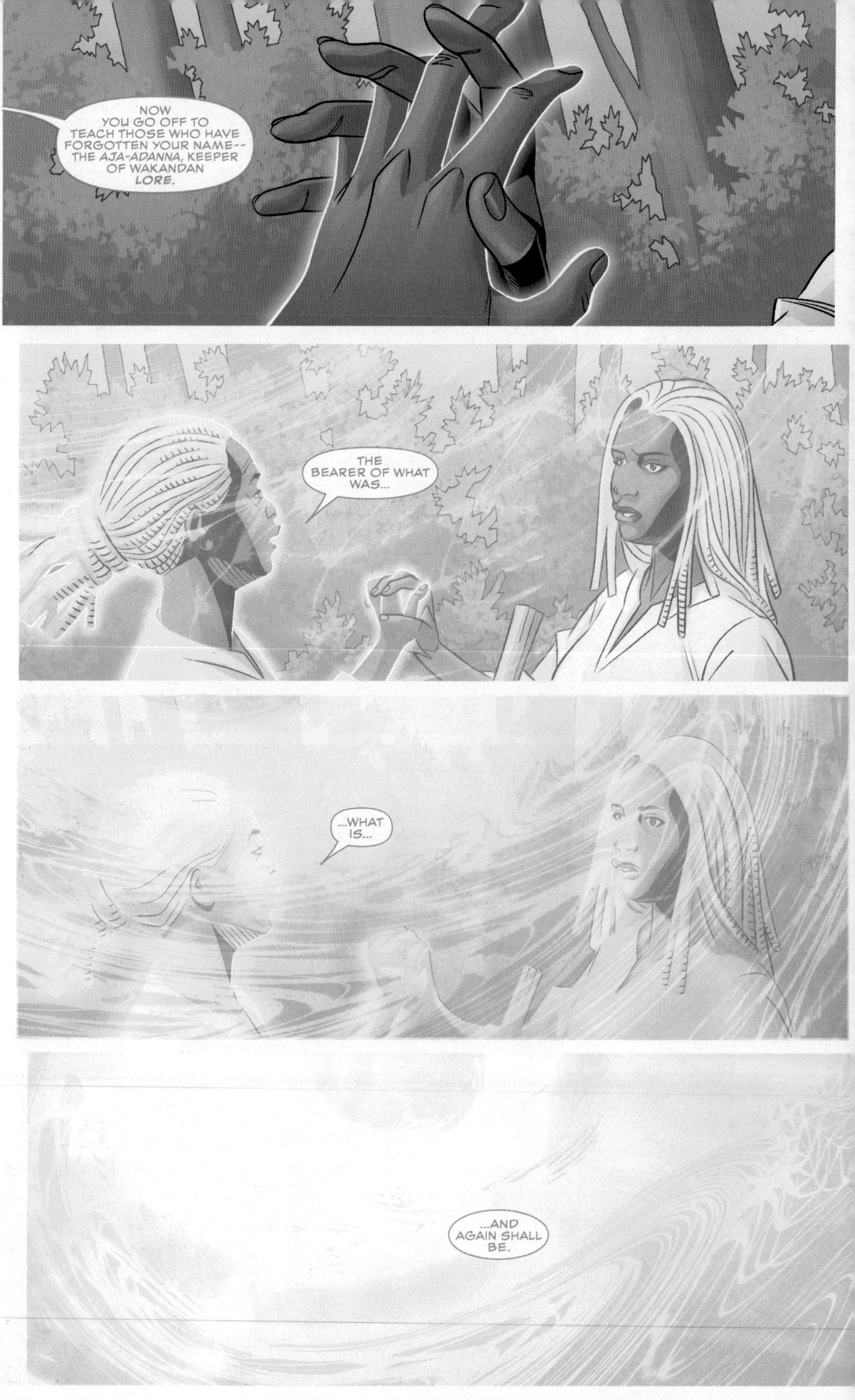
NOW YOU GO OFF TO TEACH THOSE WHO HAVE FORGOTTEN YOUR NAME-- THE AJA-ADANNA, KEEPER OF WAKANDAN LORE.
THE BEARER OF WHAT WAS...
...WHAT IS...
...AND AGAIN SHALL BE.

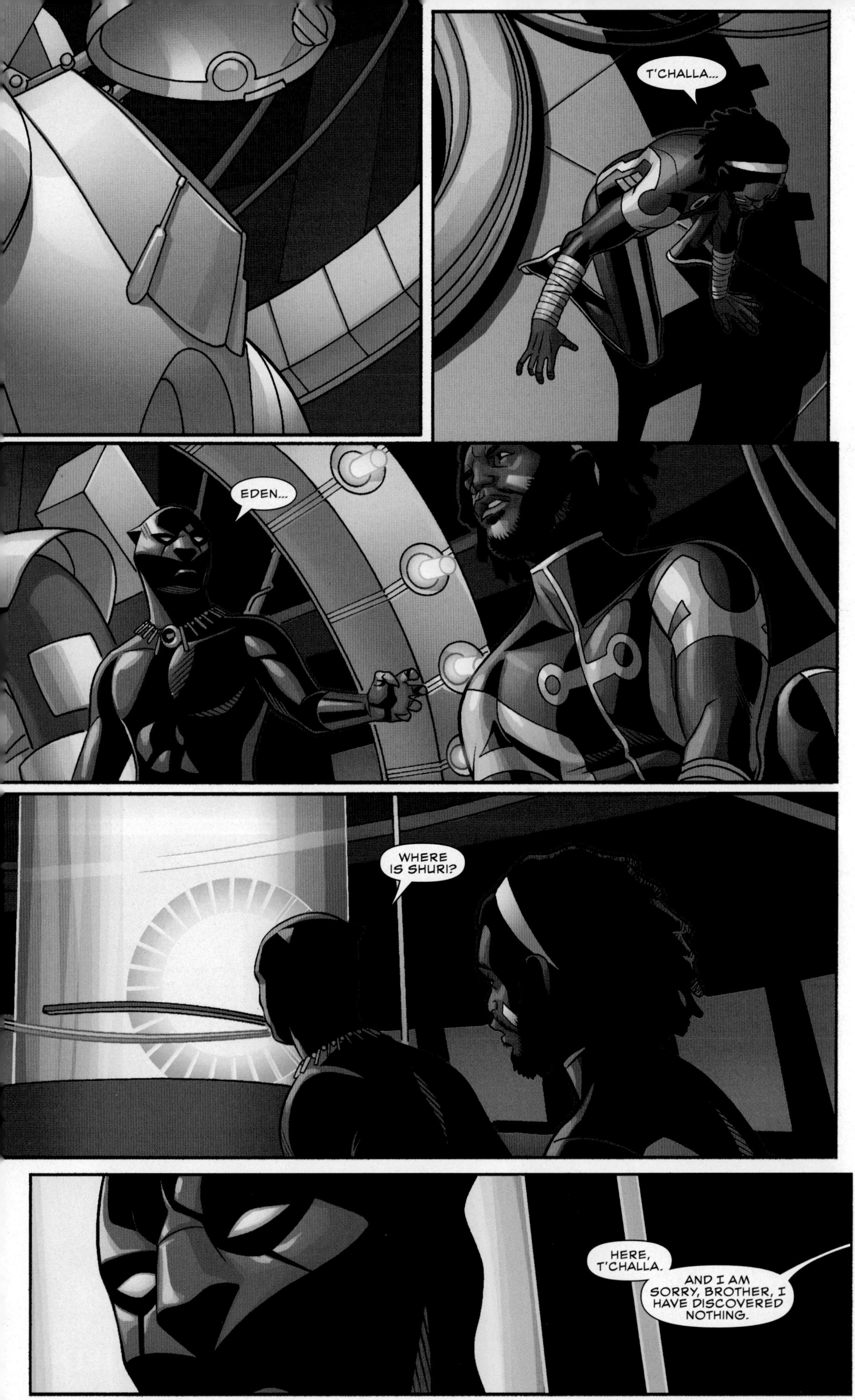

T'CHALLA...
EDEN...
WHERE IS SHURI?
HERE, T'CHALLA.
AND I AM SORRY, BROTHER, I HAVE DISCOVERED NOTHING.

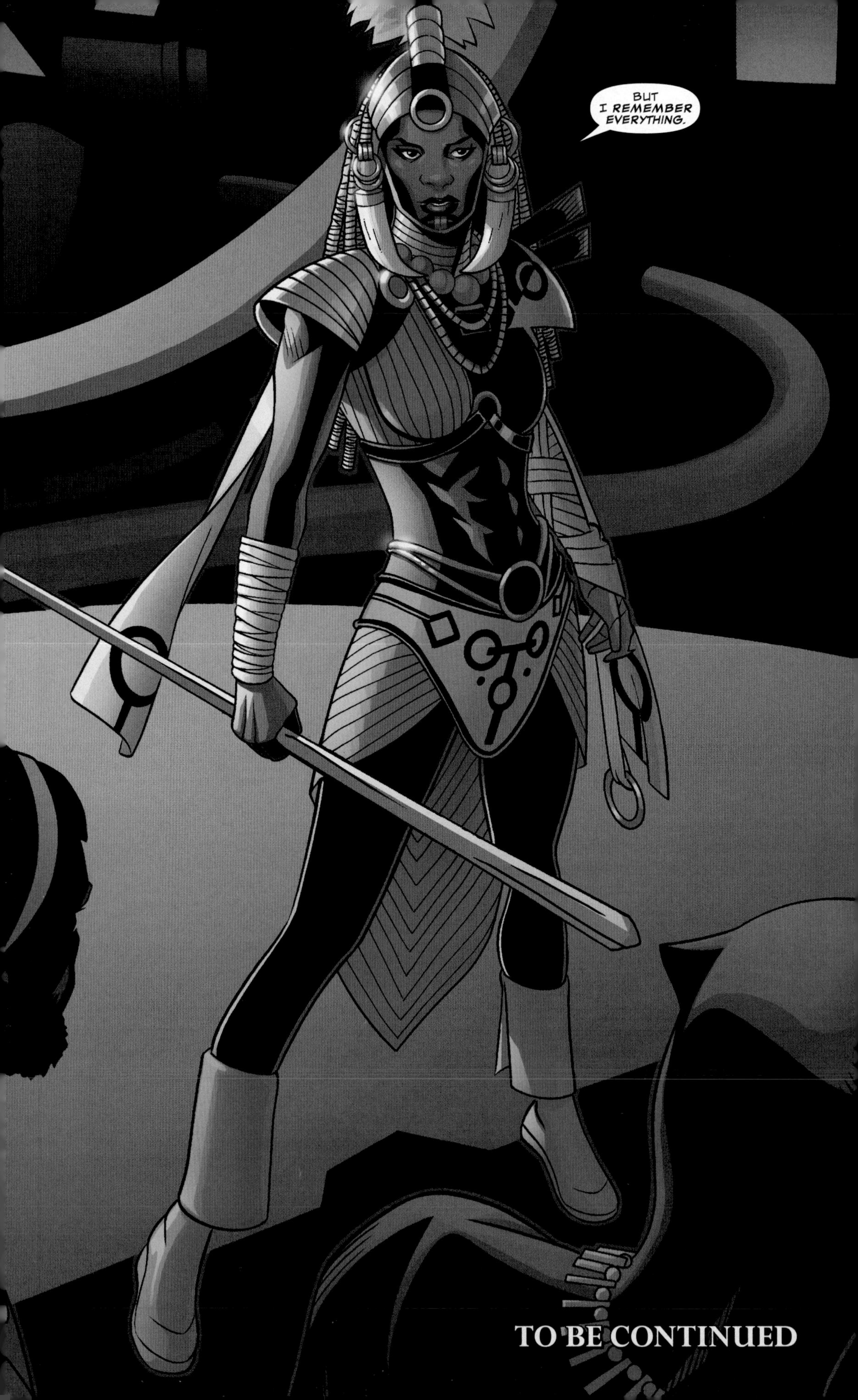
BUT I REMEMBER EVERYTHING.
TO BE CONTINUED

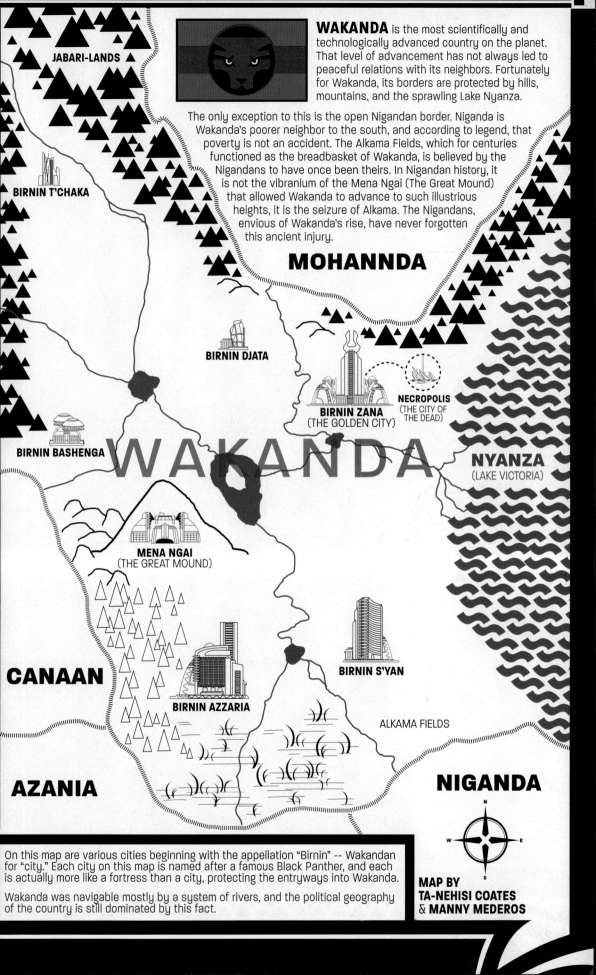

WAKANDA is the most scientifically and technologically advanced country on the planet. That level of advancement has not always led to peaceful relations with its neighbors. Fortunately for Wakanda, its borders are protected by hills, mountains, and the sprawling Lake Nyanza.

The only exception to this is the open Nigandan border. Niganda is Wakanda's poorer neighbor to the south, and according to legend, that poverty is not an accident. The Alkama Fields, which for centuries functioned as the breadbasket of Wakanda, is believed by the Nigandans to have once been theirs. In Nigandan history, it is not the vibranium of the Mena Ngai (The Great Mound) that allowed Wakanda to advance to such illustrious heights, it is the seizure of Alkama. The Nigandans, envious of Wakanda's rise, have never forgotten this ancient injury.

JABARI-LANDS

BIRNIN T'CHAKA

MOHANNDA

BIRNIN DJATA

BIRNIN ZANA
(THE GOLDEN CITY)

NECROPOLIS
(THE CITY OF
THE DEAD)

BIRNIN BASHENGA

WAKANDA

NYANZA
(LAKE VICTORIA)

MENA NGAI
(THE GREAT MOUND)

BIRNIN S'YAN

CANAAN

BIRNIN AZZARIA

ALKAMA FIELDS

AZANIA

NIGANDA

On this map are various cities beginning with the appellation "Birnin" -- Wakandan for "city." Each city on this map is named after a famous Black Panther, and each is actually more like a fortress than a city, protecting the entryways into Wakanda.

Wakanda was navigable mostly by a system of rivers, and the political geography of the country is still dominated by this fact.

N
W E
S

MAP BY
TA-NEHISI COATES
& MANNY MEDEROS

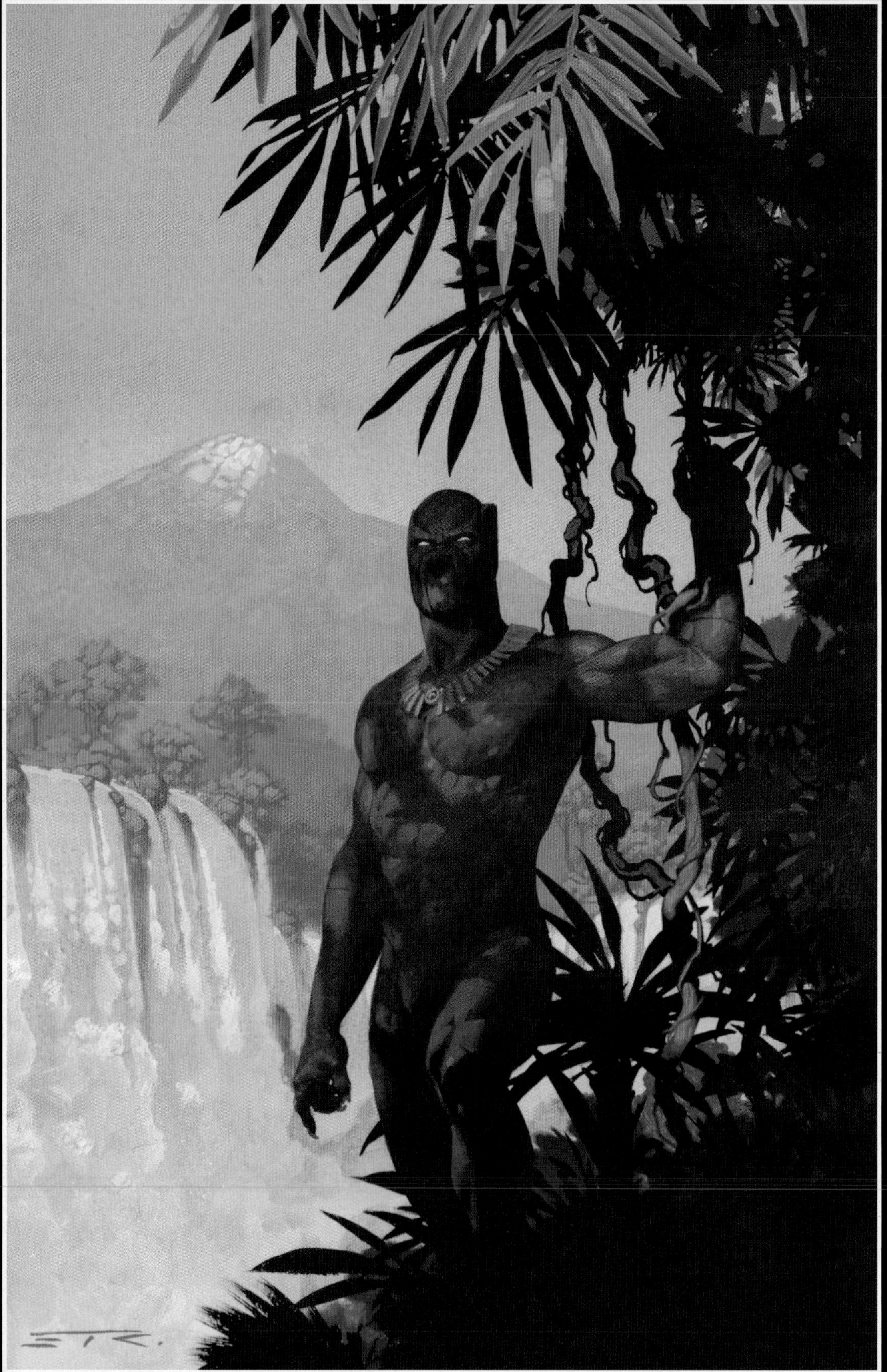

#5 VARIANT BY **ESAD RIBIC**

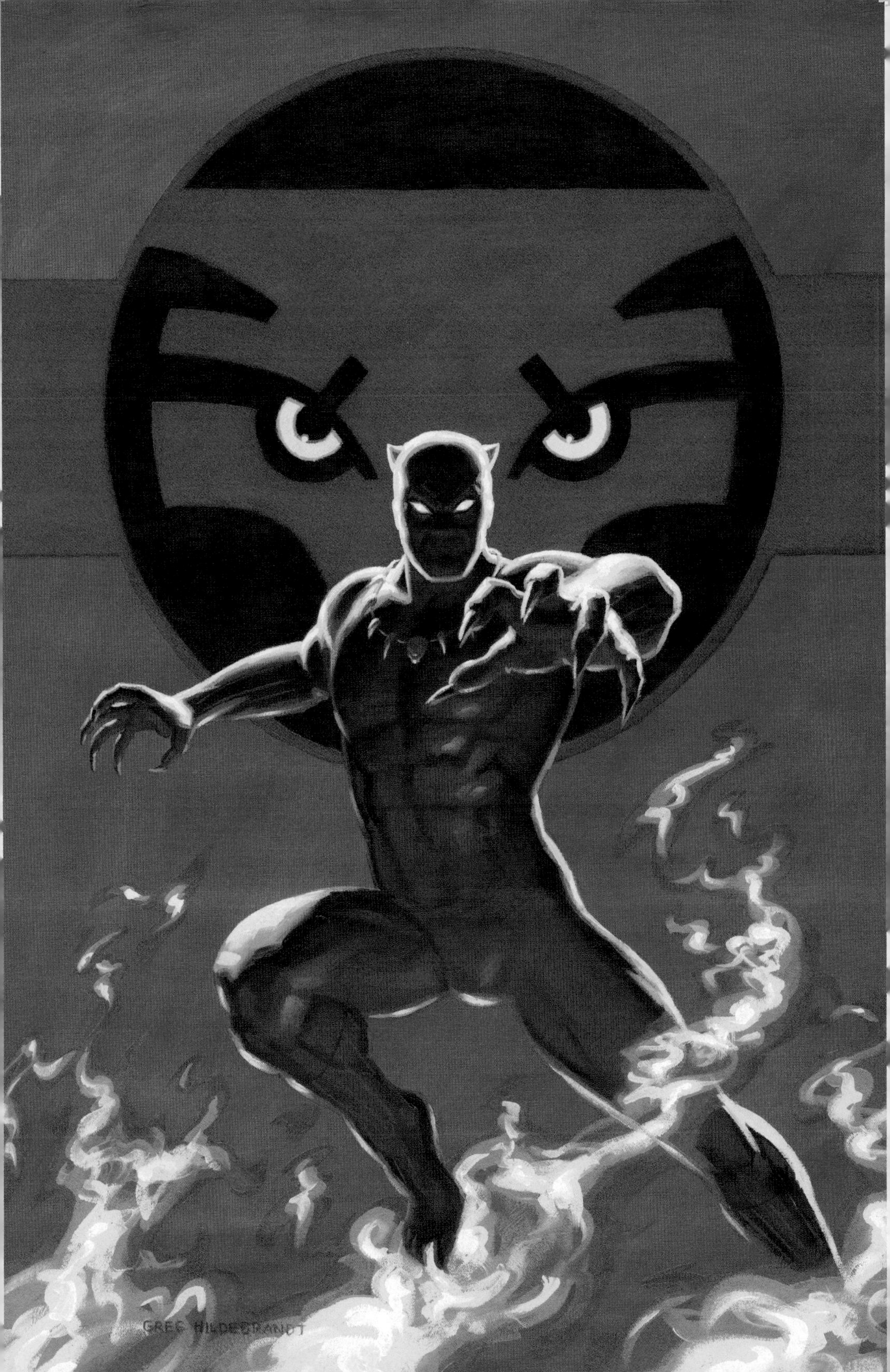
GREG HILDEBRANDT

#5 CLASSIC VARIANT BY **GREG HILDEBRANDT**

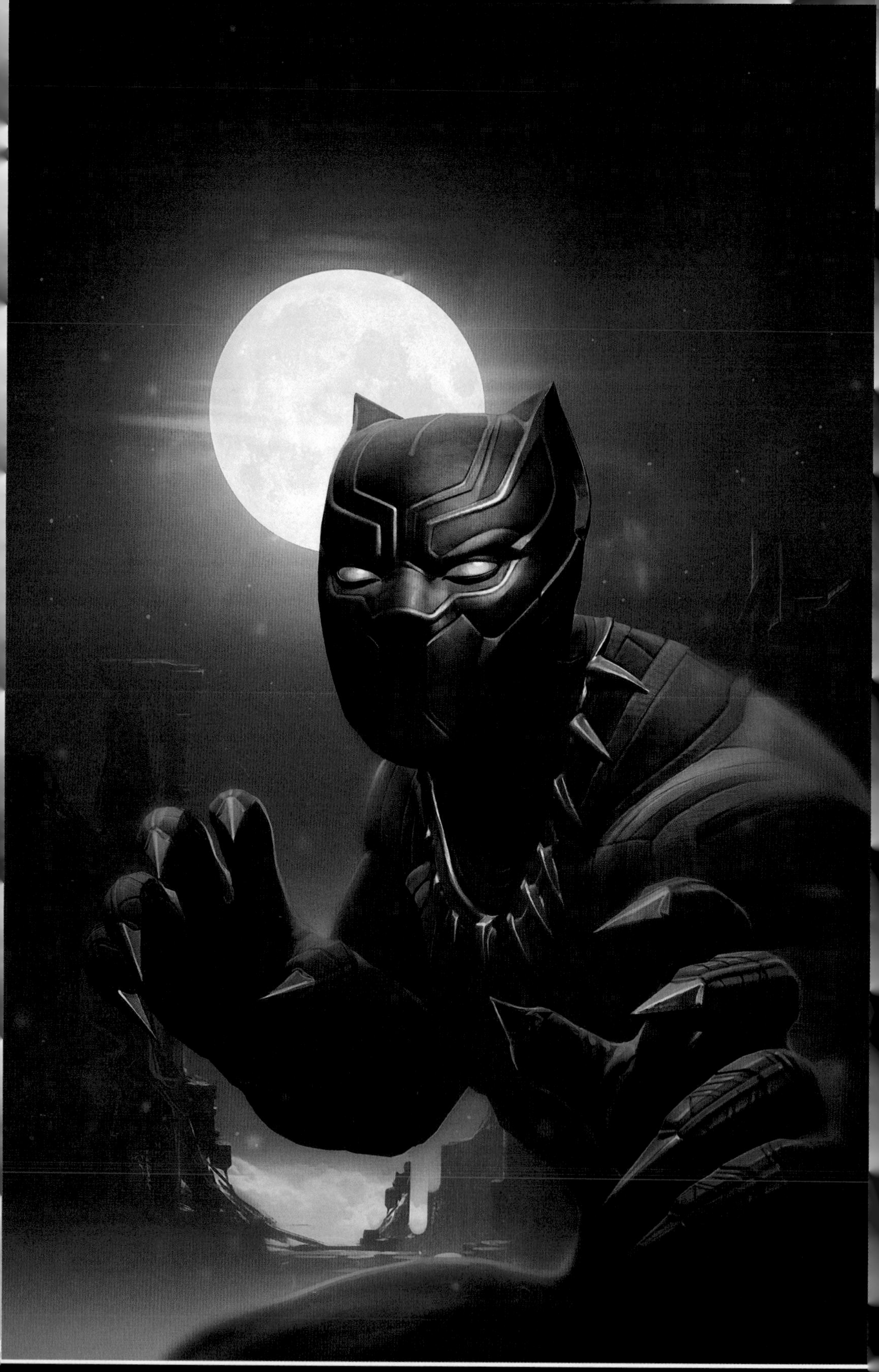

#5 CONTEST OF CHAMPIONS GAME VARIANT
BY **KABAM** WITH **GABRIEL FRIZZERA**

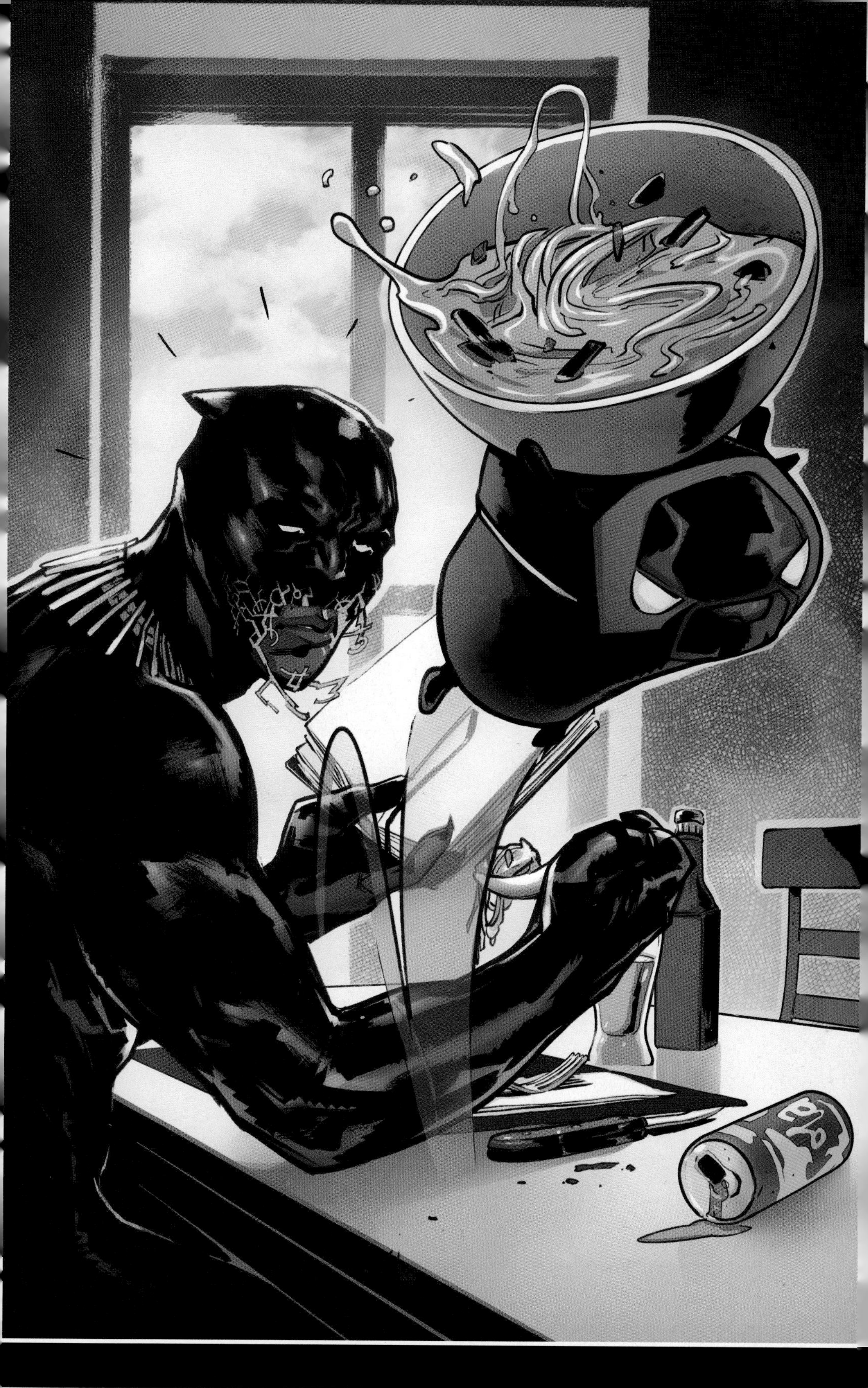

#5 MARVEL TSUM TSUM TAKEOVER VARIANT
BY **SARA PICHELLI** & **JASON KEITH**

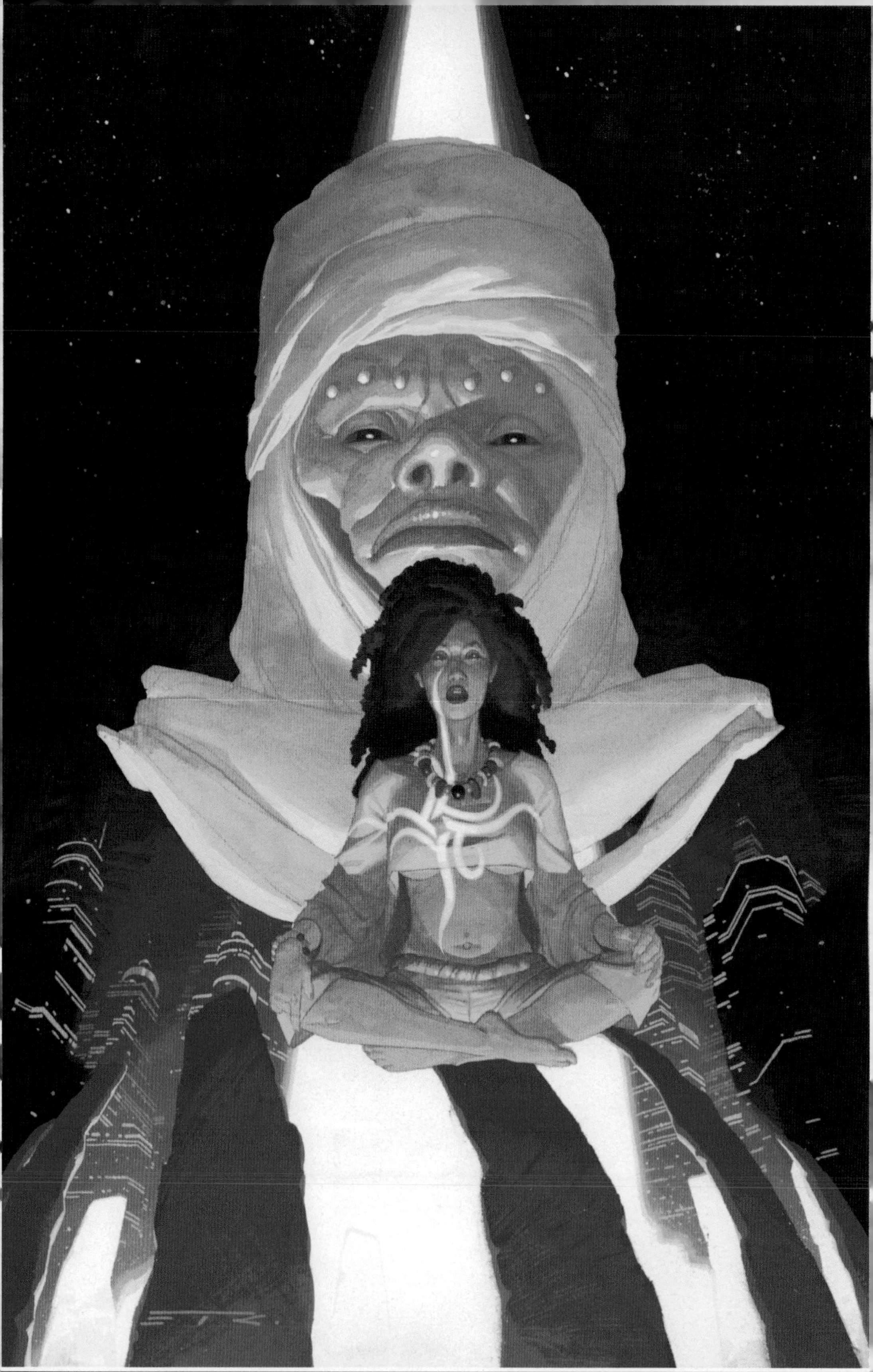

#6 VARIANT BY **ESAD RIBIC**

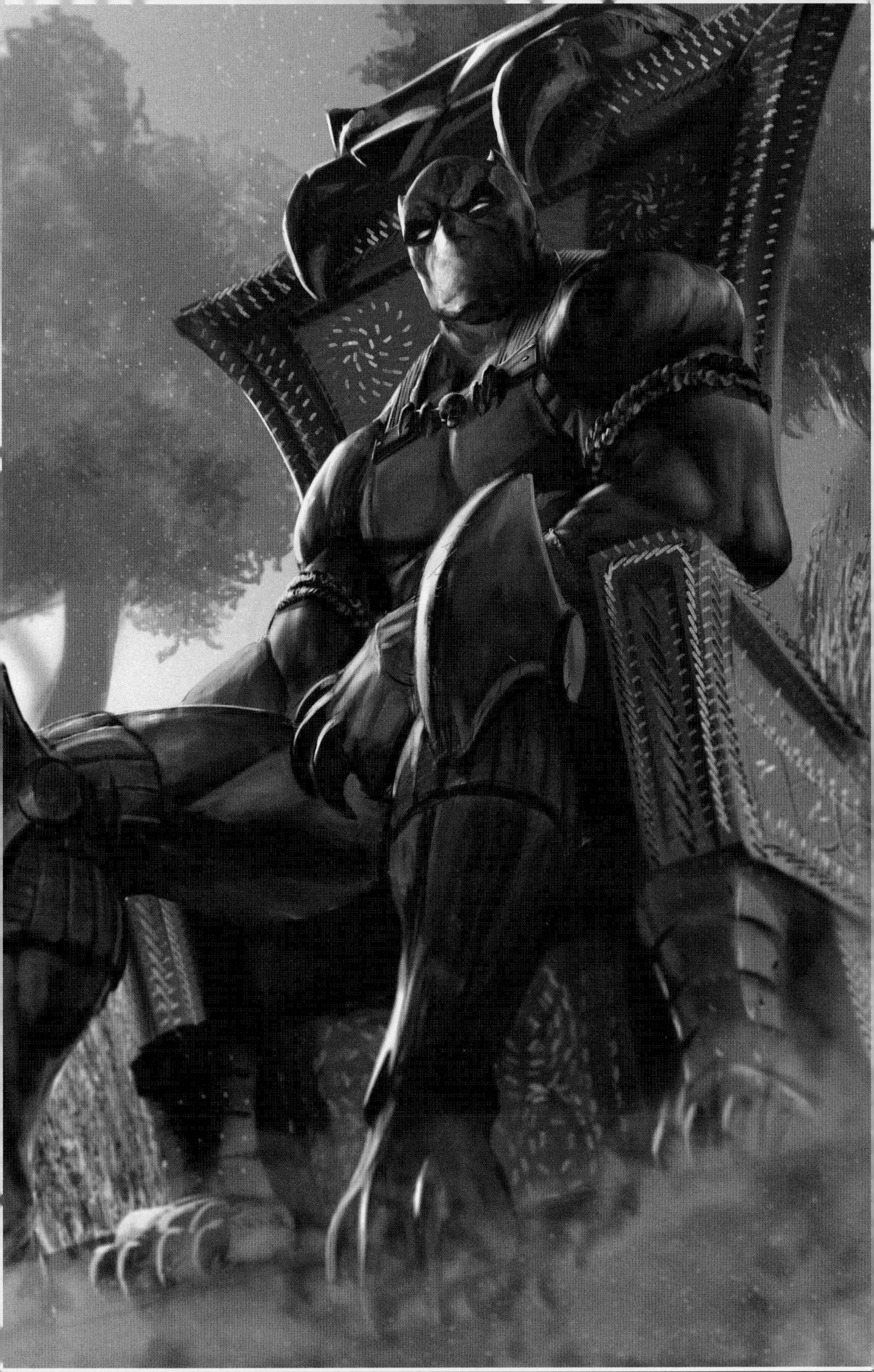

#6 VARIANT BY **UDON**

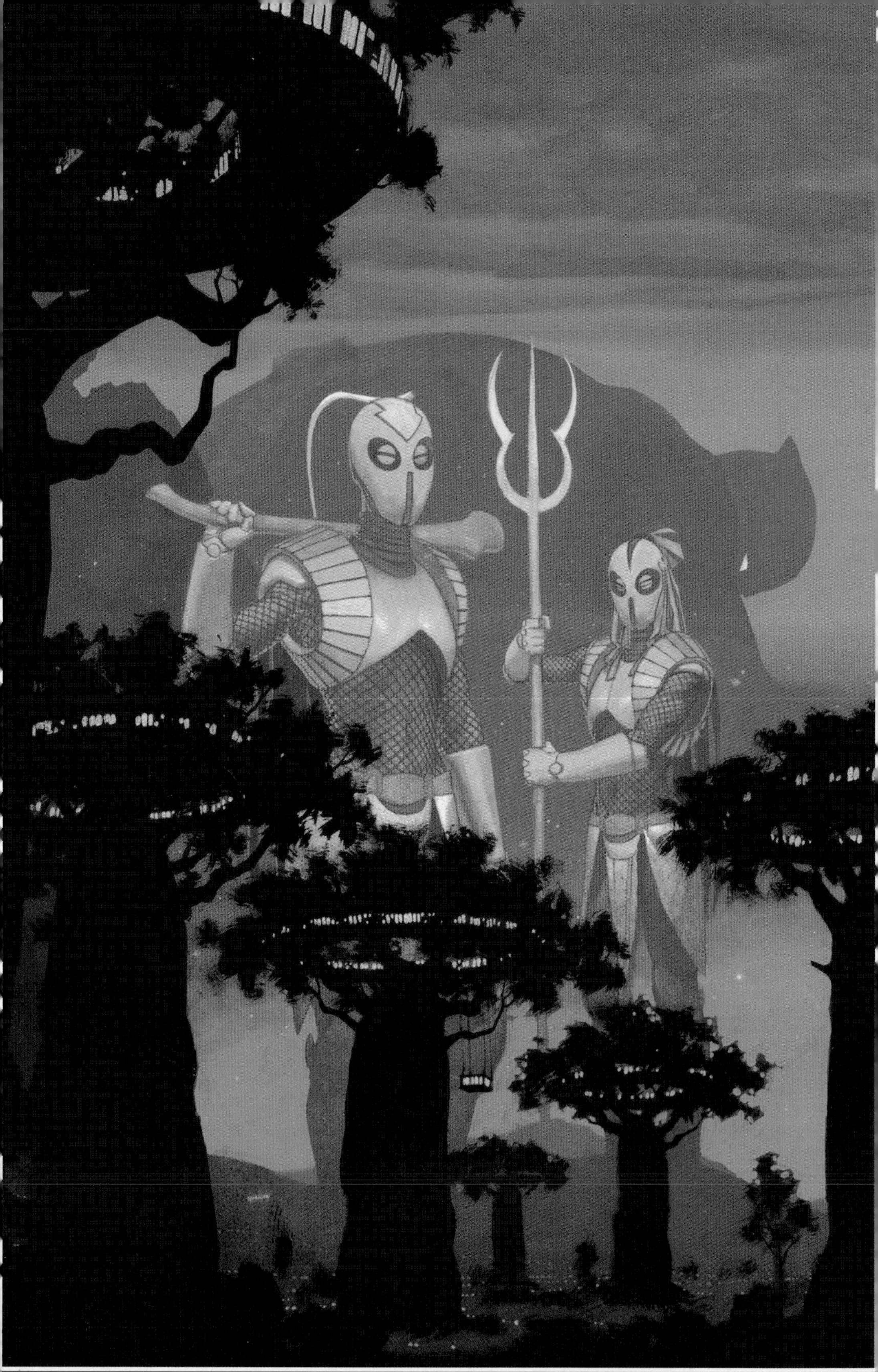

#7 VARIANT BY **ESAD RIBIC**

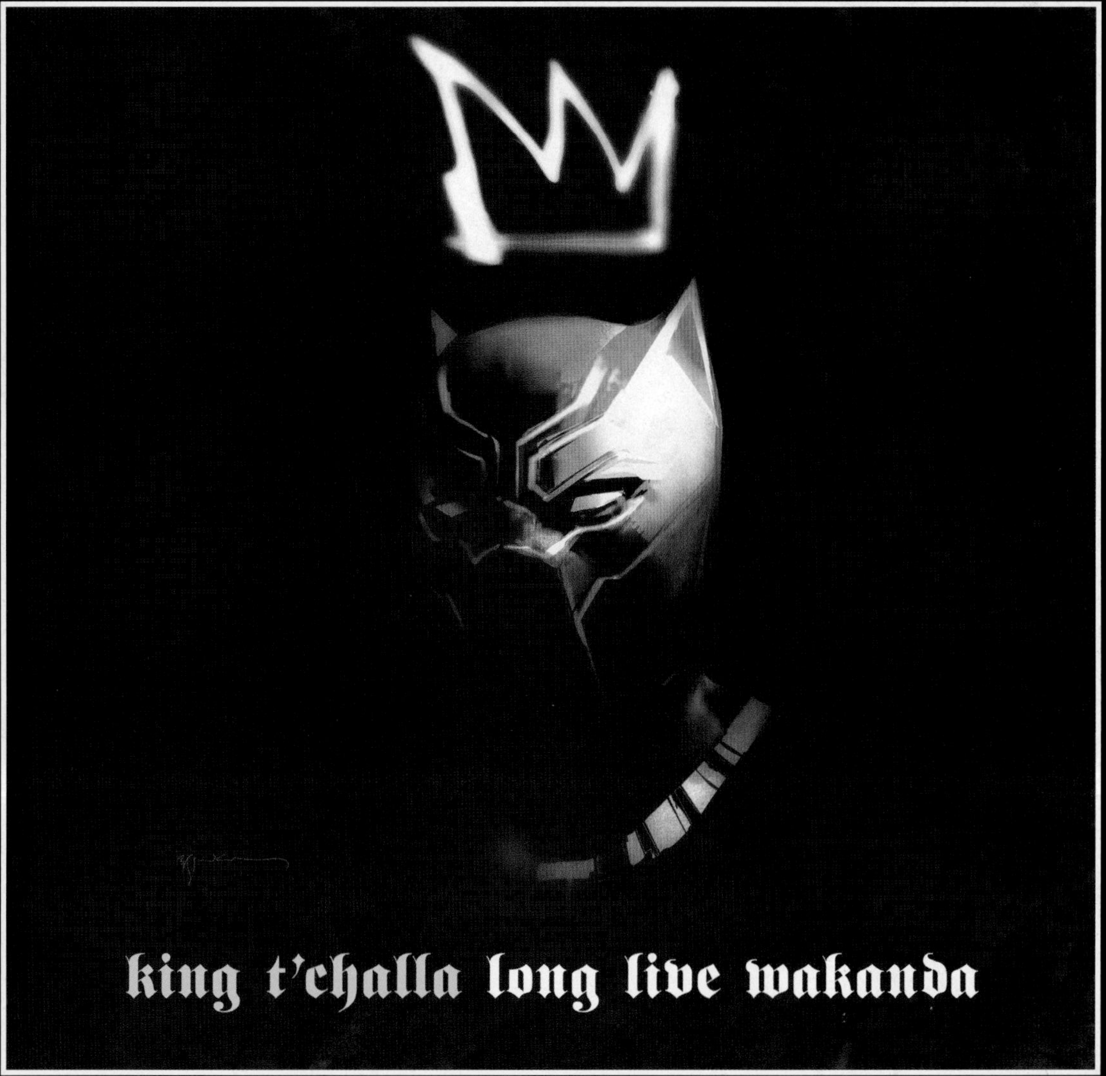
king t'challa long live wakanda

#7 HIP-HOP VARIANT BY **BILL SIENKIEWICZ**

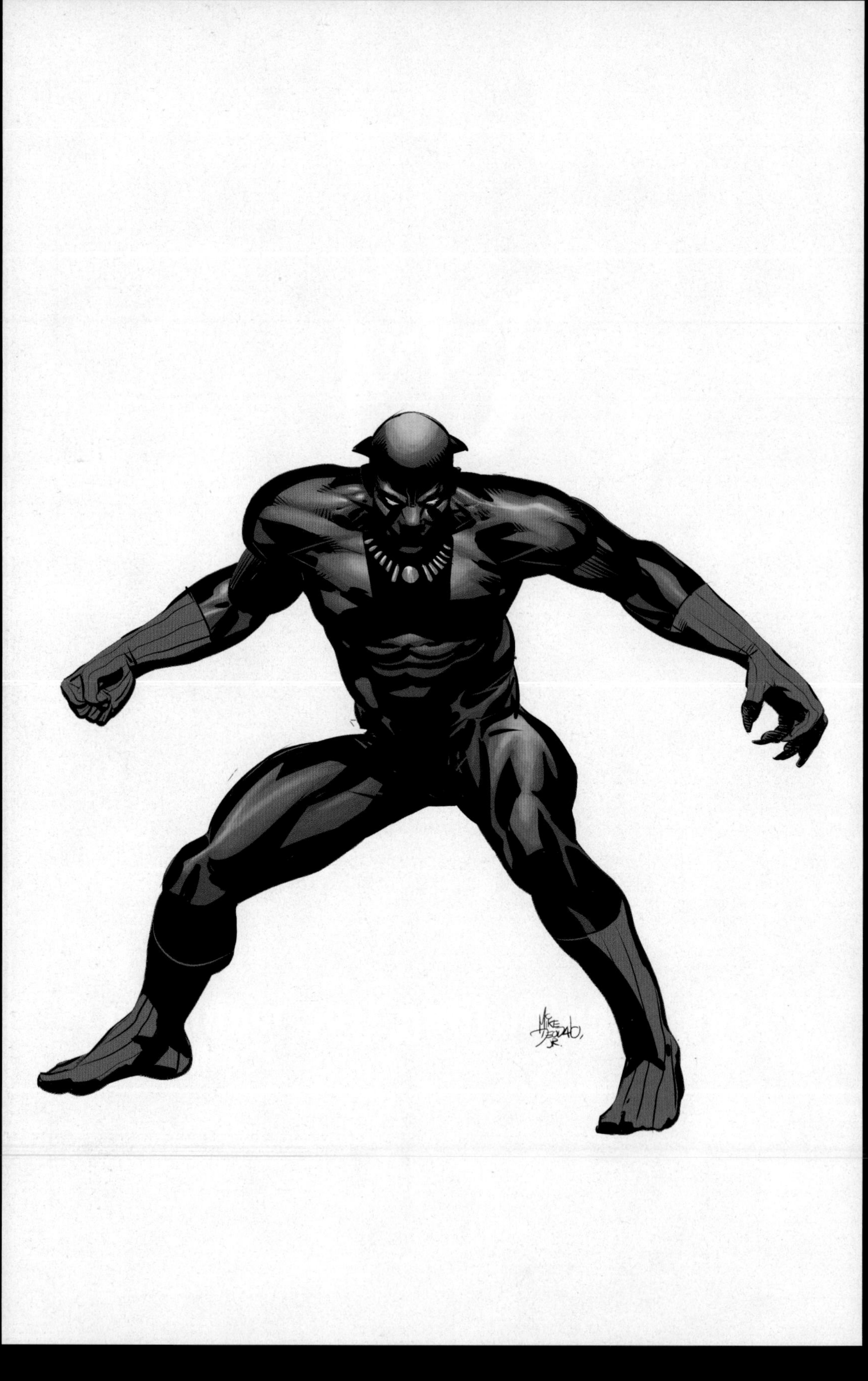

#7 TEASER VARIANT BY **MIKE DEDOATO** & **FRANK MARTIN**

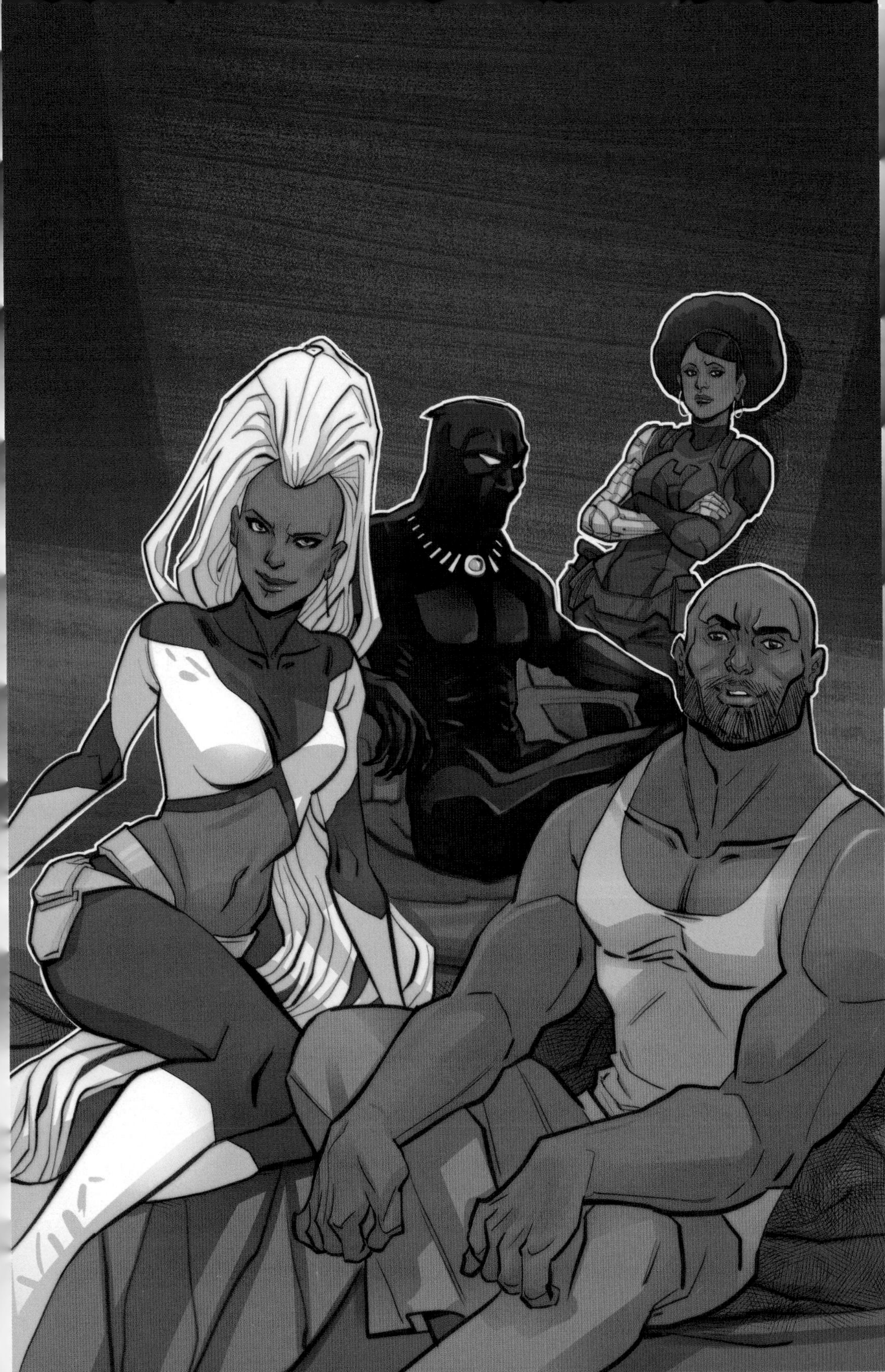

#7 VARIANT BY **MARGUERITE SAUVAGE**

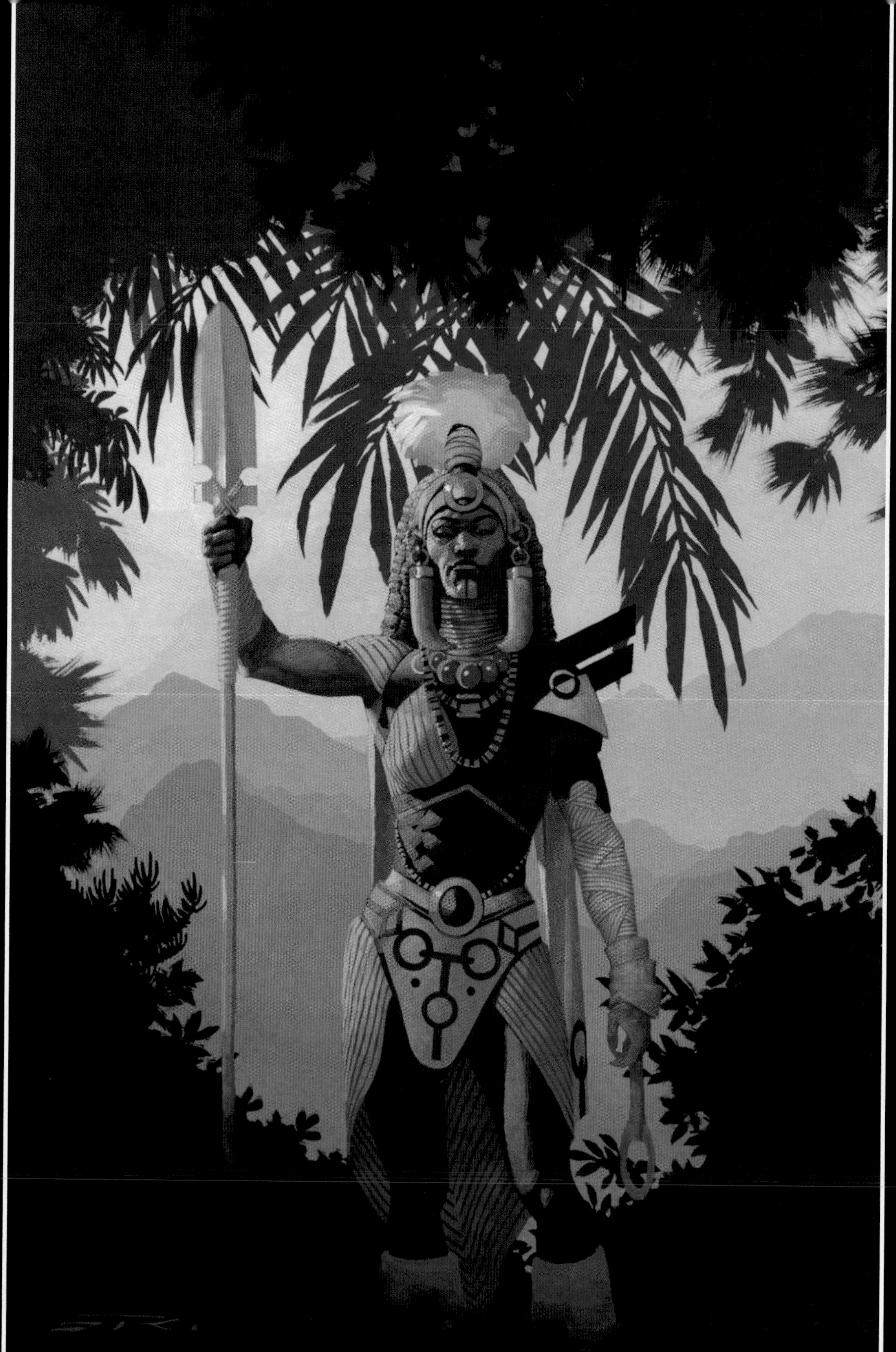

#8 VARIANT BY **ESAD RIBIC**

PAGE 1

PANEL 1
Open up with T'Challa. Mask off. Suit on. He's chained on the floor. ZEKE STANE is seated and over him. ANDREA and ANDREAS VON STRUCKER, VANISHER, and several SUN-TOUCHERS in the same room. It's a big room like a warehouse. The VON STRUCKERS are standing above, on a metal platform.

> **ZEKE STANE**
> I always thought I'd make a great king. I mean, I've got all the right attributes.

> **ZEKE STANE**
> Wise beyond my years.

> **ZEKE STANE**
> A regal mien.

PANEL 2
ZEKE STANE kicks T'CHALLA. T'CHALLA looks pained.

> **ZEKE STANE**
> A love of wanton cruelty.

PANEL 3
Pause here for a second. A shot of T'CHALLA. I want to pace this just right. It feels like there should be a beat here, before T'CHALLA turns the tables. T'CHALLA now looks like he might know something.

> **NO DIALOGUE**

PANEL 4
T'CHALLA on the floor, looking up at ZEKE STANE. More confident now. Almost smiling perhaps--but sinisterly.

> **T'CHALLA**
> Ezekiel Stane...

> **T'CHALLA**
> ...You are no longer useful to me.

PANEL 5
ZEKE STANE looking puzzled.

> **NO DIALOGUE**

PANEL 6
ZEKE STANE now figuring it all out.

> **ZEKE STANE**
> Holy Hell...

#7 PAGE 1 SCRIPT BY **TA-NEHISI COATES**
ART BY **CHRIS SPROUSE** & **KARL STORY**

PAGE 2

PANEL 1
Big splash panel. MANIFOLD opening a portal. We see STORM, LUKE CAGE, and MISTY KNIGHT bursting through. We see some of TETU's Sun-Touchers falling back under assault. ZEKE STANE and the SUN-TOUCHERS are falling back from the attack.

ZEKE STANE
Incoming!

PAGE 3

PANEL 1
Focus on MISTY KNIGHT side-kicking a SUN-TOUCHER. STORM flying overhead.

MISTY KNIGHT
What, no red, black and green? No Kwanzaa cake? I come back home, and this is reception I get?

PANEL 2
STORM using wind to blow several of the SUN-TOUCHERS backwards. MISTY KNIGHT fighting below.

STORM
Still better than the the knife-wielding thugs I found in Harlem, Misty. You do remember, don't you?

MISTY KNIGHT
I resent the term "thug."

PANEL 3
Now LUKE CAGE with like five dudes hanging on him.

LUKE CAGE
That's 'cause you a thug.

PANEL 4
MISTY KNIGHT pummels some other dude.

MISTY KNIGHT
For life.

PAGE 4

PANEL 1
VANISHER teleports in front of MISTY KNIGHT and LUKE CAGE.

VANISHER
Laugh now, bums.

PANEL 2
VANISHER teleports again and hits MISTY several times. Can we make this panel look like a constant motion of teleporting and fighting with VANISHER getting the upper hand?

VANISHER
You'll all be crying once the Vanisher's through.

PANEL 3
Another panel with VANISHER teleporting into the air and punching STORM.

NO DIALOGUE

PANEL 4
ANDREA and ANDREAS join hands and fire a concussive bolt, hitting STORM who is grounded. They are standing on a platform above the fray.

ANDREAS
Look who's joined us, Andrea!

ANDREA
Why it's the Kaffir-queen!

PANEL 5
LUKE CAGE crashes into the platform causing the VON STRUCKER twins to stumble to the ground.

LUKE CAGE
No, it's the Kaffir-crew.

ART BY **CHRIS SPROUSE** & **KARL STORY**

PAGE 5

PANEL 1
MISTY KNIGHT, now recovering. MANIFOLD attacking THE VANISHER. LUKE CAGE in the background fighting.

MISTY KNIGHT
I don't think you get to say that.

LUKE CAGE
What—Kaffir?

MISTY KNIGHT
No, *crew*. The name sucks.

PANEL 2
ZEKE STANE fires at MISTY KNIGHT and LUKE CAGE below.

ZEKE STANE
Here's a name for all of you--
rigor mortis.

PANEL 3
T'CHALLA, from the ground, leg-sweeps ZEKE STANE to the ground. His hands are still bound.

NO DIALOGUE

PANEL 4
T'CHALLA is now standing and facing off with ZEKE STANE looking ready to go.

ZEKE STANE
Seriously?

ZEKE STANE
Literally with both hands
behind your back?

PANEL 5
T'CHALLA looking mean at ZEKE STANE.

T'CHALLA
Yes.

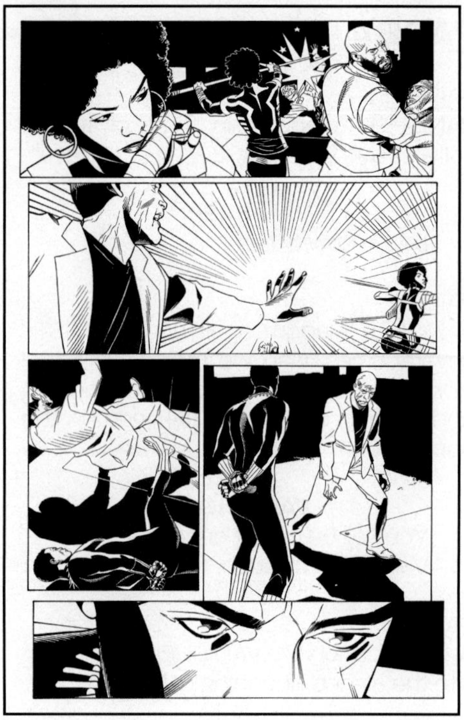

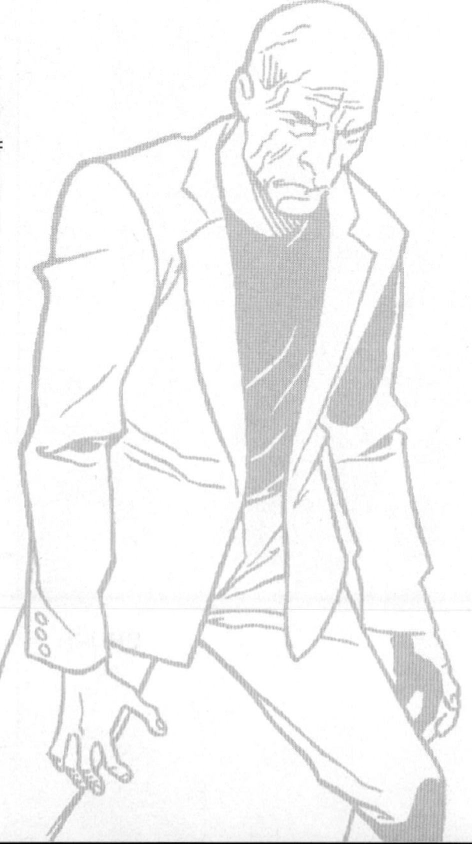

#7 PAGE 5 SCRIPT BY **TA-NEHISI COATES**
ART BY **CHRIS SPROUSE** & **KARL STORY**

SKETCHES
BY BRIAN STELFREEZE

SHURI

SKETCHES
BY BRIAN STELFREEZE

TA-NEHISI mentioned the idea of chainmail and I started riffing off of that. It led me to a cycle-style leather jacket reinforced with a single spun vibranium thread. The hood configuration gives them head protection when full-on battle time.

The necklace/sword is serpentine links that snap into place with a flick of the wrist, or it can work as a slashing whip. The shield also converts to a ridged body when it slides into its offensive position.

-STELFREEZE

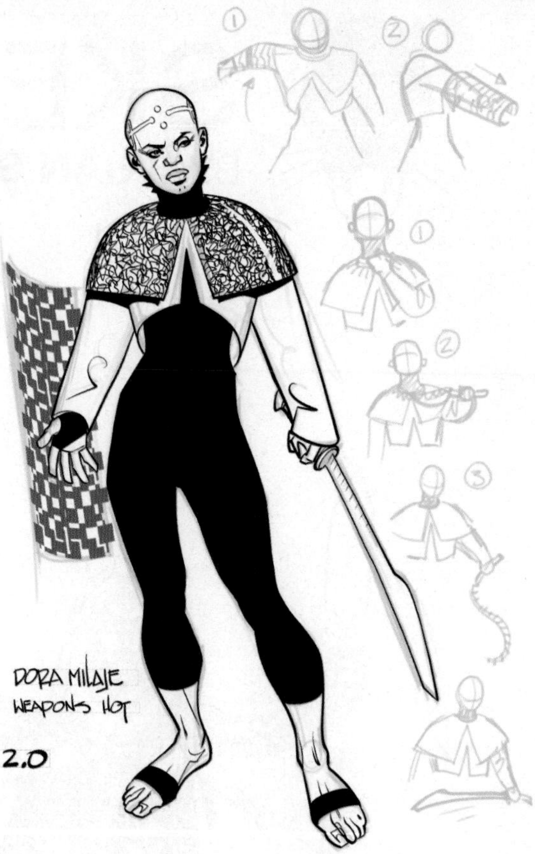

DORA MILAJE
WEAPONS HOT

DORA MILAJE 2.0

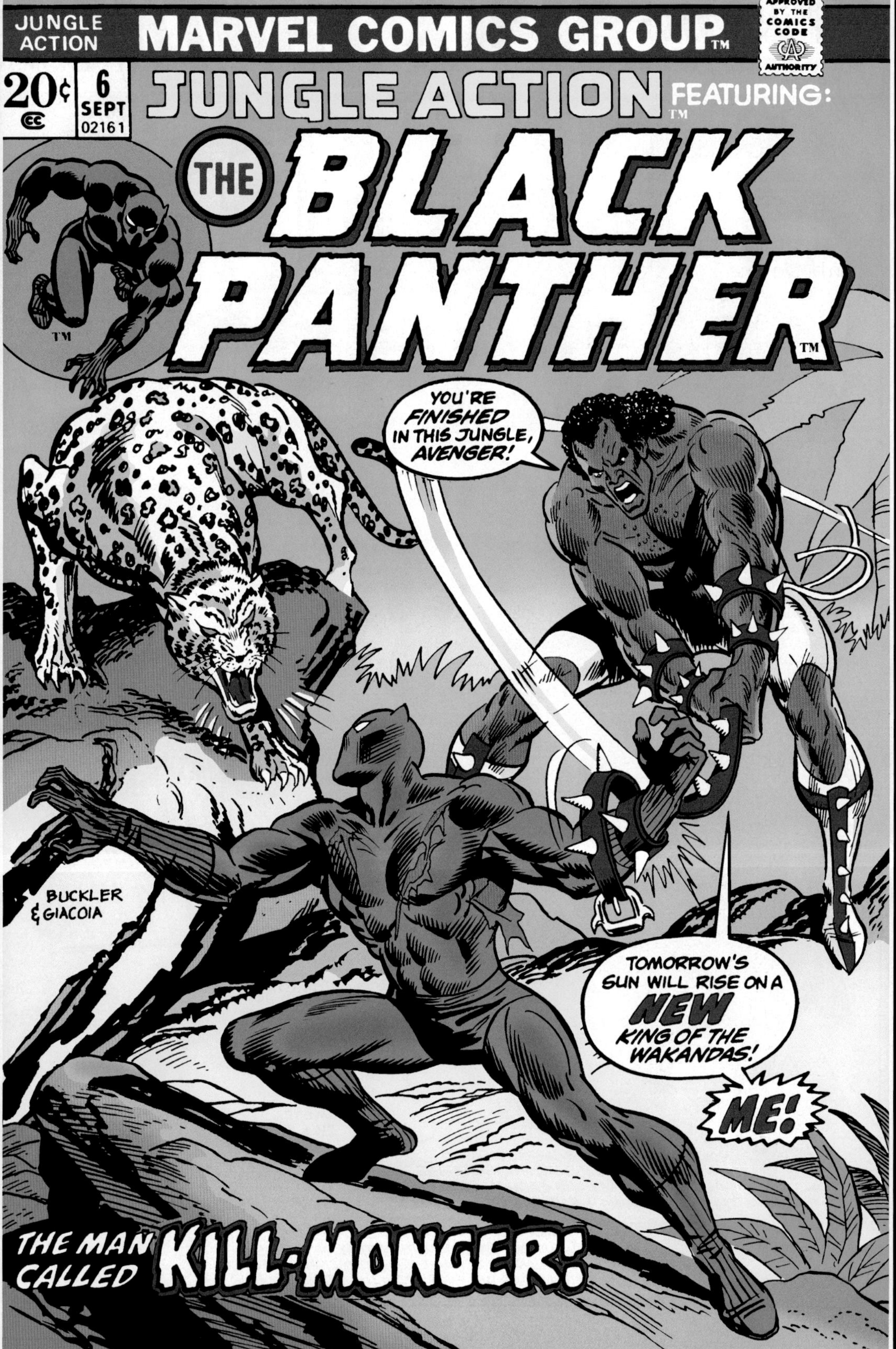
JUNGLE ACTION
MARVEL COMICS GROUP
APPROVED BY THE COMICS CODE AUTHORITY
20¢
6 SEPT 02161
JUNGLE ACTION FEATURING:
THE BLACK PANTHER
YOU'RE FINISHED IN THIS JUNGLE, AVENGER!
BUCKLER & GIACOIA
TOMORROW'S SUN WILL RISE ON A NEW KING OF THE WAKANDAS!
ME!
THE MAN CALLED KILL-MONGER!

NOW PRESENTING THE OPENING CHAPTERS OF THE CLASSIC "PANTHER'S RAGE," FEATURING KILLMONGER'S FIRST APPEARANCE!

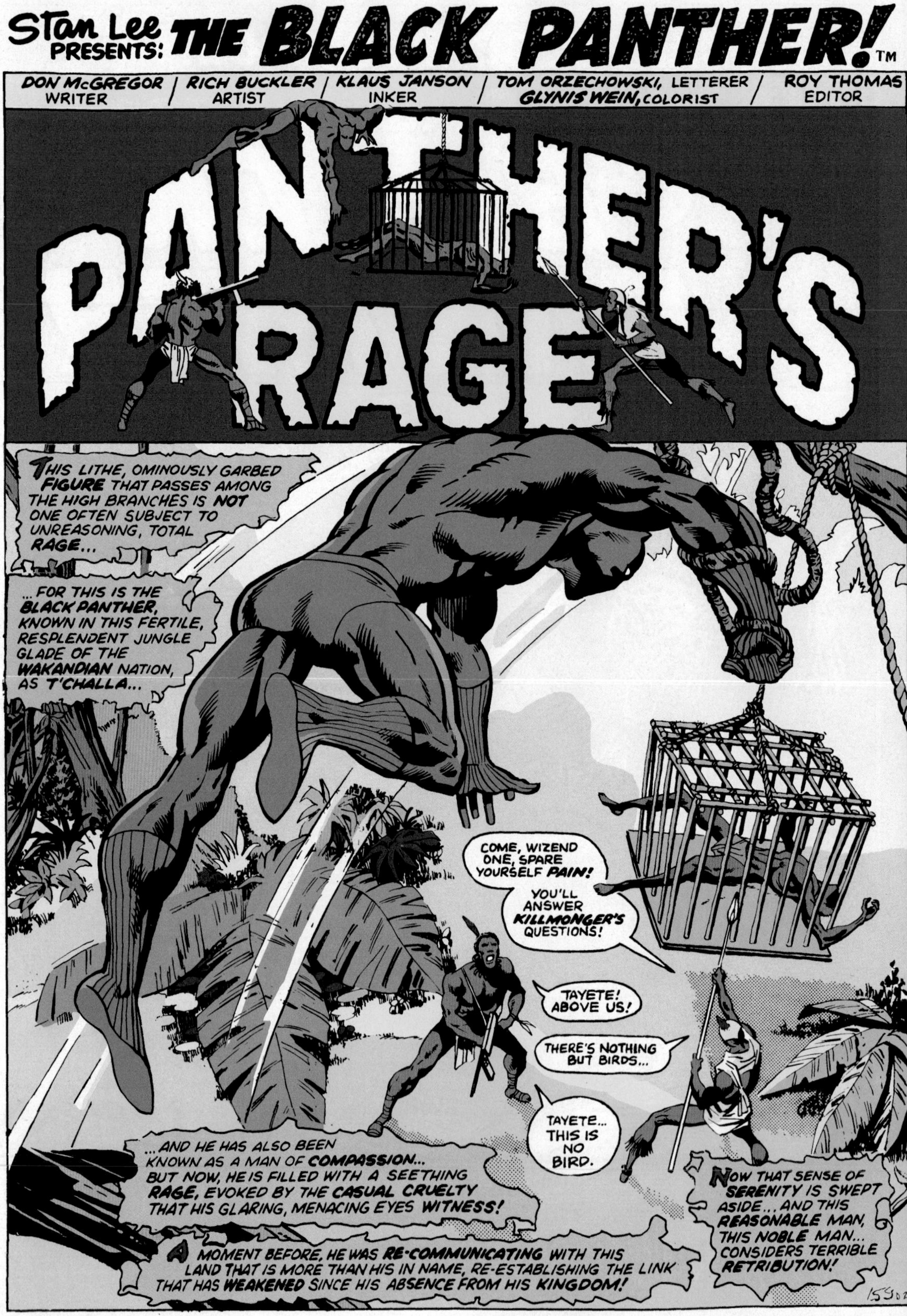
Stan Lee PRESENTS: THE BLACK PANTHER!™
DON McGREGOR WRITER / RICH BUCKLER ARTIST / KLAUS JANSON INKER / TOM ORZECHOWSKI, LETTERER GLYNIS WEIN, COLORIST / ROY THOMAS EDITOR
PANTHER'S RAGE
THIS LITHE, OMINOUSLY GARBED FIGURE THAT PASSES AMONG THE HIGH BRANCHES IS NOT ONE OFTEN SUBJECT TO UNREASONING, TOTAL RAGE...
...FOR THIS IS THE BLACK PANTHER, KNOWN IN THIS FERTILE, RESPLENDENT JUNGLE GLADE OF THE WAKANDIAN NATION, AS T'CHALLA...
COME, WIZEND ONE, SPARE YOURSELF PAIN!
YOU'LL ANSWER KILLMONGER'S QUESTIONS!
TAYETE! ABOVE US!
THERE'S NOTHING BUT BIRDS...
TAYETE... THIS IS NO BIRD.
...AND HE HAS ALSO BEEN KNOWN AS A MAN OF COMPASSION... BUT NOW, HE IS FILLED WITH A SEETHING RAGE, EVOKED BY THE CASUAL CRUELTY THAT HIS GLARING, MENACING EYES WITNESS!
A MOMENT BEFORE, HE WAS RE-COMMUNICATING WITH THIS LAND THAT IS MORE THAN HIS IN NAME, RE-ESTABLISHING THE LINK THAT HAS WEAKENED SINCE HIS ABSENCE FROM HIS KINGDOM!
NOW THAT SENSE OF SERENITY IS SWEPT ASIDE... AND THIS REASONABLE MAN, THIS NOBLE MAN... CONSIDERS TERRIBLE RETRIBUTION!

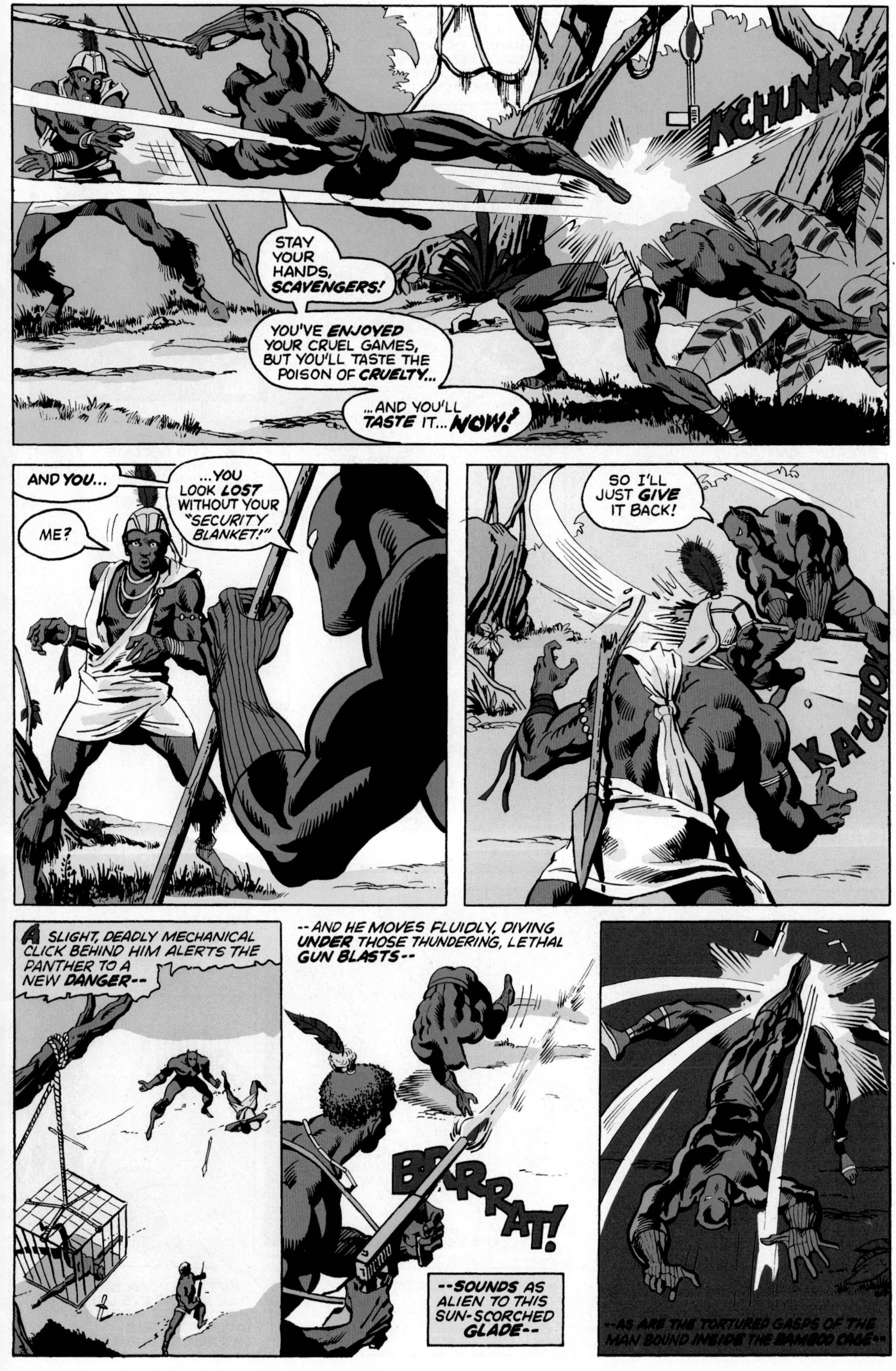
KCHUNK!
STAY YOUR HANDS, SCAVENGERS!
YOU'VE ENJOYED YOUR CRUEL GAMES, BUT YOU'LL TASTE THE POISON OF CRUELTY...
...AND YOU'LL TASTE IT... NOW!
AND YOU...
...YOU LOOK LOST WITHOUT YOUR "SECURITY BLANKET!"
ME?
SO I'LL JUST GIVE IT BACK!
KA-CHOK
A SLIGHT, DEADLY MECHANICAL CLICK BEHIND HIM ALERTS THE PANTHER TO A NEW DANGER--
--AND HE MOVES FLUIDLY, DIVING UNDER THOSE THUNDERING, LETHAL GUN BLASTS--
BRRRAT!
--SOUNDS AS ALIEN TO THIS SUN-SCORCHED GLADE--
--AS ARE THE TORTURED GASPS OF THE MAN BOUND INSIDE THE BAMBOO CAGE--

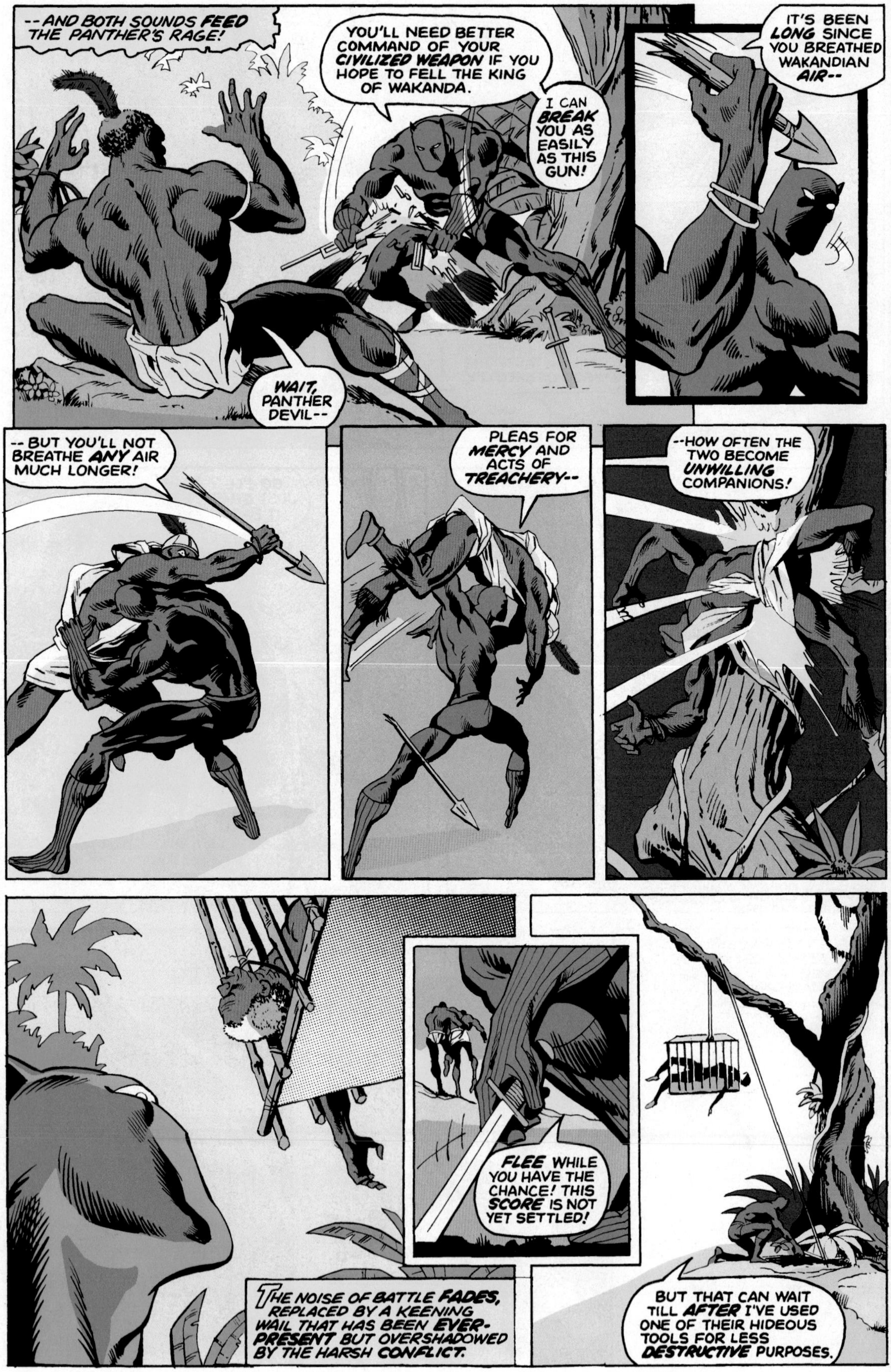
--AND BOTH SOUNDS FEED THE PANTHER'S RAGE!
YOU'LL NEED BETTER COMMAND OF YOUR CIVILIZED WEAPON IF YOU HOPE TO FELL THE KING OF WAKANDA.
I CAN BREAK YOU AS EASILY AS THIS GUN!
WAIT, PANTHER DEVIL--
IT'S BEEN LONG SINCE YOU BREATHED WAKANDIAN AIR--
-- BUT YOU'LL NOT BREATHE ANY AIR MUCH LONGER!
PLEAS FOR MERCY AND ACTS OF TREACHERY--
--HOW OFTEN THE TWO BECOME UNWILLING COMPANIONS!
FLEE WHILE YOU HAVE THE CHANCE! THIS SCORE IS NOT YET SETTLED!
THE NOISE OF BATTLE FADES, REPLACED BY A KEENING WAIL THAT HAS BEEN EVER-PRESENT BUT OVERSHADOWED BY THE HARSH CONFLICT.
BUT THAT CAN WAIT TILL AFTER I'VE USED ONE OF THEIR HIDEOUS TOOLS FOR LESS DESTRUCTIVE PURPOSES.

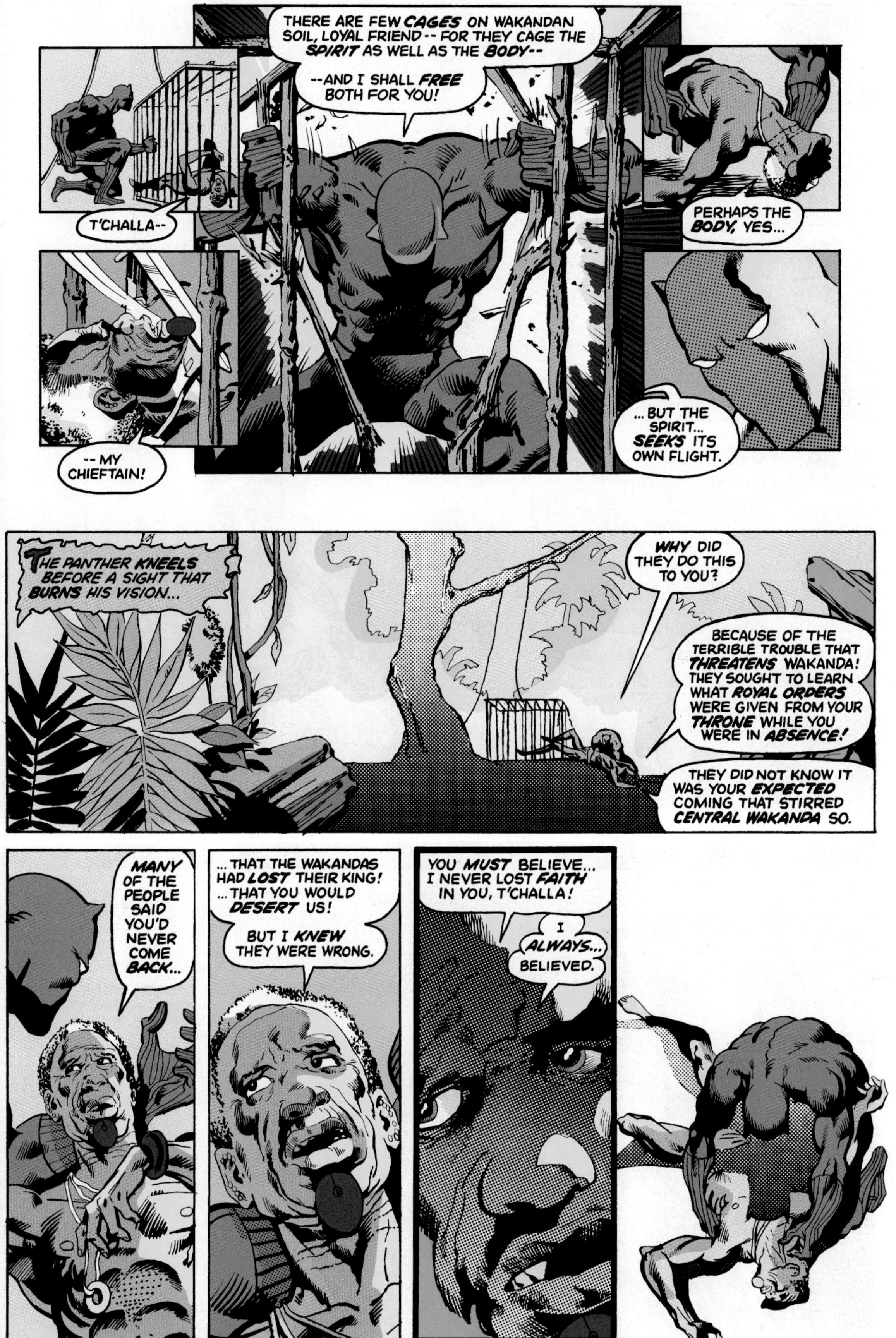
THERE ARE FEW CAGES ON WAKANDAN SOIL, LOYAL FRIEND -- FOR THEY CAGE THE SPIRIT AS WELL AS THE BODY--
--AND I SHALL FREE BOTH FOR YOU!
T'CHALLA--
-- MY CHIEFTAIN!
PERHAPS THE BODY, YES...
... BUT THE SPIRIT... SEEKS ITS OWN FLIGHT.
THE PANTHER KNEELS BEFORE A SIGHT THAT BURNS HIS VISION...
WHY DID THEY DO THIS TO YOU?
BECAUSE OF THE TERRIBLE TROUBLE THAT THREATENS WAKANDA! THEY SOUGHT TO LEARN WHAT ROYAL ORDERS WERE GIVEN FROM YOUR THRONE WHILE YOU WERE IN ABSENCE!
THEY DID NOT KNOW IT WAS YOUR EXPECTED COMING THAT STIRRED CENTRAL WAKANDA SO.
MANY OF THE PEOPLE SAID YOU'D NEVER COME BACK...
... THAT THE WAKANDAS HAD LOST THEIR KING! ... THAT YOU WOULD DESERT US!
BUT I KNEW THEY WERE WRONG.
YOU MUST BELIEVE... I NEVER LOST FAITH IN YOU, T'CHALLA!
I ALWAYS... BELIEVED.

IT IS A LONG *TREK* BACK INTO THE CENTER OF THE *WAKANDA* VILLAGE...

...AND AS THE *PANTHER* STEPS OUT OF THE LUSH *FOLIAGE* INTO THE *SUN-BURNT DUST* SURROUNDING THE WOOD AND STRAW HUTS, ANOTHER DISTURBING THOUGHT *CLAIMS* HIM:

HE *HAS* BEEN AWAY *TOO* LONG.

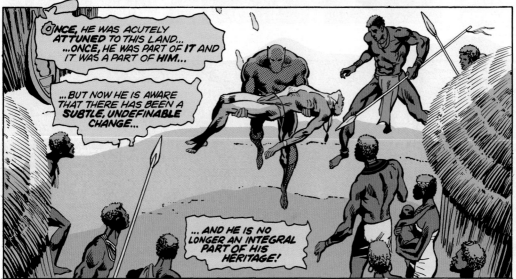

*O*NCE, HE WAS ACUTELY *ATTUNED* TO THIS LAND... ...ONCE, HE WAS PART OF *IT* AND IT WAS A PART OF *HIM*...

...BUT NOW HE IS AWARE THAT THERE HAS BEEN A *SUBTLE, UNDEFINABLE* CHANGE...

...AND HE IS NO LONGER AN *INTEGRAL* PART OF HIS *HERITAGE!*

*T*HE KNOWLEDGE OF THIS AND OF THE *DESTROYED HUMANITY* HE HOLDS IN HIS ARMS IS *REFLECTED* IN HIS WALK.

A SOMBER WAKE FORMS THIS *SILENT* PROCESSION, ALL MUTE WITH ONE *EMOTION:*

MOURNING!

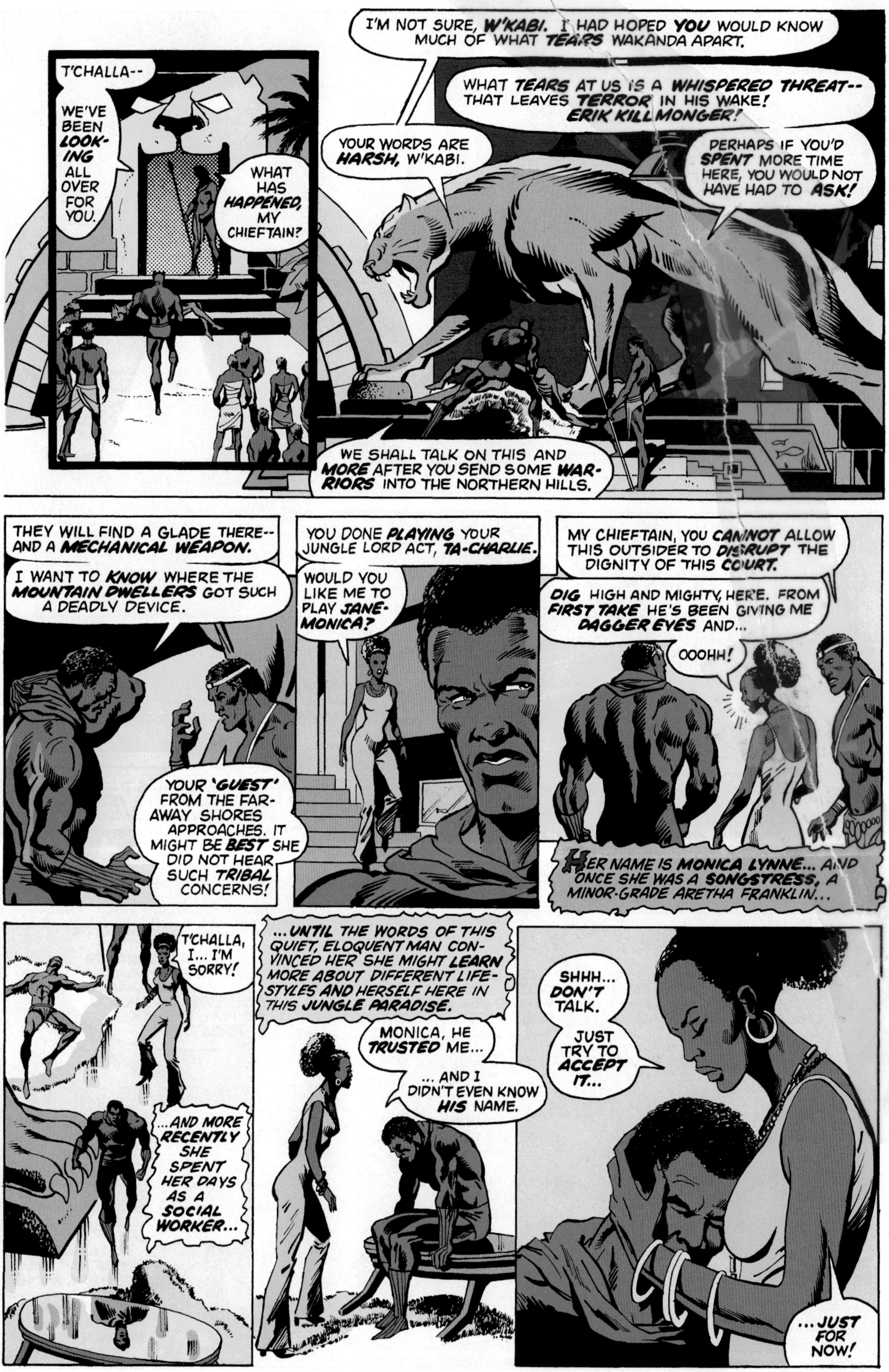
T'CHALLA--
WE'VE BEEN LOOKING ALL OVER FOR YOU.
WHAT HAS HAPPENED, MY CHIEFTAIN?
I'M NOT SURE, W'KABI. I HAD HOPED YOU WOULD KNOW MUCH OF WHAT TEARS WAKANDA APART.
YOUR WORDS ARE HARSH, W'KABI.
WHAT TEARS AT US IS A WHISPERED THREAT-- THAT LEAVES TERROR IN HIS WAKE! ERIK KILLMONGER!
PERHAPS IF YOU'D SPENT MORE TIME HERE, YOU WOULD NOT HAVE HAD TO ASK!
WE SHALL TALK ON THIS AND MORE AFTER YOU SEND SOME WARRIORS INTO THE NORTHERN HILLS.
THEY WILL FIND A GLADE THERE-- AND A MECHANICAL WEAPON.
I WANT TO KNOW WHERE THE MOUNTAIN DWELLERS GOT SUCH A DEADLY DEVICE.
YOUR 'GUEST' FROM THE FAR-AWAY SHORES APPROACHES. IT MIGHT BE BEST SHE DID NOT HEAR SUCH TRIBAL CONCERNS!
YOU DONE PLAYING YOUR JUNGLE LORD ACT, TA-CHARLIE.
WOULD YOU LIKE ME TO PLAY JANE-MONICA?
MY CHIEFTAIN, YOU CANNOT ALLOW THIS OUTSIDER TO DISRUPT THE DIGNITY OF THIS COURT.
DIG HIGH AND MIGHTY, HERE. FROM FIRST TAKE HE'S BEEN GIVING ME DAGGER EYES AND...
OOOHH!
HER NAME IS MONICA LYNNE... AND ONCE SHE WAS A SONGSTRESS, A MINOR-GRADE ARETHA FRANKLIN...
T'CHALLA, I... I'M SORRY!
...AND MORE RECENTLY SHE SPENT HER DAYS AS A SOCIAL WORKER...
...UNTIL THE WORDS OF THIS QUIET, ELOQUENT MAN CONVINCED HER SHE MIGHT LEARN MORE ABOUT DIFFERENT LIFE-STYLES AND HERSELF HERE IN THIS JUNGLE PARADISE.
MONICA, HE TRUSTED ME...
... AND I DIDN'T EVEN KNOW HIS NAME.
SHHH... DON'T TALK.
JUST TRY TO ACCEPT IT...
...JUST FOR NOW!

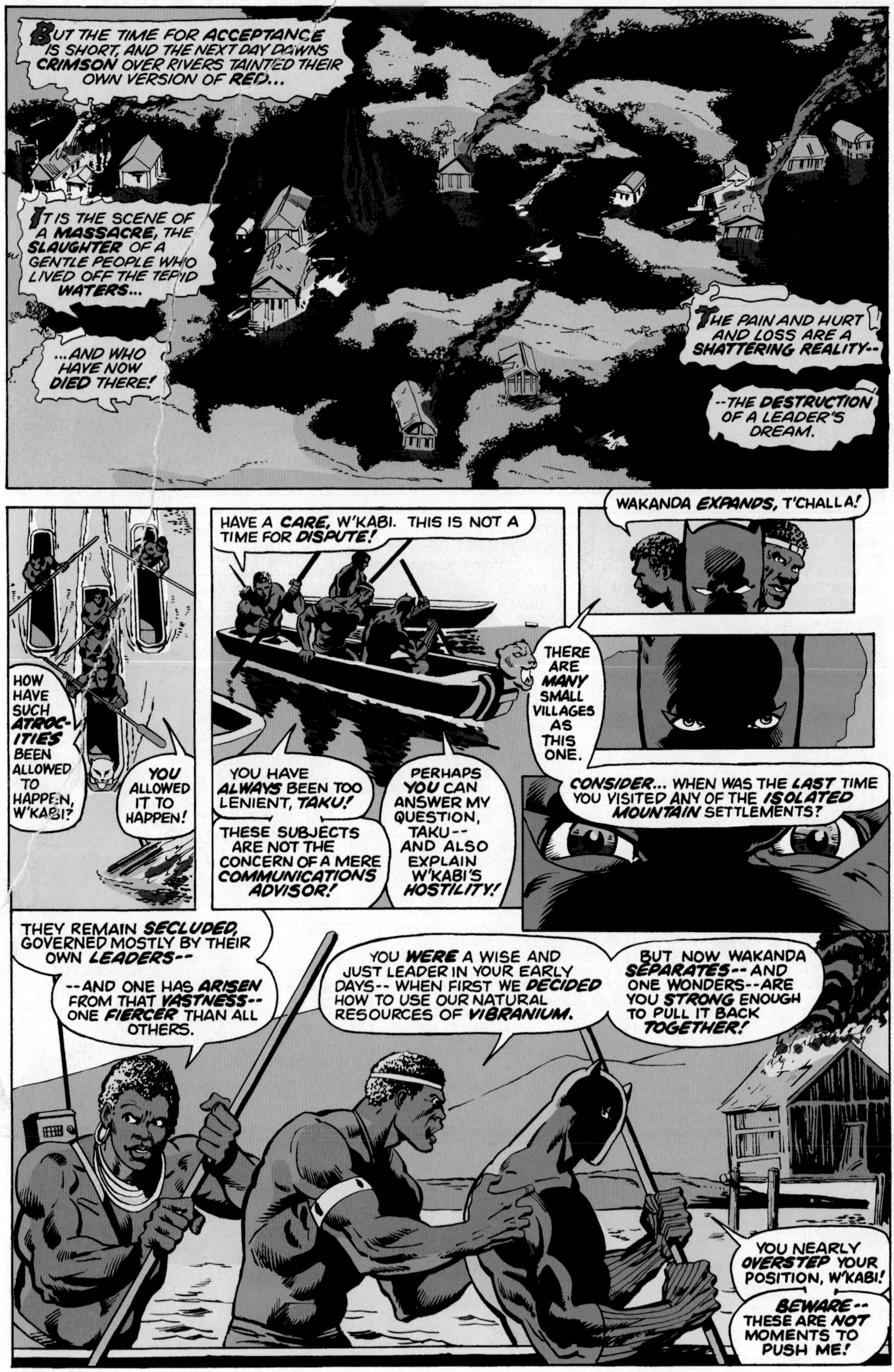

BUT THE TIME FOR ACCEPTANCE IS SHORT, AND THE NEXT DAY DAWNS CRIMSON OVER RIVERS TAINTED THEIR OWN VERSION OF RED...
IT IS THE SCENE OF A MASSACRE, THE SLAUGHTER OF A GENTLE PEOPLE WHO LIVED OFF THE TEPID WATERS...
...AND WHO HAVE NOW DIED THERE!
THE PAIN AND HURT AND LOSS ARE A SHATTERING REALITY--
--THE DESTRUCTION OF A LEADER'S DREAM.
HOW HAVE SUCH ATROCITIES BEEN ALLOWED TO HAPPEN, W'KABI?
YOU ALLOWED IT TO HAPPEN!
HAVE A CARE, W'KABI. THIS IS NOT A TIME FOR DISPUTE!
YOU HAVE ALWAYS BEEN TOO LENIENT, TAKU!
THESE SUBJECTS ARE NOT THE CONCERN OF A MERE COMMUNICATIONS ADVISOR!
PERHAPS YOU CAN ANSWER MY QUESTION, TAKU-- AND ALSO EXPLAIN W'KABI'S HOSTILITY!
WAKANDA EXPANDS, T'CHALLA!
THERE ARE MANY SMALL VILLAGES AS THIS ONE.
CONSIDER... WHEN WAS THE LAST TIME YOU VISITED ANY OF THE ISOLATED MOUNTAIN SETTLEMENTS?
THEY REMAIN SECLUDED, GOVERNED MOSTLY BY THEIR OWN LEADERS--
--AND ONE HAS ARISEN FROM THAT VASTNESS-- ONE FIERCER THAN ALL OTHERS.
YOU WERE A WISE AND JUST LEADER IN YOUR EARLY DAYS-- WHEN FIRST WE DECIDED HOW TO USE OUR NATURAL RESOURCES OF VIBRANIUM.
BUT NOW WAKANDA SEPARATES-- AND ONE WONDERS--ARE YOU STRONG ENOUGH TO PULL IT BACK TOGETHER!
YOU NEARLY OVERSTEP YOUR POSITION, W'KABI!
BEWARE-- THESE ARE NOT MOMENTS TO PUSH ME!

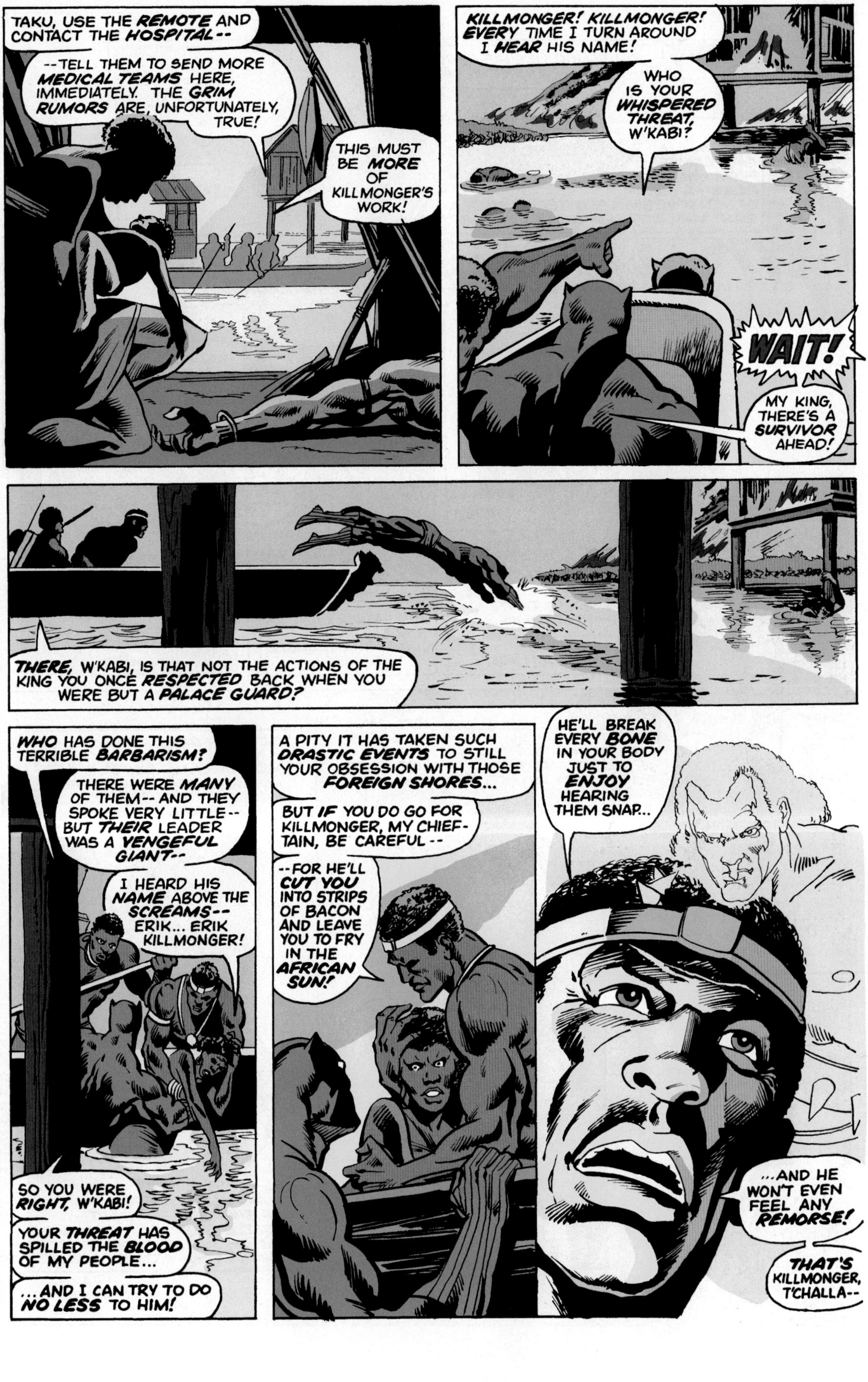
TAKU, USE THE REMOTE AND CONTACT THE HOSPITAL--
--TELL THEM TO SEND MORE MEDICAL TEAMS HERE, IMMEDIATELY. THE GRIM RUMORS ARE, UNFORTUNATELY, TRUE!
THIS MUST BE MORE OF KILLMONGER'S WORK!
KILLMONGER! KILLMONGER! EVERY TIME I TURN AROUND I HEAR HIS NAME!
WHO IS YOUR WHISPERED THREAT, W'KABI?
WAIT!
MY KING, THERE'S A SURVIVOR AHEAD!
THERE, W'KABI, IS THAT NOT THE ACTIONS OF THE KING YOU ONCE RESPECTED BACK WHEN YOU WERE BUT A PALACE GUARD?
WHO HAS DONE THIS TERRIBLE BARBARISM?
THERE WERE MANY OF THEM-- AND THEY SPOKE VERY LITTLE-- BUT THEIR LEADER WAS A VENGEFUL GIANT--
I HEARD HIS NAME ABOVE THE SCREAMS-- ERIK... ERIK KILLMONGER!
SO YOU WERE RIGHT, W'KABI!
YOUR THREAT HAS SPILLED THE BLOOD OF MY PEOPLE...
...AND I CAN TRY TO DO NO LESS TO HIM!
A PITY IT HAS TAKEN SUCH DRASTIC EVENTS TO STILL YOUR OBSESSION WITH THOSE FOREIGN SHORES...
BUT IF YOU DO GO FOR KILLMONGER, MY CHIEF-TAIN, BE CAREFUL --
--FOR HE'LL CUT YOU INTO STRIPS OF BACON AND LEAVE YOU TO FRY IN THE AFRICAN SUN!
HE'LL BREAK EVERY BONE IN YOUR BODY JUST TO ENJOY HEARING THEM SNAP...
...AND HE WON'T EVEN FEEL ANY REMORSE!
THAT'S KILLMONGER, T'CHALLA--

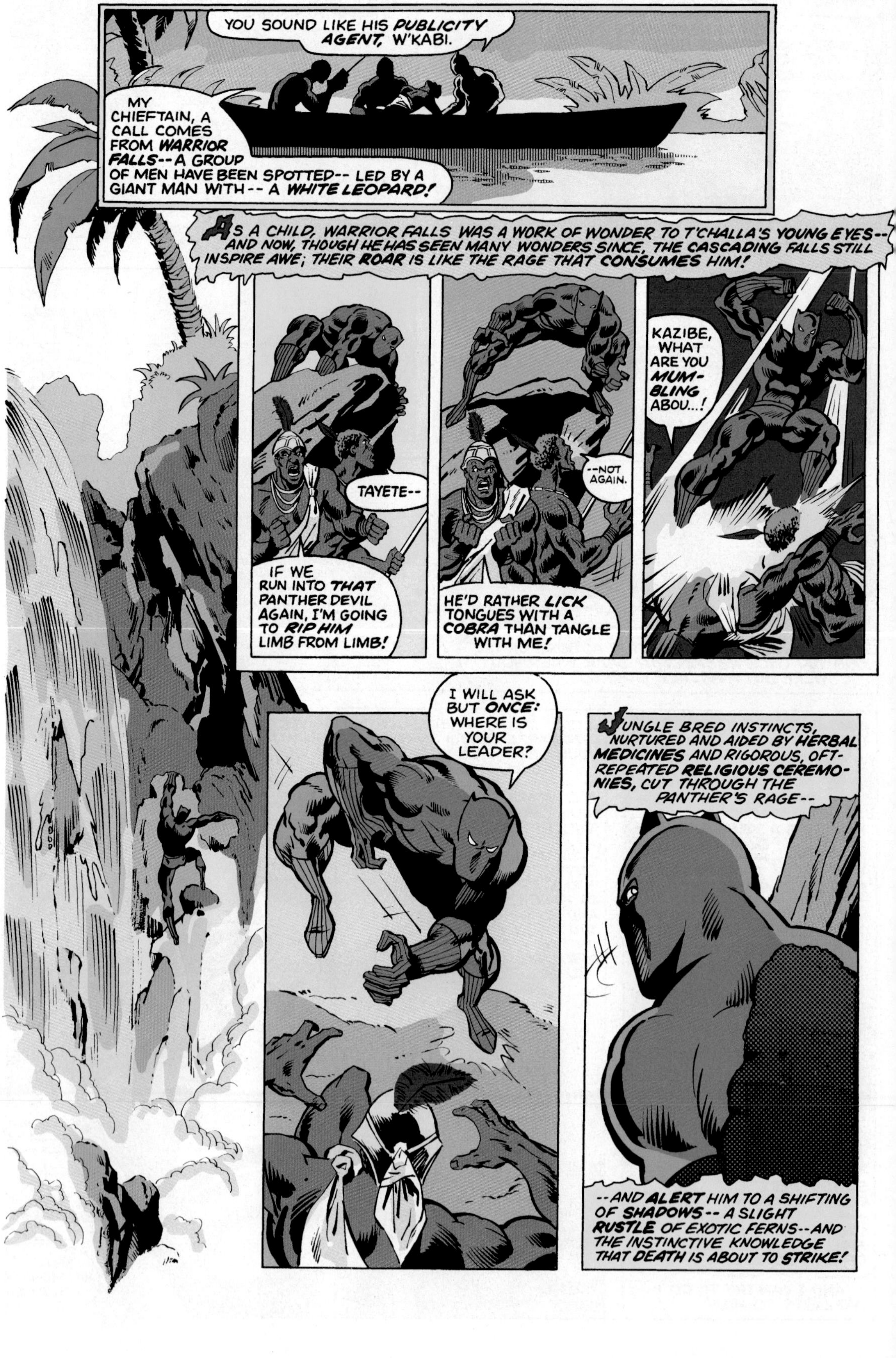
YOU SOUND LIKE HIS PUBLICITY AGENT, W'KABI.
MY CHIEFTAIN, A CALL COMES FROM WARRIOR FALLS--A GROUP OF MEN HAVE BEEN SPOTTED-- LED BY A GIANT MAN WITH -- A WHITE LEOPARD!
AS A CHILD, WARRIOR FALLS WAS A WORK OF WONDER TO T'CHALLA'S YOUNG EYES--AND NOW, THOUGH HE HAS SEEN MANY WONDERS SINCE, THE CASCADING FALLS STILL INSPIRE AWE; THEIR ROAR IS LIKE THE RAGE THAT CONSUMES HIM!
TAYETE--
IF WE RUN INTO THAT PANTHER DEVIL AGAIN, I'M GOING TO RIP HIM LIMB FROM LIMB!
--NOT AGAIN.
HE'D RATHER LICK TONGUES WITH A COBRA THAN TANGLE WITH ME!
KAZIBE, WHAT ARE YOU MUMBLING ABOU...!
I WILL ASK BUT ONCE: WHERE IS YOUR LEADER?
JUNGLE BRED INSTINCTS, NURTURED AND AIDED BY HERBAL MEDICINES AND RIGOROUS, OFT-REPEATED RELIGIOUS CEREMONIES, CUT THROUGH THE PANTHER'S RAGE--
--AND ALERT HIM TO A SHIFTING OF SHADOWS-- A SLIGHT RUSTLE OF EXOTIC FERNS--AND THE INSTINCTIVE KNOWLEDGE THAT DEATH IS ABOUT TO STRIKE!

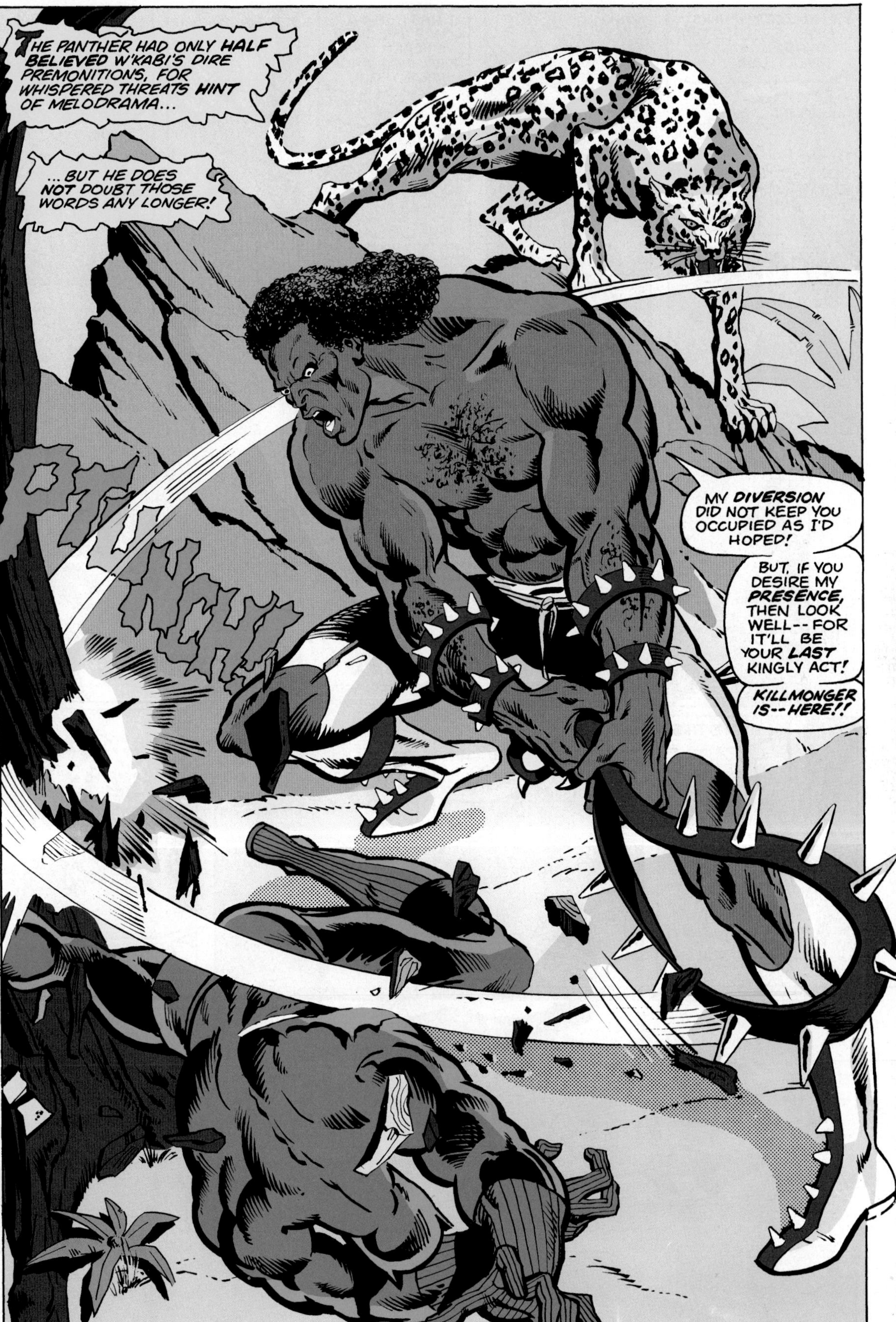
THE PANTHER HAD ONLY HALF BELIEVED W'KABI'S DIRE PREMONITIONS, FOR WHISPERED THREATS HINT OF MELODRAMA...
...BUT HE DOES NOT DOUBT THOSE WORDS ANY LONGER!
PTCHNCH!
MY DIVERSION DID NOT KEEP YOU OCCUPIED AS I'D HOPED!
BUT, IF YOU DESIRE MY PRESENCE, THEN LOOK WELL--FOR IT'LL BE YOUR LAST KINGLY ACT!
KILLMONGER IS--HERE!!

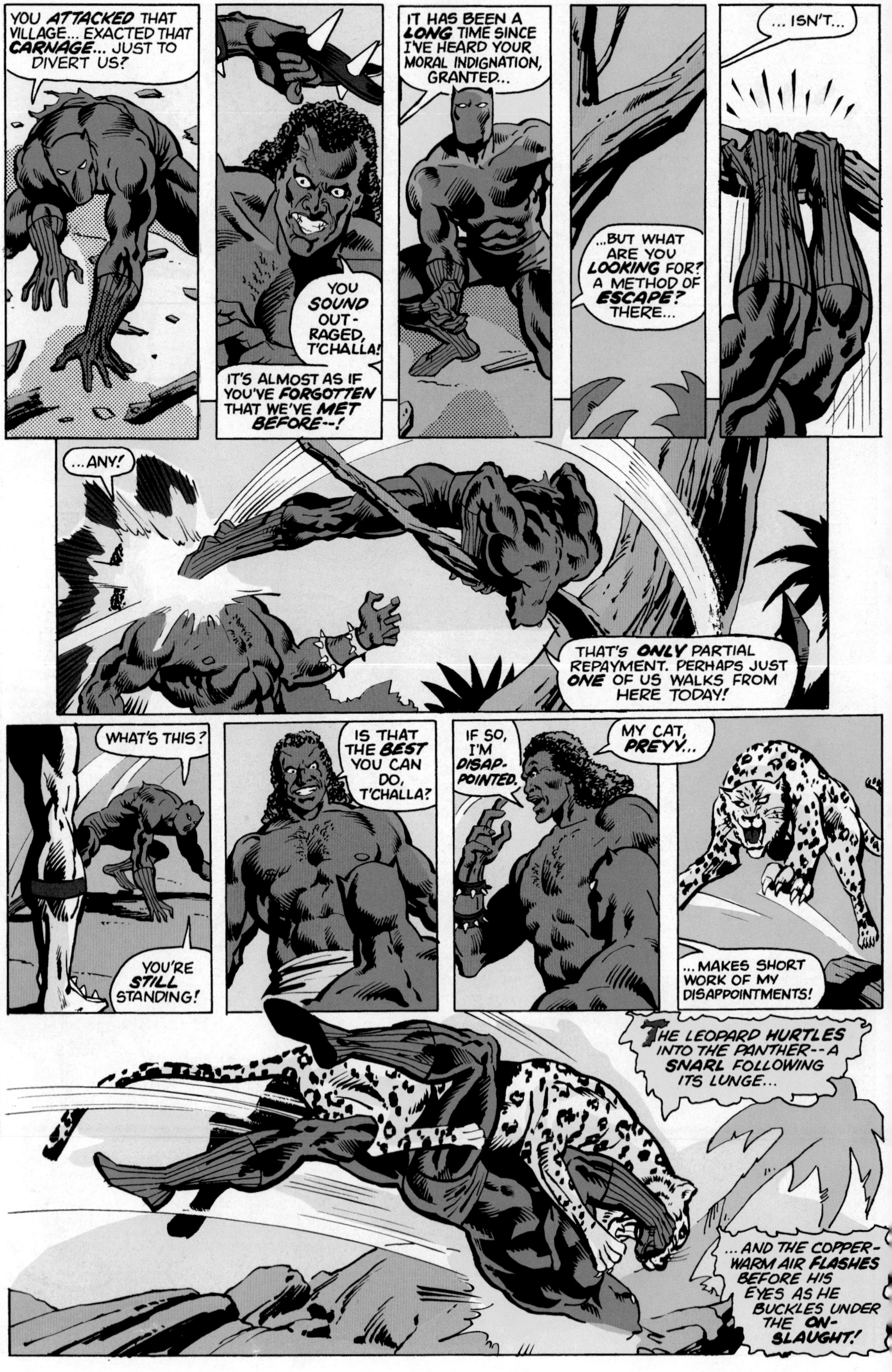
YOU ATTACKED THAT VILLAGE... EXACTED THAT CARNAGE... JUST TO DIVERT US?
YOU SOUND OUT-RAGED, T'CHALLA!
IT'S ALMOST AS IF YOU'VE FORGOTTEN THAT WE'VE MET BEFORE--!
IT HAS BEEN A LONG TIME SINCE I'VE HEARD YOUR MORAL INDIGNATION, GRANTED...
...BUT WHAT ARE YOU LOOKING FOR? A METHOD OF ESCAPE? THERE...
... ISN'T...
...ANY!
THAT'S ONLY PARTIAL REPAYMENT. PERHAPS JUST ONE OF US WALKS FROM HERE TODAY!
WHAT'S THIS?
YOU'RE STILL STANDING!
IS THAT THE BEST YOU CAN DO, T'CHALLA?
IF SO, I'M DISAP-POINTED.
MY CAT, PREYY...
...MAKES SHORT WORK OF MY DISAPPOINTMENTS!
THE LEOPARD HURTLES INTO THE PANTHER--A SNARL FOLLOWING ITS LUNGE...
...AND THE COPPER-WARM AIR FLASHES BEFORE HIS EYES AS HE BUCKLES UNDER THE ON-SLAUGHT!

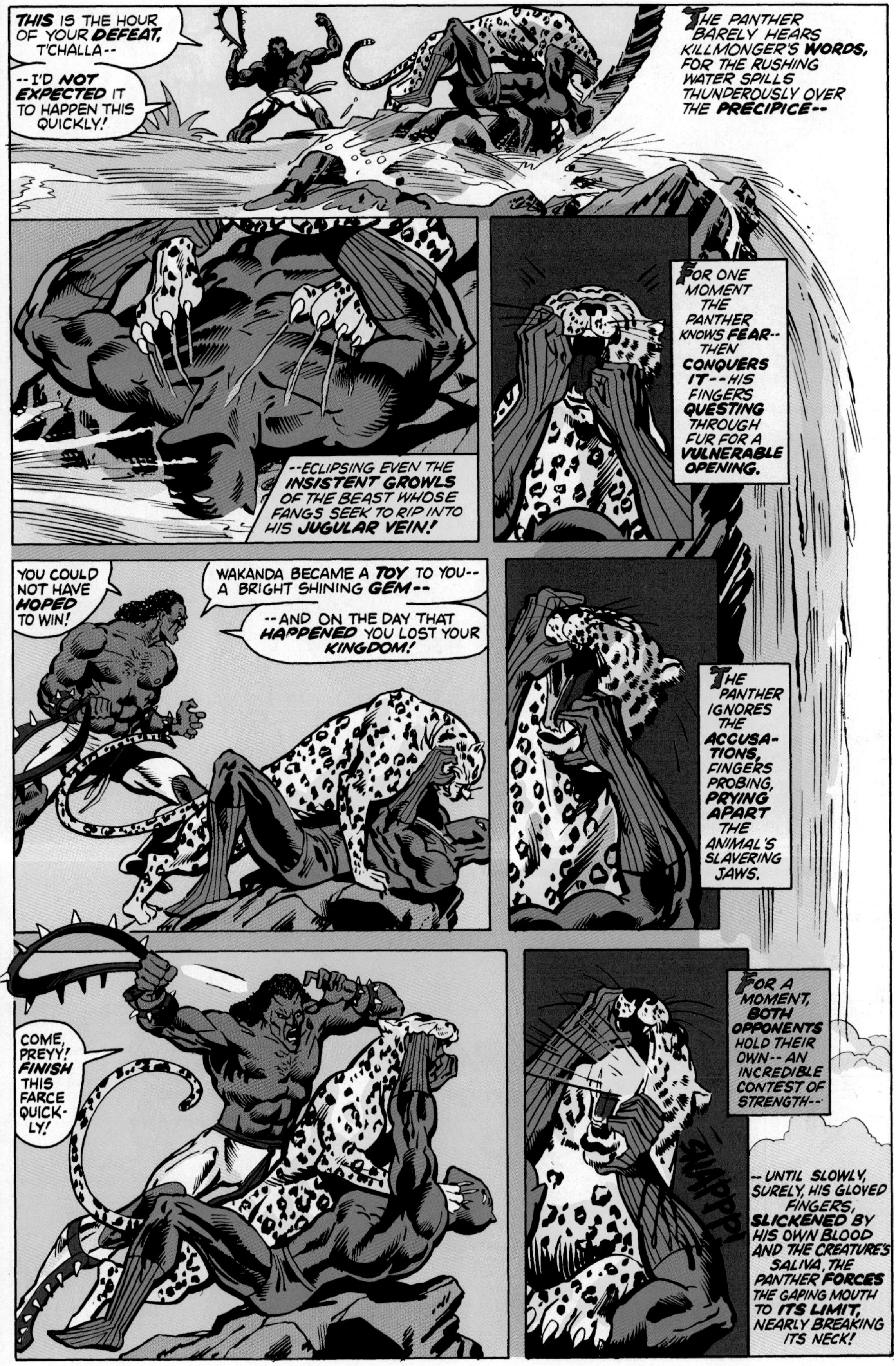
THIS IS THE HOUR OF YOUR DEFEAT, T'CHALLA--
--I'D NOT EXPECTED IT TO HAPPEN THIS QUICKLY!
THE PANTHER BARELY HEARS KILLMONGER'S WORDS, FOR THE RUSHING WATER SPILLS THUNDEROUSLY OVER THE PRECIPICE--
--ECLIPSING EVEN THE INSISTENT GROWLS OF THE BEAST WHOSE FANGS SEEK TO RIP INTO HIS JUGULAR VEIN!
FOR ONE MOMENT THE PANTHER KNOWS FEAR-- THEN CONQUERS IT--HIS FINGERS QUESTING THROUGH FUR FOR A VULNERABLE OPENING.
YOU COULD NOT HAVE HOPED TO WIN!
WAKANDA BECAME A TOY TO YOU-- A BRIGHT SHINING GEM--
--AND ON THE DAY THAT HAPPENED YOU LOST YOUR KINGDOM!
THE PANTHER IGNORES THE ACCUSATIONS, FINGERS PROBING, PRYING APART THE ANIMAL'S SLAVERING JAWS.
COME, PREYY! FINISH THIS FARCE QUICKLY!
FOR A MOMENT, BOTH OPPONENTS HOLD THEIR OWN-- AN INCREDIBLE CONTEST OF STRENGTH--
SNAPP!
--UNTIL SLOWLY, SURELY, HIS GLOVED FINGERS, SLICKENED BY HIS OWN BLOOD AND THE CREATURE'S SALIVA, THE PANTHER FORCES THE GAPING MOUTH TO ITS LIMIT, NEARLY BREAKING ITS NECK!

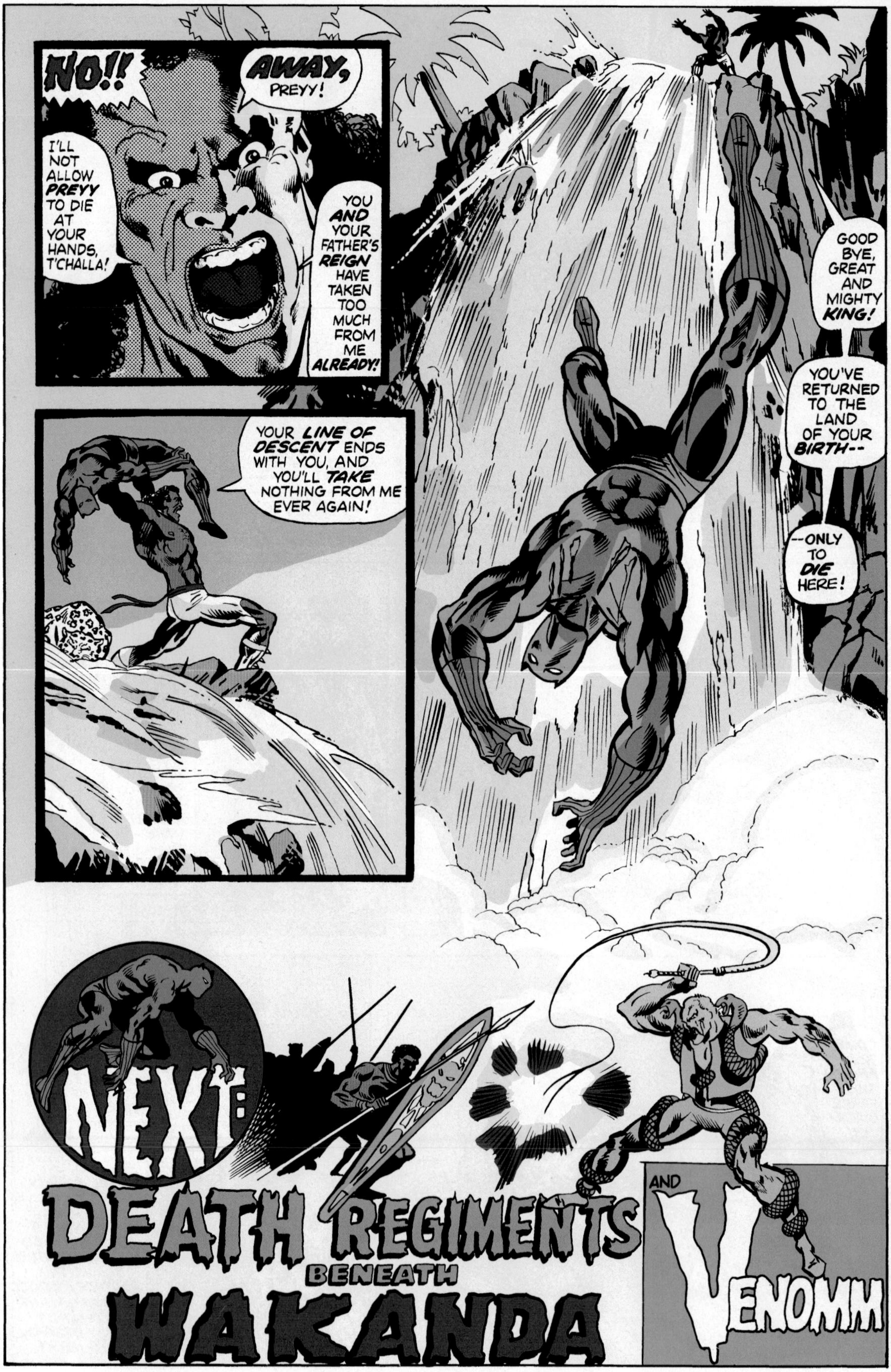
NO!!
AWAY, PREYY!
I'LL NOT ALLOW PREYY TO DIE AT YOUR HANDS, T'CHALLA!
YOU AND YOUR FATHER'S REIGN HAVE TAKEN TOO MUCH FROM ME ALREADY!
YOUR LINE OF DESCENT ENDS WITH YOU, AND YOU'LL TAKE NOTHING FROM ME EVER AGAIN!
GOOD BYE, GREAT AND MIGHTY KING!
YOU'VE RETURNED TO THE LAND OF YOUR BIRTH--
--ONLY TO DIE HERE!
NEXT:
DEATH REGIMENTS BENEATH WAKANDA
AND VENOMM

MAP OF THE LAND OF THE WAKANDA

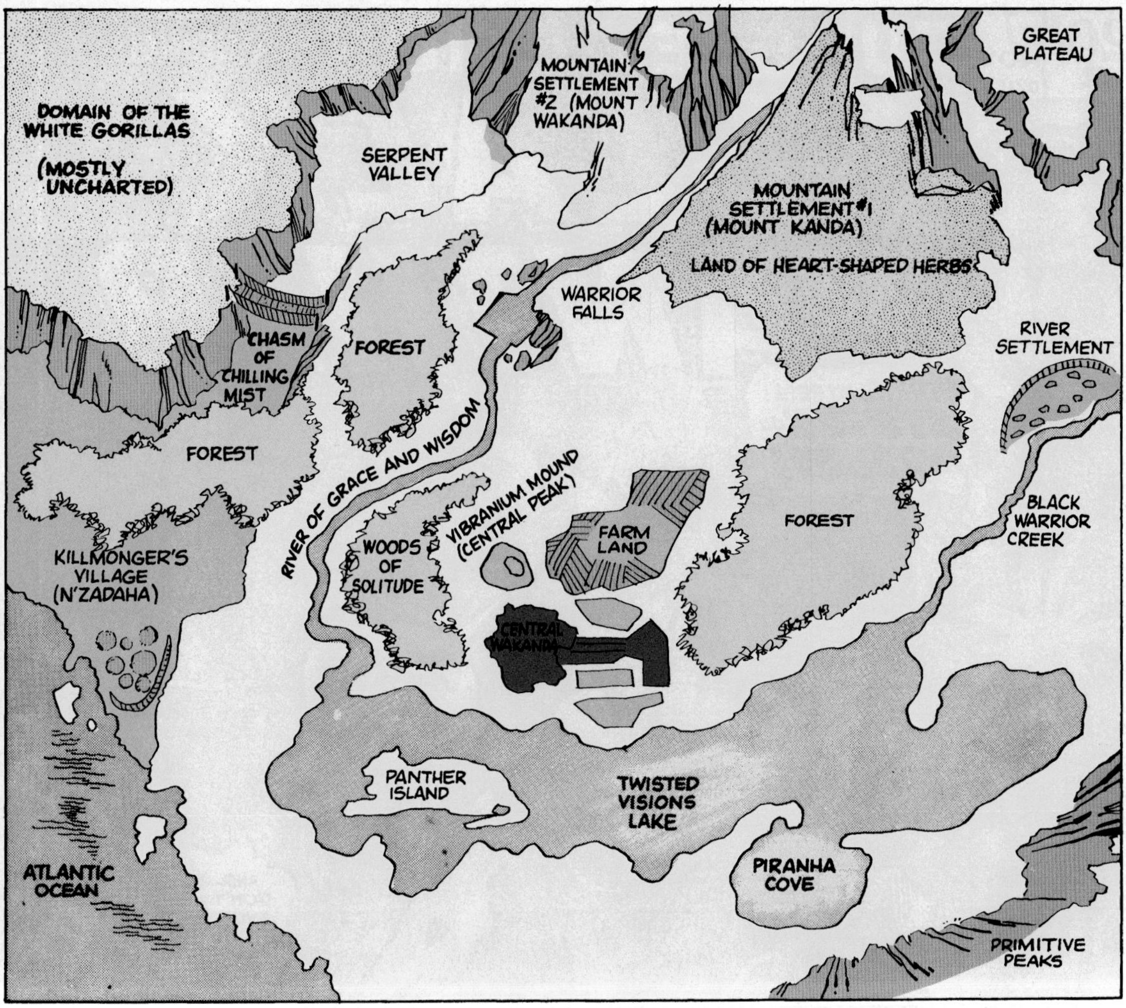

DOMAIN OF THE WHITE GORILLAS
(MOSTLY UNCHARTED)
SERPENT VALLEY
MOUNTAIN SETTLEMENT #2 (MOUNT WAKANDA)
GREAT PLATEAU
MOUNTAIN SETTLEMENT #1 (MOUNT KANDA)
LAND OF HEART-SHAPED HERBS
WARRIOR FALLS
CHASM OF CHILLING MIST
FOREST
RIVER SETTLEMENT
FOREST
RIVER OF GRACE AND WISDOM
VIBRANIUM MOUND (CENTRAL PEAK)
FARM LAND
FOREST
BLACK WARRIOR CREEK
KILLMONGER'S VILLAGE (N'ZADAHA)
WOODS OF SOLITUDE
CENTRAL WAKANDA
PANTHER ISLAND
TWISTED VISIONS LAKE
PIRANHA COVE
ATLANTIC OCEAN
PRIMITIVE PEAKS

CENTRAL WAKANDA

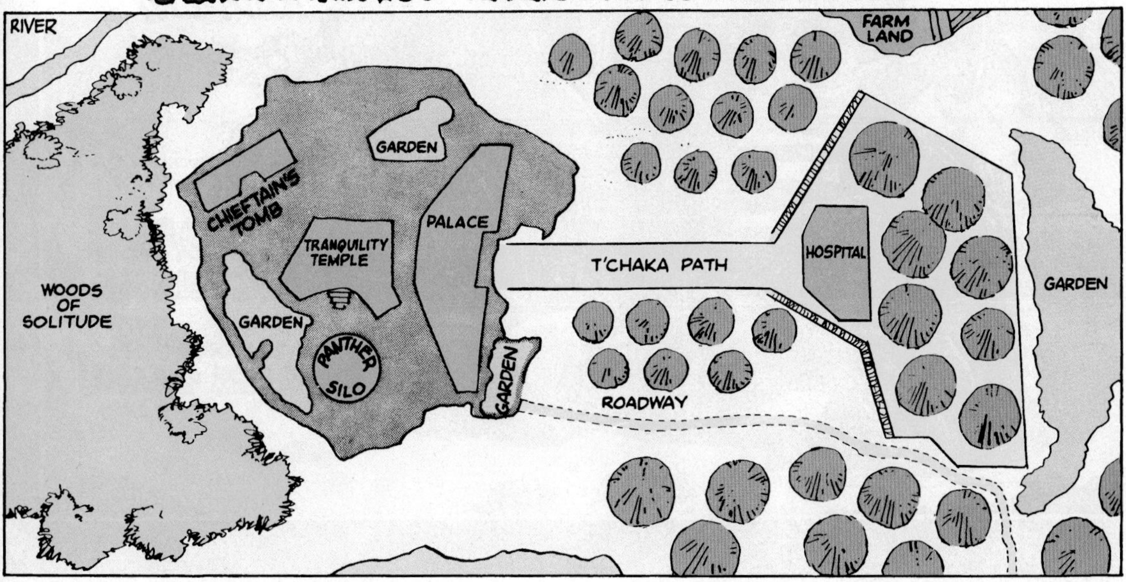

RIVER
FARM LAND
GARDEN
CHIEFTAIN'S TOMB
TRANQUILITY TEMPLE
PALACE
T'CHAKA PATH
HOSPITAL
WOODS OF SOLITUDE
GARDEN
PANTHER SILO
GARDEN
GARDEN
ROADWAY

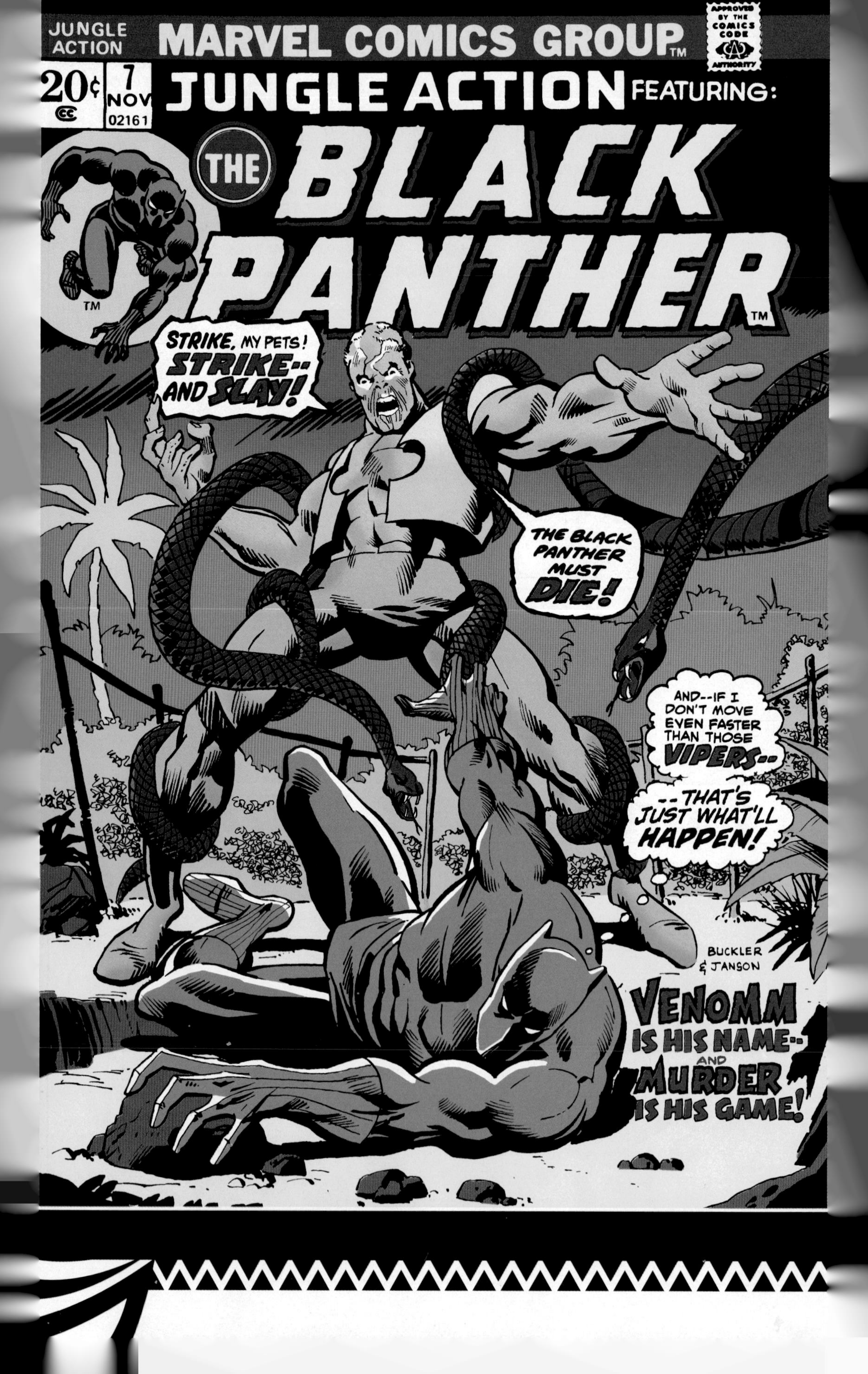

JUNGLE ACTION
MARVEL COMICS GROUP
APPROVED BY THE COMICS CODE AUTHORITY
20¢
7 NOV
02161
JUNGLE ACTION FEATURING:
THE BLACK PANTHER
STRIKE, MY PETS! STRIKE-- AND SLAY!
THE BLACK PANTHER MUST DIE!
AND--IF I DON'T MOVE EVEN FASTER THAN THOSE VIPERS--
--THAT'S JUST WHAT'LL HAPPEN!
BUCKLER & JANSON
VENOMM IS HIS NAME-- AND MURDER IS HIS GAME!

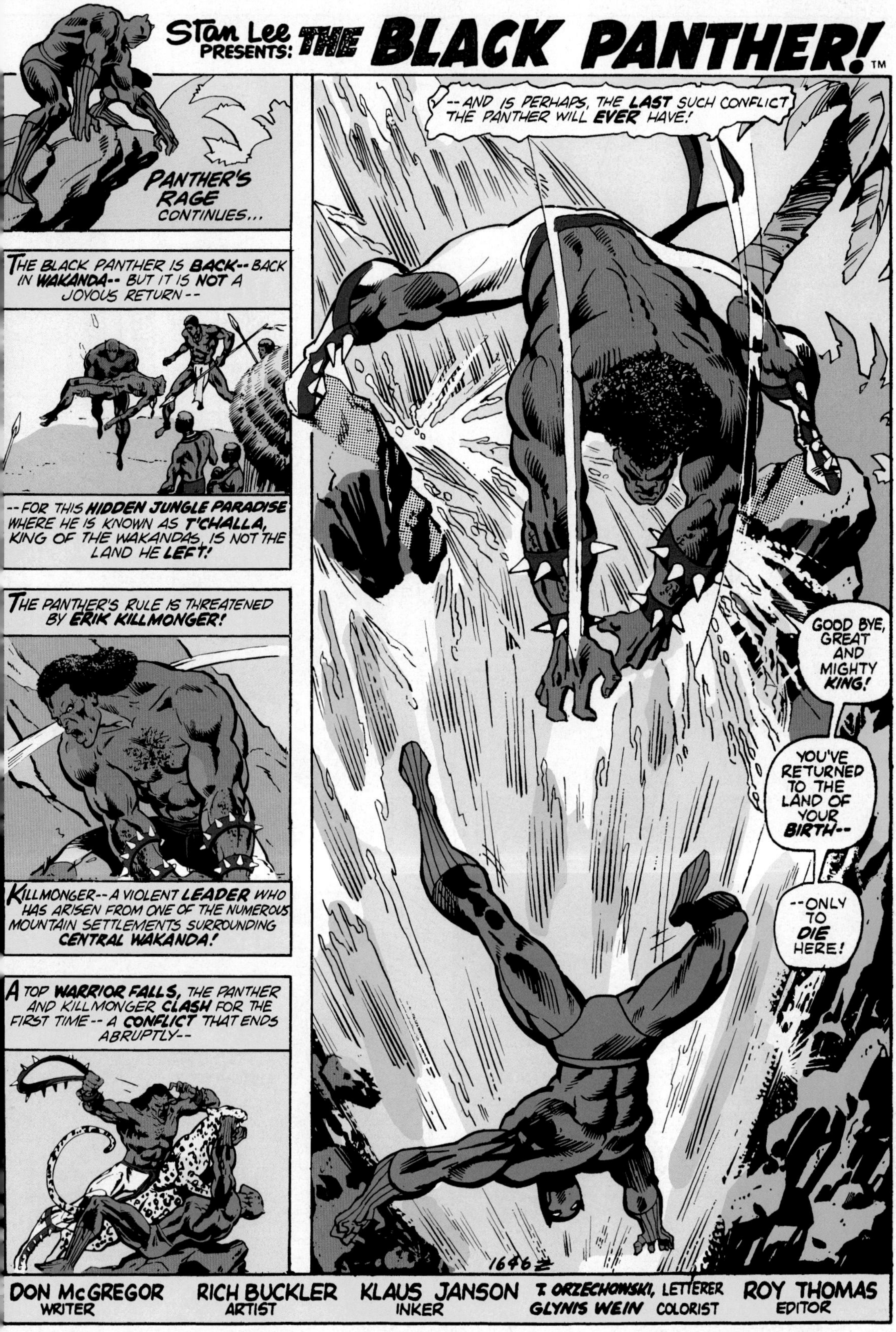
Stan Lee PRESENTS: THE BLACK PANTHER!™
PANTHER'S RAGE CONTINUES...
THE BLACK PANTHER IS BACK-- BACK IN WAKANDA-- BUT IT IS NOT A JOYOUS RETURN--
--FOR THIS HIDDEN JUNGLE PARADISE WHERE HE IS KNOWN AS T'CHALLA, KING OF THE WAKANDAS, IS NOT THE LAND HE LEFT!
THE PANTHER'S RULE IS THREATENED BY ERIK KILLMONGER!
KILLMONGER-- A VIOLENT LEADER WHO HAS ARISEN FROM ONE OF THE NUMEROUS MOUNTAIN SETTLEMENTS SURROUNDING CENTRAL WAKANDA!
A TOP WARRIOR FALLS, THE PANTHER AND KILLMONGER CLASH FOR THE FIRST TIME-- A CONFLICT THAT ENDS ABRUPTLY--
--AND IS PERHAPS, THE LAST SUCH CONFLICT THE PANTHER WILL EVER HAVE!
GOOD BYE, GREAT AND MIGHTY KING!
YOU'VE RETURNED TO THE LAND OF YOUR BIRTH--
--ONLY TO DIE HERE!
DON McGREGOR WRITER
RICH BUCKLER ARTIST
KLAUS JANSON INKER
T. ORZECHOWSKI, LETTERER
GLYNIS WEIN COLORIST
ROY THOMAS EDITOR

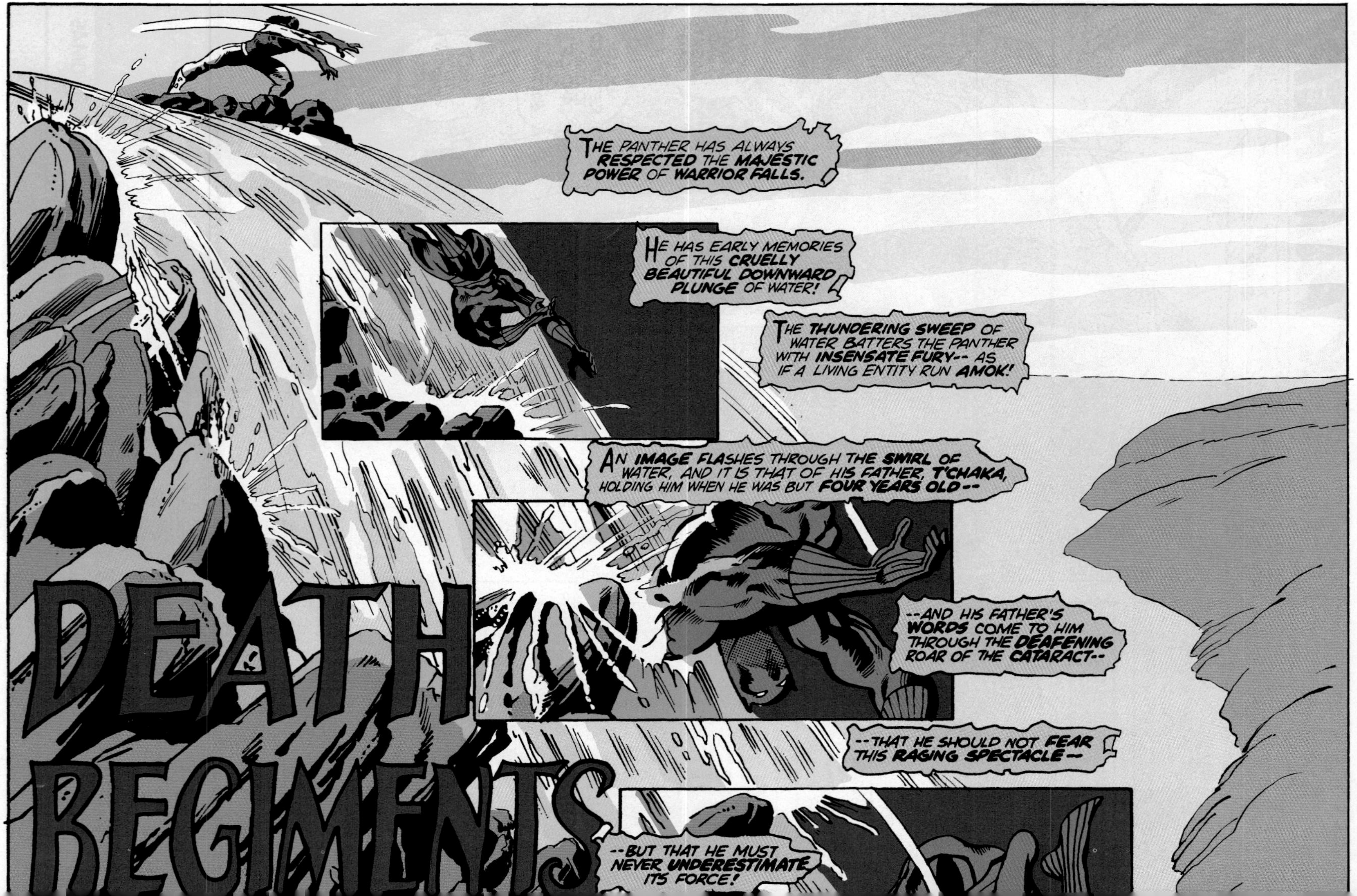
THE PANTHER HAS ALWAYS RESPECTED THE MAJESTIC POWER OF WARRIOR FALLS.
HE HAS EARLY MEMORIES OF THIS CRUELLY BEAUTIFUL DOWNWARD PLUNGE OF WATER!
THE THUNDERING SWEEP OF WATER BATTERS THE PANTHER WITH INSENSATE FURY-- AS IF A LIVING ENTITY RUN AMOK!
AN IMAGE FLASHES THROUGH THE SWIRL OF WATER, AND IT IS THAT OF HIS FATHER, T'CHAKA, HOLDING HIM WHEN HE WAS BUT FOUR YEARS OLD--
--AND HIS FATHER'S WORDS COME TO HIM THROUGH THE DEAFENING ROAR OF THE CATARACT--
--THAT HE SHOULD NOT FEAR THIS RAGING SPECTACLE--
--BUT THAT HE MUST NEVER UNDERESTIMATE ITS FORCE!
DEATH REGIMENTS

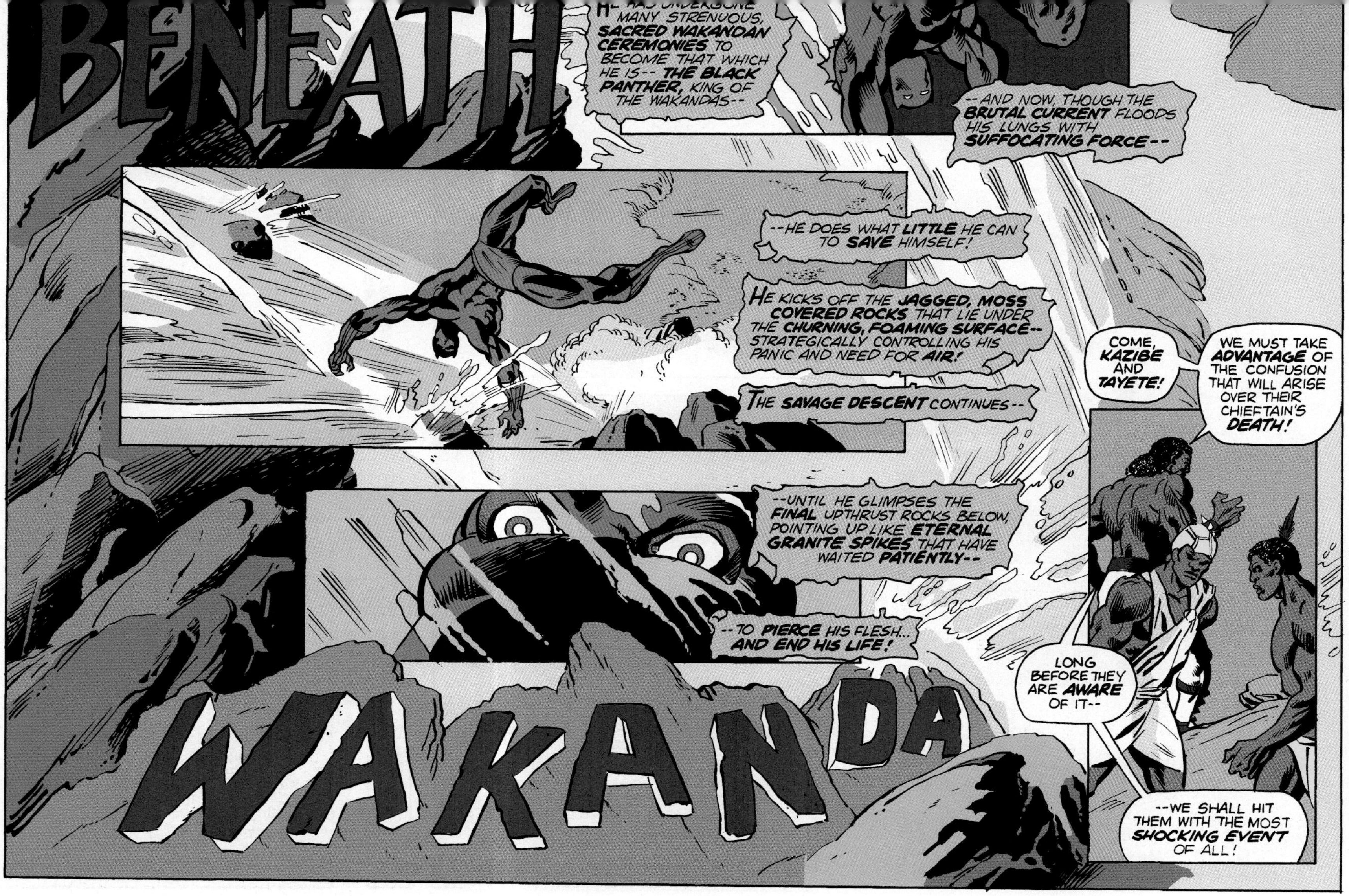
BENEATH
MANY STRENUOUS, SACRED WAKANDAN CEREMONIES TO BECOME THAT WHICH HE IS-- THE BLACK PANTHER, KING OF THE WAKANDAS--
--AND NOW, THOUGH THE BRUTAL CURRENT FLOODS HIS LUNGS WITH SUFFOCATING FORCE--
--HE DOES WHAT LITTLE HE CAN TO SAVE HIMSELF!
HE KICKS OFF THE JAGGED, MOSS COVERED ROCKS THAT LIE UNDER THE CHURNING, FOAMING SURFACE--STRATEGICALLY CONTROLLING HIS PANIC AND NEED FOR AIR!
THE SAVAGE DESCENT CONTINUES--
--UNTIL HE GLIMPSES THE FINAL UPTHRUST ROCKS BELOW, POINTING UP LIKE ETERNAL GRANITE SPIKES THAT HAVE WAITED PATIENTLY--
--TO PIERCE HIS FLESH... AND END HIS LIFE!
WAKANDA
COME, KAZIBE AND TAYETE!
WE MUST TAKE ADVANTAGE OF THE CONFUSION THAT WILL ARISE OVER THEIR CHIEFTAIN'S DEATH!
LONG BEFORE THEY ARE AWARE OF IT--
--WE SHALL HIT THEM WITH THE MOST SHOCKING EVENT OF ALL!

MONICA LYNNE LOOKS FOR THE FIRST TIME UPON THE *RIVER OF GRACE AND WISDOM*--

--AND THE *LYRICAL SINGER* SHE ONCE WAS SEES UNDER THE *IDYLLIC*, SMOOTHLY FLOWING *CURRENT*--

--AND SHE *UNDERSTANDS* WHY THE RIVER WAS SO *NAMED*.

SHE LISTENS TO THE *MOVEMENT* OF THE WATER THE WAY SHE WANTED OTHERS TO LISTEN TO HER *SONGS*--

--TO *HEAR* THE WORDS -- TO REALLY *LISTEN*.

AND THEN THERE WAS A MAN WHO *DID* LISTEN... AND THAT IS WHY SHE IS *HERE*!

YOU WILL FIND THE WATER MOST *WARM* AND *PLEASING* AT THIS SPOT, MISS LYNNE.

IT'S A *BEAUTIFUL* PLACE. I *THANK YOU* FOR BRINGING ME HERE.

BUT, *TANZIKA*, WHY IS IT I GET SO MANY *BAD VIBES* FROM YOU?

YOU TALK MOST *STRANGELY*... MISS LYNNE!

CALL ME MONICA.

I'LL BE *AWAITING* YOU UP IN THE *AMBER PAGODA*.

IF YOU SHOULD *NEED* ANYTHING, JUST *CALL*...

... MISS LYNNE.

THE WATER IS *WARM* AND EASES HER SENSE OF *ALIENATION*...

... BUT ONLY FOR *A MOMENT!*

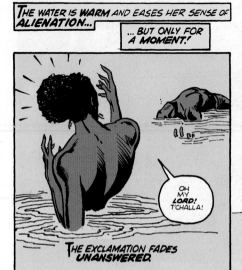

OH MY *LORD!* T'CHALLA!

THE EXCLAMATION FADES *UNANSWERED*.

TEARS FILL MONICA'S EYES--

--AND SHE *FEARS* THAT THE MAN WHO *HAD LISTENED*-- WILL NEVER *HEAR* ANYTHING... AGAIN!

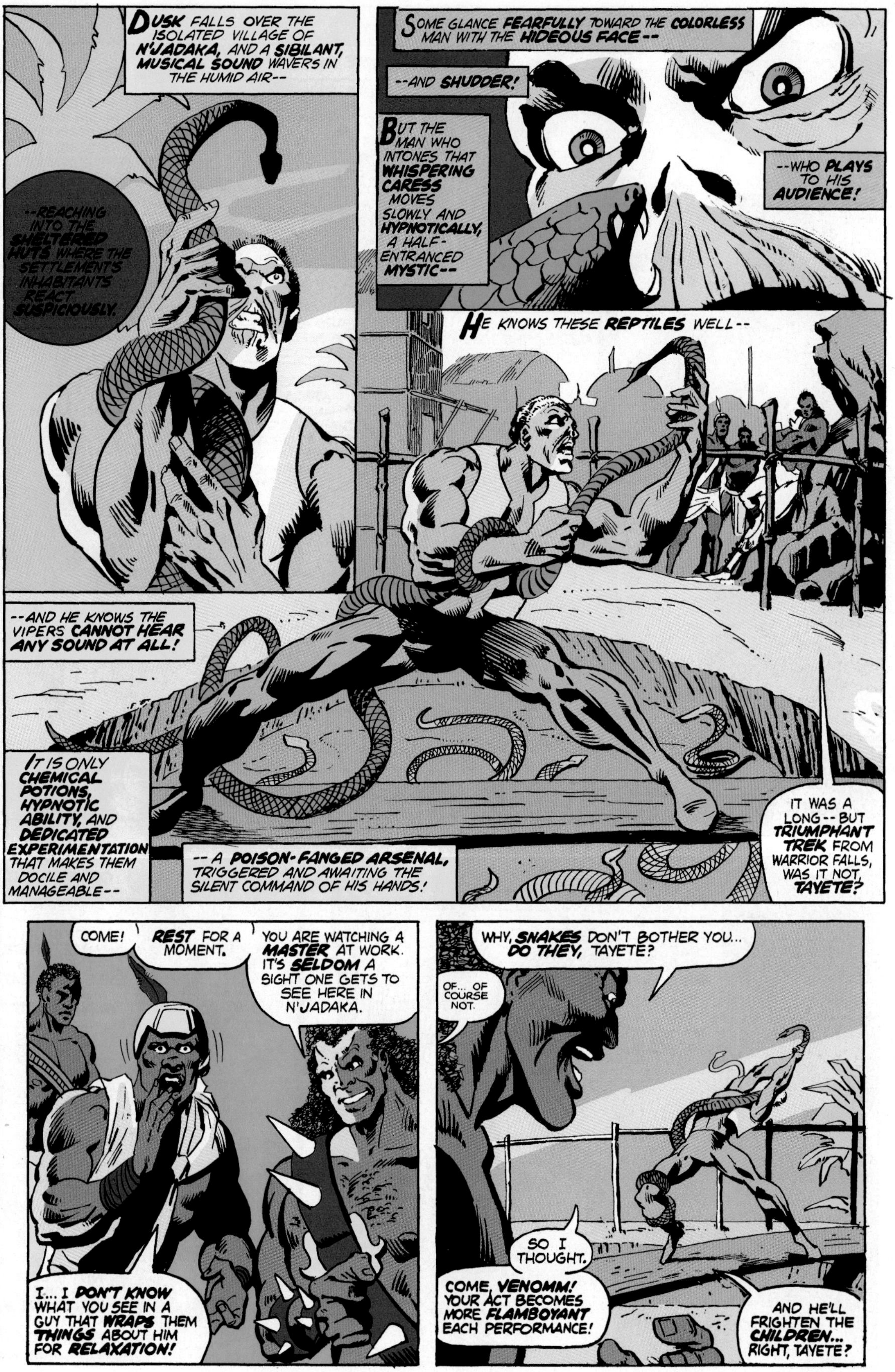
DUSK FALLS OVER THE ISOLATED VILLAGE OF N'JADAKA, AND A SIBILANT, MUSICAL SOUND WAVERS IN THE HUMID AIR--
--REACHING INTO THE SHELTERED HUTS WHERE THE SETTLEMENT'S INHABITANTS REACT SUSPICIOUSLY.
SOME GLANCE FEARFULLY TOWARD THE COLORLESS MAN WITH THE HIDEOUS FACE--
--AND SHUDDER!
BUT THE MAN WHO INTONES THAT WHISPERING CARESS MOVES SLOWLY AND HYPNOTICALLY, A HALF-ENTRANCED MYSTIC--
--WHO PLAYS TO HIS AUDIENCE!
HE KNOWS THESE REPTILES WELL--
--AND HE KNOWS THE VIPERS CANNOT HEAR ANY SOUND AT ALL!
IT IS ONLY CHEMICAL POTIONS, HYPNOTIC ABILITY, AND DEDICATED EXPERIMENTATION THAT MAKES THEM DOCILE AND MANAGEABLE--
--A POISON-FANGED ARSENAL, TRIGGERED AND AWAITING THE SILENT COMMAND OF HIS HANDS!
IT WAS A LONG--BUT TRIUMPHANT TREK FROM WARRIOR FALLS, WAS IT NOT, TAYETE?
COME!
REST FOR A MOMENT.
YOU ARE WATCHING A MASTER AT WORK. IT'S SELDOM A SIGHT ONE GETS TO SEE HERE IN N'JADAKA.
I... I DON'T KNOW WHAT YOU SEE IN A GUY THAT WRAPS THEM THINGS ABOUT HIM FOR RELAXATION!
WHY, SNAKES DON'T BOTHER YOU... DO THEY, TAYETE?
OF... OF COURSE NOT.
SO I THOUGHT.
COME, VENOMM! YOUR ACT BECOMES MORE FLAMBOYANT EACH PERFORMANCE!
AND HE'LL FRIGHTEN THE CHILDREN... RIGHT, TAYETE?

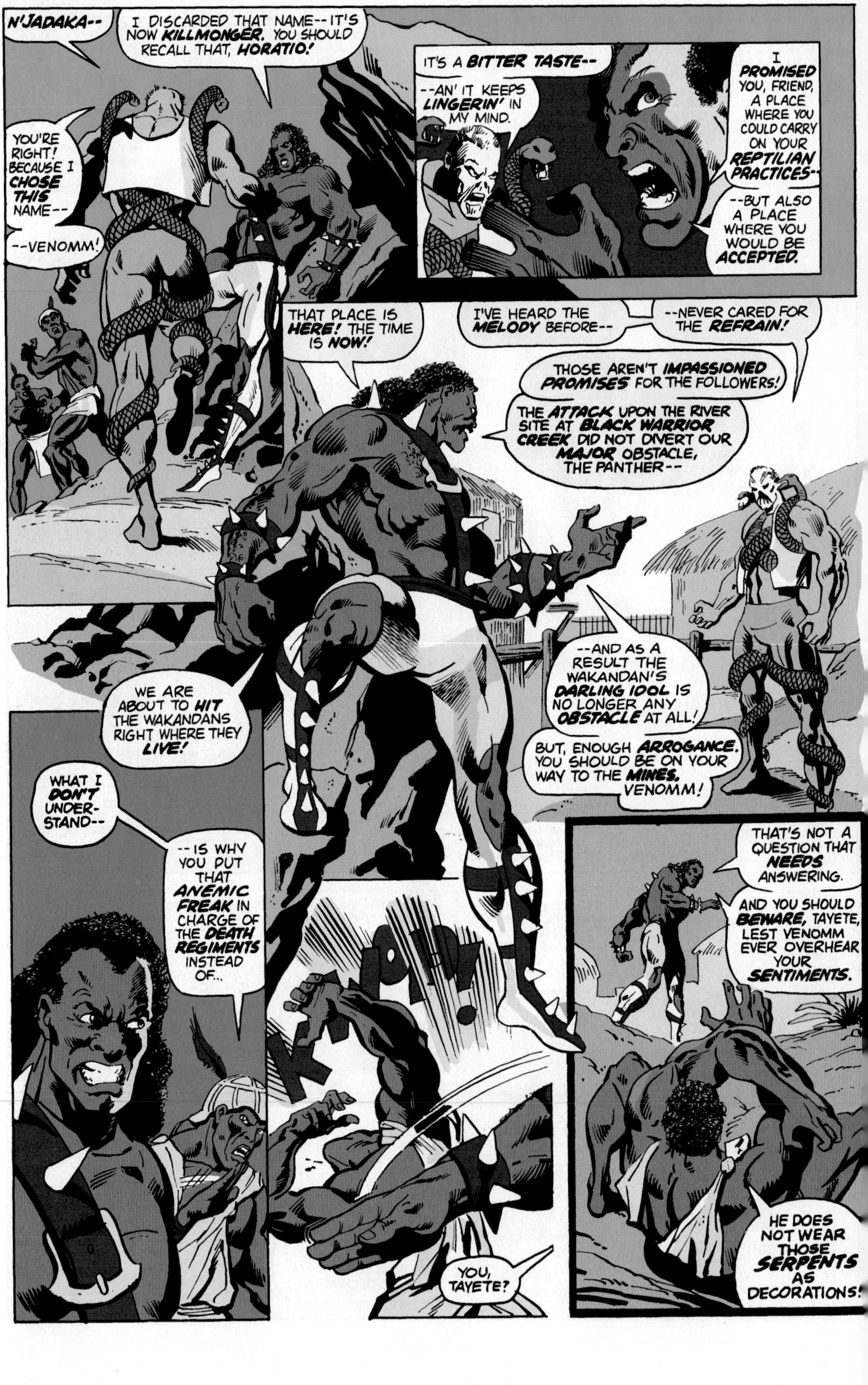
N'JADAKA--
I DISCARDED THAT NAME--IT'S NOW KILLMONGER. YOU SHOULD RECALL THAT, HORATIO!
YOU'RE RIGHT! BECAUSE I CHOSE THIS NAME--
--VENOMM!
IT'S A BITTER TASTE--
--AN' IT KEEPS LINGERIN' IN MY MIND.
I PROMISED YOU, FRIEND, A PLACE WHERE YOU COULD CARRY ON YOUR REPTILIAN PRACTICES--
--BUT ALSO A PLACE WHERE YOU WOULD BE ACCEPTED.
THAT PLACE IS HERE! THE TIME IS NOW!
I'VE HEARD THE MELODY BEFORE--
--NEVER CARED FOR THE REFRAIN!
THOSE AREN'T IMPASSIONED PROMISES FOR THE FOLLOWERS!
THE ATTACK UPON THE RIVER SITE AT BLACK WARRIOR CREEK DID NOT DIVERT OUR MAJOR OBSTACLE, THE PANTHER--
--AND AS A RESULT THE WAKANDAN'S DARLING IDOL IS NO LONGER ANY OBSTACLE AT ALL!
BUT, ENOUGH ARROGANCE. YOU SHOULD BE ON YOUR WAY TO THE MINES, VENOMM!
WE ARE ABOUT TO HIT THE WAKANDANS RIGHT WHERE THEY LIVE!
WHAT I DON'T UNDER-STAND--
--IS WHY YOU PUT THAT ANEMIC FREAK IN CHARGE OF THE DEATH REGIMENTS INSTEAD OF...
YOU, TAYETE?
THAT'S NOT A QUESTION THAT NEEDS ANSWERING.
AND YOU SHOULD BEWARE, TAYETE, LEST VENOMM EVER OVERHEAR YOUR SENTIMENTS.
HE DOES NOT WEAR THOSE SERPENTS AS DECORATIONS!

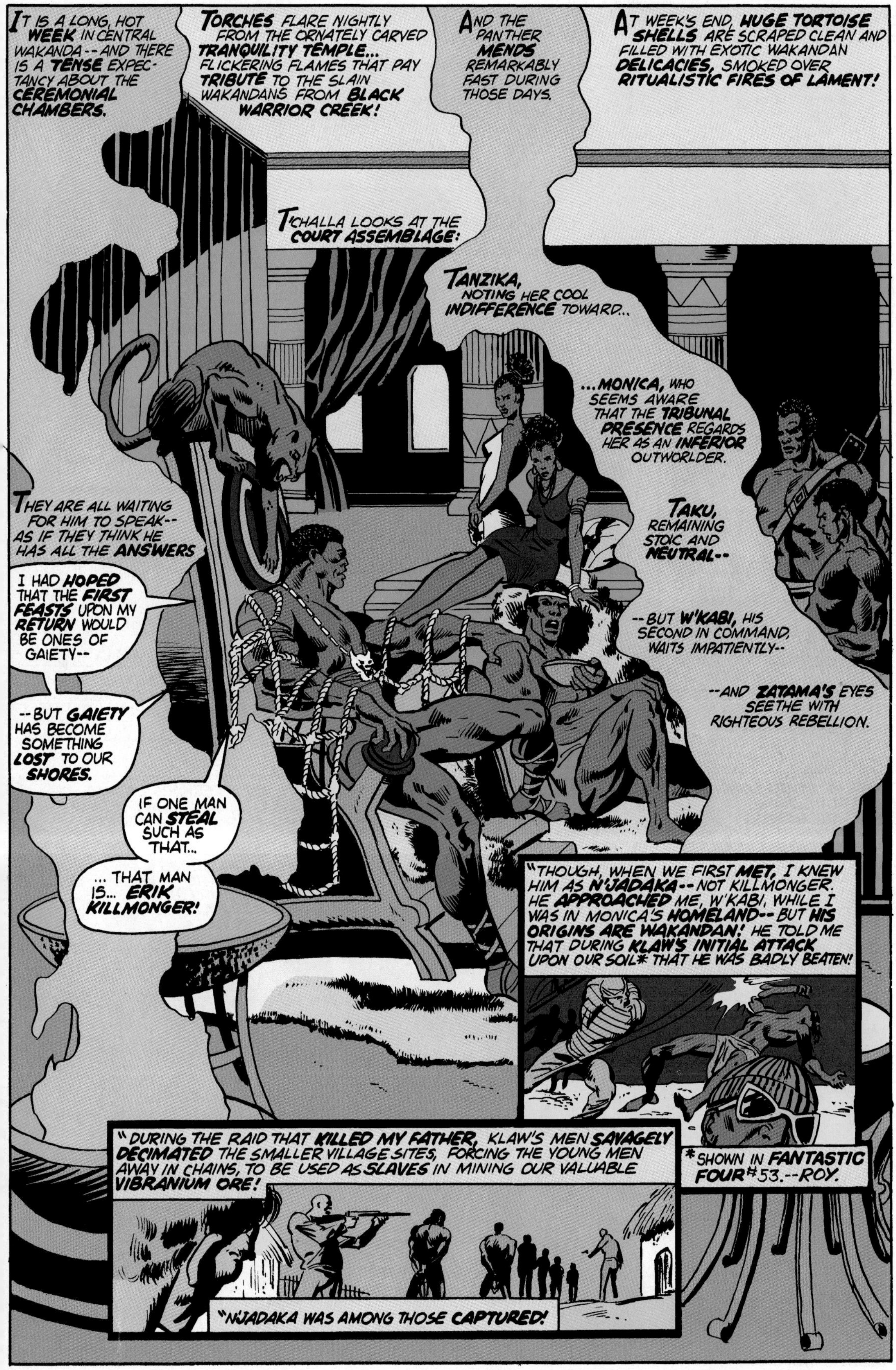

IT IS A LONG, HOT WEEK IN CENTRAL WAKANDA--AND THERE IS A TENSE EXPECTANCY ABOUT THE CEREMONIAL CHAMBERS.
TORCHES FLARE NIGHTLY FROM THE ORNATELY CARVED TRANQUILITY TEMPLE... FLICKERING FLAMES THAT PAY TRIBUTE TO THE SLAIN WAKANDANS FROM BLACK WARRIOR CREEK!
AND THE PANTHER MENDS REMARKABLY FAST DURING THOSE DAYS.
AT WEEK'S END, HUGE TORTOISE SHELLS ARE SCRAPED CLEAN AND FILLED WITH EXOTIC WAKANDAN DELICACIES, SMOKED OVER RITUALISTIC FIRES OF LAMENT!
T'CHALLA LOOKS AT THE COURT ASSEMBLAGE:
TANZIKA, NOTING HER COOL INDIFFERENCE TOWARD...
...MONICA, WHO SEEMS AWARE THAT THE TRIBUNAL PRESENCE REGARDS HER AS AN INFERIOR OUTWORLDER.
TAKU, REMAINING STOIC AND NEUTRAL--
--BUT W'KABI, HIS SECOND IN COMMAND, WAITS IMPATIENTLY--
--AND ZATAMA'S EYES SEETHE WITH RIGHTEOUS REBELLION.
THEY ARE ALL WAITING FOR HIM TO SPEAK-- AS IF THEY THINK HE HAS ALL THE ANSWERS
I HAD HOPED THAT THE FIRST FEASTS UPON MY RETURN WOULD BE ONES OF GAIETY--
--BUT GAIETY HAS BECOME SOMETHING LOST TO OUR SHORES.
IF ONE MAN CAN STEAL SUCH AS THAT...
...THAT MAN IS... ERIK KILLMONGER!
"THOUGH, WHEN WE FIRST MET, I KNEW HIM AS N'JADAKA--NOT KILLMONGER. HE APPROACHED ME, W'KABI, WHILE I WAS IN MONICA'S HOMELAND--BUT HIS ORIGINS ARE WAKANDAN! HE TOLD ME THAT DURING KLAW'S INITIAL ATTACK UPON OUR SOIL* THAT HE WAS BADLY BEATEN!
"DURING THE RAID THAT KILLED MY FATHER, KLAW'S MEN SAVAGELY DECIMATED THE SMALLER VILLAGE SITES, FORCING THE YOUNG MEN AWAY IN CHAINS, TO BE USED AS SLAVES IN MINING OUR VALUABLE VIBRANIUM ORE!
*SHOWN IN FANTASTIC FOUR #53.--ROY.
"N'JADAKA WAS AMONG THOSE CAPTURED!

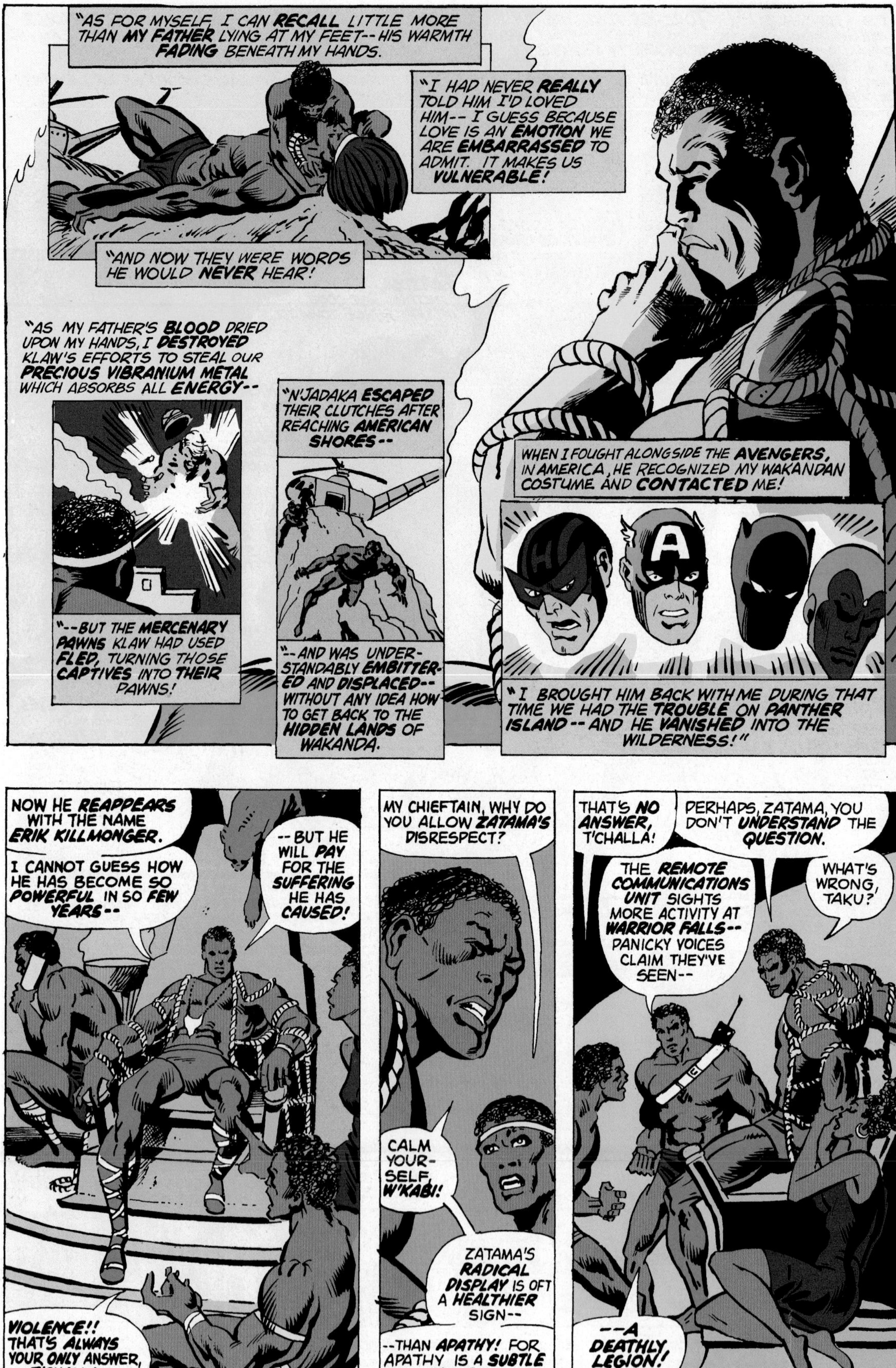
"AS FOR MYSELF, I CAN RECALL LITTLE MORE THAN MY FATHER LYING AT MY FEET-- HIS WARMTH FADING BENEATH MY HANDS.
"I HAD NEVER REALLY TOLD HIM I'D LOVED HIM-- I GUESS BECAUSE LOVE IS AN EMOTION WE ARE EMBARRASSED TO ADMIT. IT MAKES US VULNERABLE!
"AND NOW THEY WERE WORDS HE WOULD NEVER HEAR!
"AS MY FATHER'S BLOOD DRIED UPON MY HANDS, I DESTROYED KLAW'S EFFORTS TO STEAL OUR PRECIOUS VIBRANIUM METAL WHICH ABSORBS ALL ENERGY--
"--BUT THE MERCENARY PAWNS KLAW HAD USED FLED, TURNING THOSE CAPTIVES INTO THEIR PAWNS!
"N'JADAKA ESCAPED THEIR CLUTCHES AFTER REACHING AMERICAN SHORES--
"--AND WAS UNDERSTANDABLY EMBITTERED AND DISPLACED-- WITHOUT ANY IDEA HOW TO GET BACK TO THE HIDDEN LANDS OF WAKANDA.
WHEN I FOUGHT ALONGSIDE THE AVENGERS, IN AMERICA, HE RECOGNIZED MY WAKANDAN COSTUME AND CONTACTED ME!
"I BROUGHT HIM BACK WITH ME DURING THAT TIME WE HAD THE TROUBLE ON PANTHER ISLAND -- AND HE VANISHED INTO THE WILDERNESS!"
NOW HE REAPPEARS WITH THE NAME ERIK KILLMONGER.
I CANNOT GUESS HOW HE HAS BECOME SO POWERFUL IN SO FEW YEARS--
-- BUT HE WILL PAY FOR THE SUFFERING HE HAS CAUSED!
VIOLENCE!! THAT'S ALWAYS YOUR ONLY ANSWER, T'CHALLA!
MY CHIEFTAIN, WHY DO YOU ALLOW ZATAMA'S DISRESPECT?
CALM YOURSELF, W'KABI!
ZATAMA'S RADICAL DISPLAY IS OFT A HEALTHIER SIGN--
--THAN APATHY! FOR APATHY IS A SUBTLE KILLER!
THAT'S NO ANSWER, T'CHALLA!
PERHAPS, ZATAMA, YOU DON'T UNDERSTAND THE QUESTION.
WHAT'S WRONG, TAKU?
THE REMOTE COMMUNICATIONS UNIT SIGHTS MORE ACTIVITY AT WARRIOR FALLS-- PANICKY VOICES CLAIM THEY'VE SEEN--
--A DEATHLY LEGION!

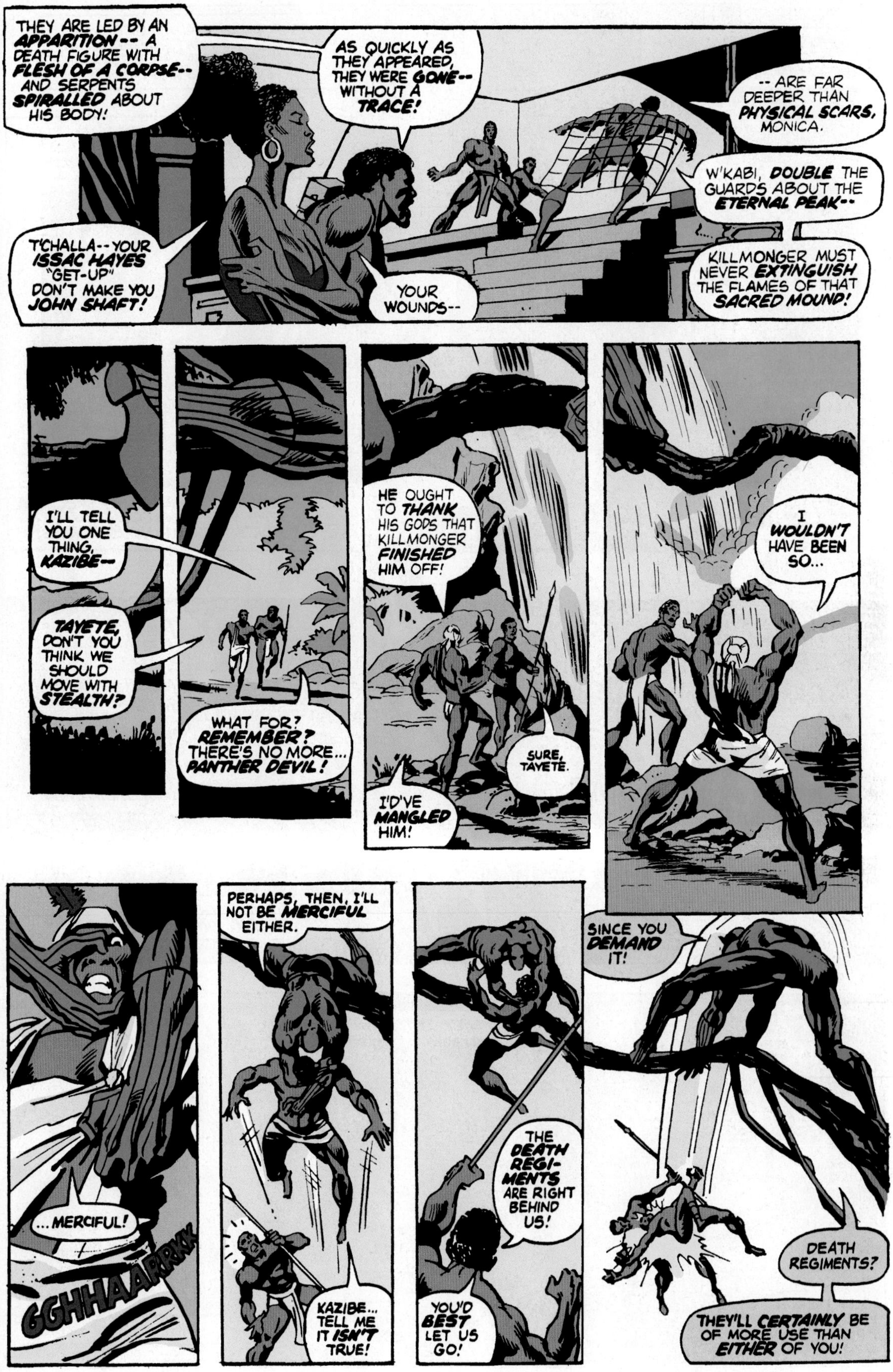
THEY ARE LED BY AN APPARITION-- A DEATH FIGURE WITH FLESH OF A CORPSE-- AND SERPENTS SPIRALLED ABOUT HIS BODY!
AS QUICKLY AS THEY APPEARED, THEY WERE GONE-- WITHOUT A TRACE!
T'CHALLA--YOUR ISSAC HAYES "GET-UP" DON'T MAKE YOU JOHN SHAFT!
YOUR WOUNDS--
-- ARE FAR DEEPER THAN PHYSICAL SCARS, MONICA.
W'KABI, DOUBLE THE GUARDS ABOUT THE ETERNAL PEAK--
KILLMONGER MUST NEVER EXTINGUISH THE FLAMES OF THAT SACRED MOUND!
I'LL TELL YOU ONE THING, KAZIBE--
TAYETE, DON'T YOU THINK WE SHOULD MOVE WITH STEALTH?
WHAT FOR? REMEMBER? THERE'S NO MORE... PANTHER DEVIL!
HE OUGHT TO THANK HIS GODS THAT KILLMONGER FINISHED HIM OFF!
SURE, TAYETE.
I'D'VE MANGLED HIM!
I WOULDN'T HAVE BEEN SO...
...MERCIFUL!
GGHHAARRKK
PERHAPS, THEN, I'LL NOT BE MERCIFUL EITHER.
KAZIBE... TELL ME IT ISN'T TRUE!
THE DEATH REGIMENTS ARE RIGHT BEHIND US!
YOU'D BEST LET US GO!
SINCE YOU DEMAND IT!
DEATH REGIMENTS?
THEY'LL CERTAINLY BE OF MORE USE THAN EITHER OF YOU!

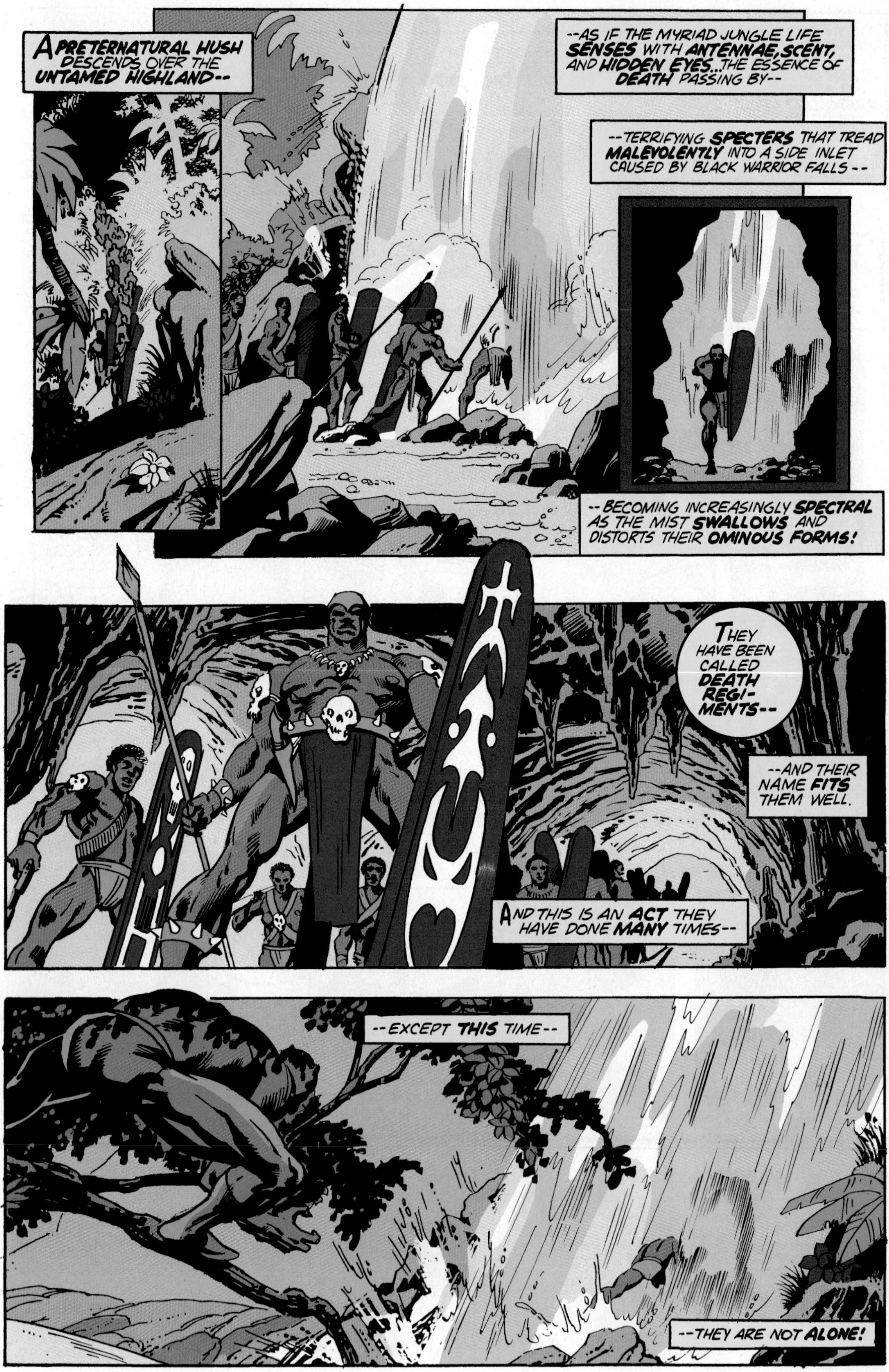
A PRETERNATURAL HUSH DESCENDS OVER THE UNTAMED HIGHLAND--
--AS IF THE MYRIAD JUNGLE LIFE SENSES WITH ANTENNAE, SCENT, AND HIDDEN EYES... THE ESSENCE OF DEATH PASSING BY--
--TERRIFYING SPECTERS THAT TREAD MALEVOLENTLY INTO A SIDE INLET CAUSED BY BLACK WARRIOR FALLS--
--BECOMING INCREASINGLY SPECTRAL AS THE MIST SWALLOWS AND DISTORTS THEIR OMINOUS FORMS!
THEY HAVE BEEN CALLED DEATH REGIMENTS--
--AND THEIR NAME FITS THEM WELL.
AND THIS IS AN ACT THEY HAVE DONE MANY TIMES--
--EXCEPT THIS TIME--
--THEY ARE NOT ALONE!

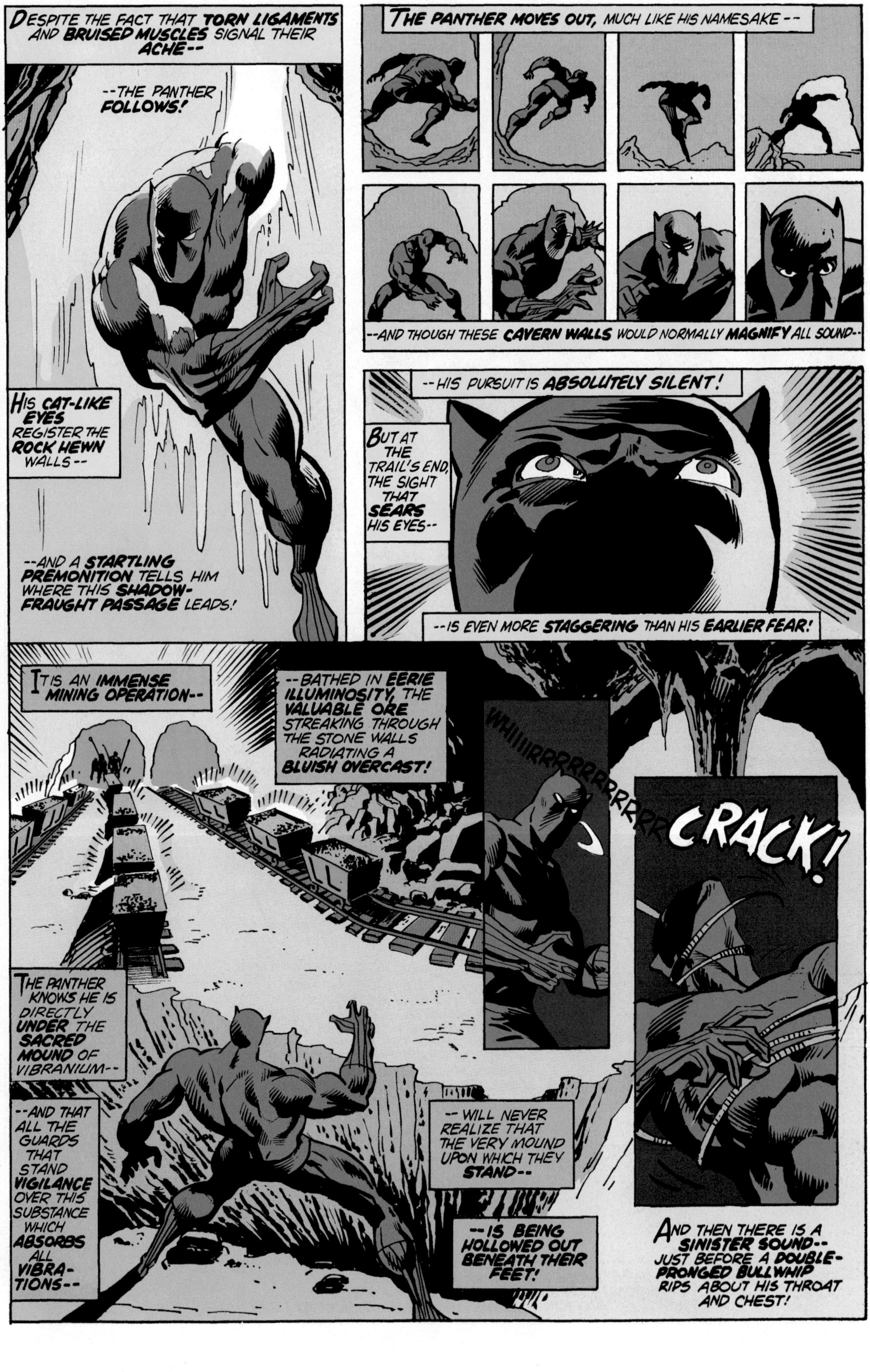
DESPITE THE FACT THAT TORN LIGAMENTS AND BRUISED MUSCLES SIGNAL THEIR ACHE--
--THE PANTHER FOLLOWS!
HIS CAT-LIKE EYES REGISTER THE ROCK HEWN WALLS--
--AND A STARTLING PREMONITION TELLS HIM WHERE THIS SHADOW-FRAUGHT PASSAGE LEADS!
THE PANTHER MOVES OUT, MUCH LIKE HIS NAMESAKE--
--AND THOUGH THESE CAVERN WALLS WOULD NORMALLY MAGNIFY ALL SOUND--
--HIS PURSUIT IS ABSOLUTELY SILENT!
BUT AT THE TRAIL'S END, THE SIGHT THAT SEARS HIS EYES--
--IS EVEN MORE STAGGERING THAN HIS EARLIER FEAR!
IT IS AN IMMENSE MINING OPERATION--
--BATHED IN EERIE ILLUMINOSITY, THE VALUABLE ORE STREAKING THROUGH THE STONE WALLS RADIATING A BLUISH OVERCAST!
THE PANTHER KNOWS HE IS DIRECTLY UNDER THE SACRED MOUND OF VIBRANIUM--
--AND THAT ALL THE GUARDS THAT STAND VIGILANCE OVER THIS SUBSTANCE WHICH ABSORBS ALL VIBRA-TIONS--
--WILL NEVER REALIZE THAT THE VERY MOUND UPON WHICH THEY STAND--
--IS BEING HOLLOWED OUT BENEATH THEIR FEET!
WHIIIIRRRRRRRRRRRRRR
CRACK!
AND THEN THERE IS A SINISTER SOUND-- JUST BEFORE A DOUBLE-PRONGED BULLWHIP RIPS ABOUT HIS THROAT AND CHEST!

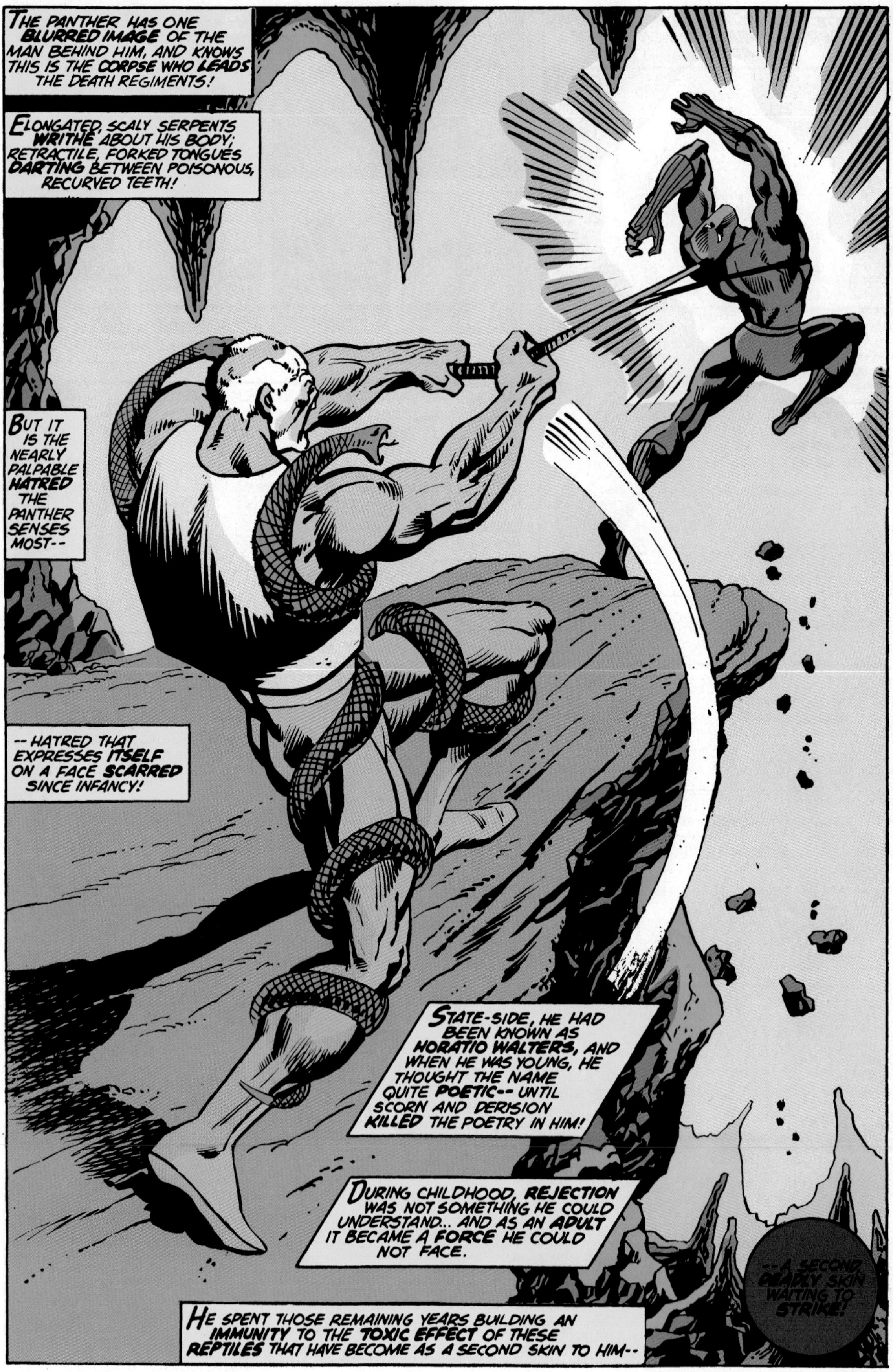
THE PANTHER HAS ONE BLURRED IMAGE OF THE MAN BEHIND HIM, AND KNOWS THIS IS THE CORPSE WHO LEADS THE DEATH REGIMENTS!
ELONGATED, SCALY SERPENTS WRITHE ABOUT HIS BODY; RETRACTILE, FORKED TONGUES DARTING BETWEEN POISONOUS, RECURVED TEETH!
BUT IT IS THE NEARLY PALPABLE HATRED THE PANTHER SENSES MOST--
--HATRED THAT EXPRESSES ITSELF ON A FACE SCARRED SINCE INFANCY!
STATE-SIDE, HE HAD BEEN KNOWN AS HORATIO WALTERS, AND WHEN HE WAS YOUNG, HE THOUGHT THE NAME QUITE POETIC-- UNTIL SCORN AND DERISION KILLED THE POETRY IN HIM!
DURING CHILDHOOD, REJECTION WAS NOT SOMETHING HE COULD UNDERSTAND... AND AS AN ADULT IT BECAME A FORCE HE COULD NOT FACE.
HE SPENT THOSE REMAINING YEARS BUILDING AN IMMUNITY TO THE TOXIC EFFECT OF THESE REPTILES THAT HAVE BECOME AS A SECOND SKIN TO HIM--
--A SECOND, DEADLY SKIN WAITING TO STRIKE!

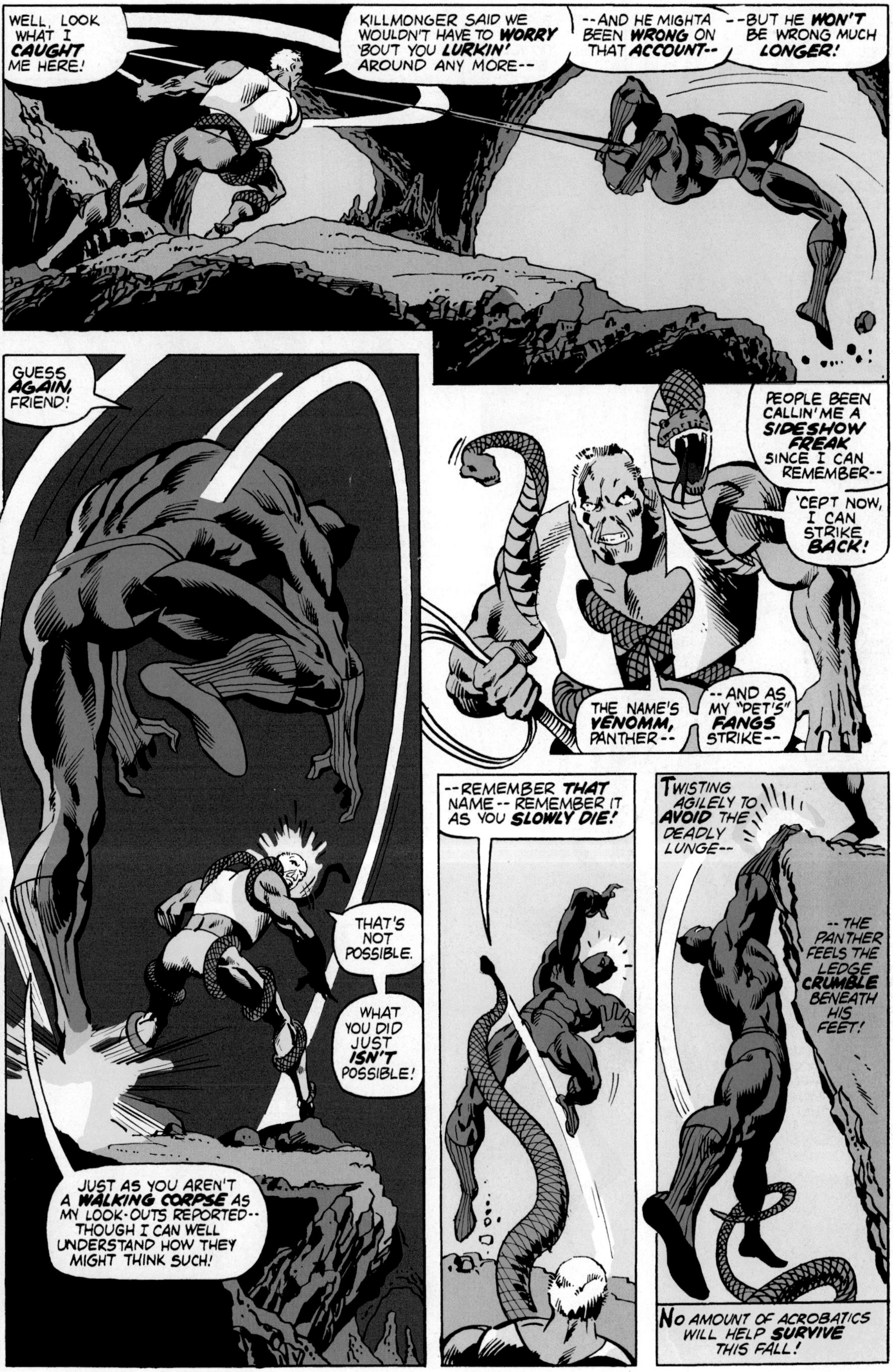
WELL, LOOK WHAT I CAUGHT ME HERE!
KILLMONGER SAID WE WOULDN'T HAVE TO WORRY 'BOUT YOU LURKIN' AROUND ANY MORE--
--AND HE MIGHTA BEEN WRONG ON THAT ACCOUNT--
--BUT HE WON'T BE WRONG MUCH LONGER!
GUESS AGAIN, FRIEND!
THAT'S NOT POSSIBLE.
WHAT YOU DID JUST ISN'T POSSIBLE!
JUST AS YOU AREN'T A WALKING CORPSE AS MY LOOK-OUTS REPORTED-- THOUGH I CAN WELL UNDERSTAND HOW THEY MIGHT THINK SUCH!
PEOPLE BEEN CALLIN' ME A SIDESHOW FREAK SINCE I CAN REMEMBER--
'CEPT NOW, I CAN STRIKE BACK!
THE NAME'S VENOMM, PANTHER--
--AND AS MY "PET'S" FANGS STRIKE--
--REMEMBER THAT NAME-- REMEMBER IT AS YOU SLOWLY DIE!
TWISTING AGILELY TO AVOID THE DEADLY LUNGE--
--THE PANTHER FEELS THE LEDGE CRUMBLE BENEATH HIS FEET!
NO AMOUNT OF ACROBATICS WILL HELP SURVIVE THIS FALL!

YOU JUST KEEP ON *SURPRIZIN'* ME!

KILLMONGER DIDN'T *EXAGGERATE* A BIT ABOUT YOU!

BUT THERE'S NOTHIN' *LEFT* TO GRAB ONTO AFTER THIS *EDGE*--!

YOU CAN TWIST YOURSELF INTO A *PRETZEL*--

BUT IT *WON'T* DO YOU A BIT 'A GOOD!

YOU'RE A *REAL* DEAD MAN THIS TIME, PANTHER!

VENOMM'S WORDS *RICOCHET* HAUNTINGLY OFF THE *CAVERN WALLS*--

--AND THEN, THE PANTHER DOES WHAT FEW OTHER MEN WOULD EVER DARE ATTEMPT!

HE LETS HIS FREE HAND SWING *AWAY* FROM HIS *LIFE-HOLD*--

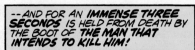

--AND FOR AN *IMMENSE THREE SECONDS* IS HELD FROM DEATH BY THE BOOT OF *THE MAN THAT INTENDS TO KILL HIM!*

AND BEFORE VENOMM CAN LIFT THAT FOOT, AND LET THE ENEMY *SPLATTER* UPON THE *STALAGMITES* BELOW--

--THE PANTHER HAS *REVERSED* POSITIONS!

DON'T BE *AFRAID* OF DYING JUST YET, VENOMM--

--THOUGH YOU MIGHT WELL *WISH* YOU *HAD* BY THE TIME I'M *FINISHED* WITH YOU!

I WON'T LET YOU *STEAL* KILLMONGER'S *PROMISE!*

I *WON'T* LET YOU *STEAL* MY *CHANCE* FOR RESPECT!

RESPECT!

SPEAK NOT TO ME OF RESPECT!

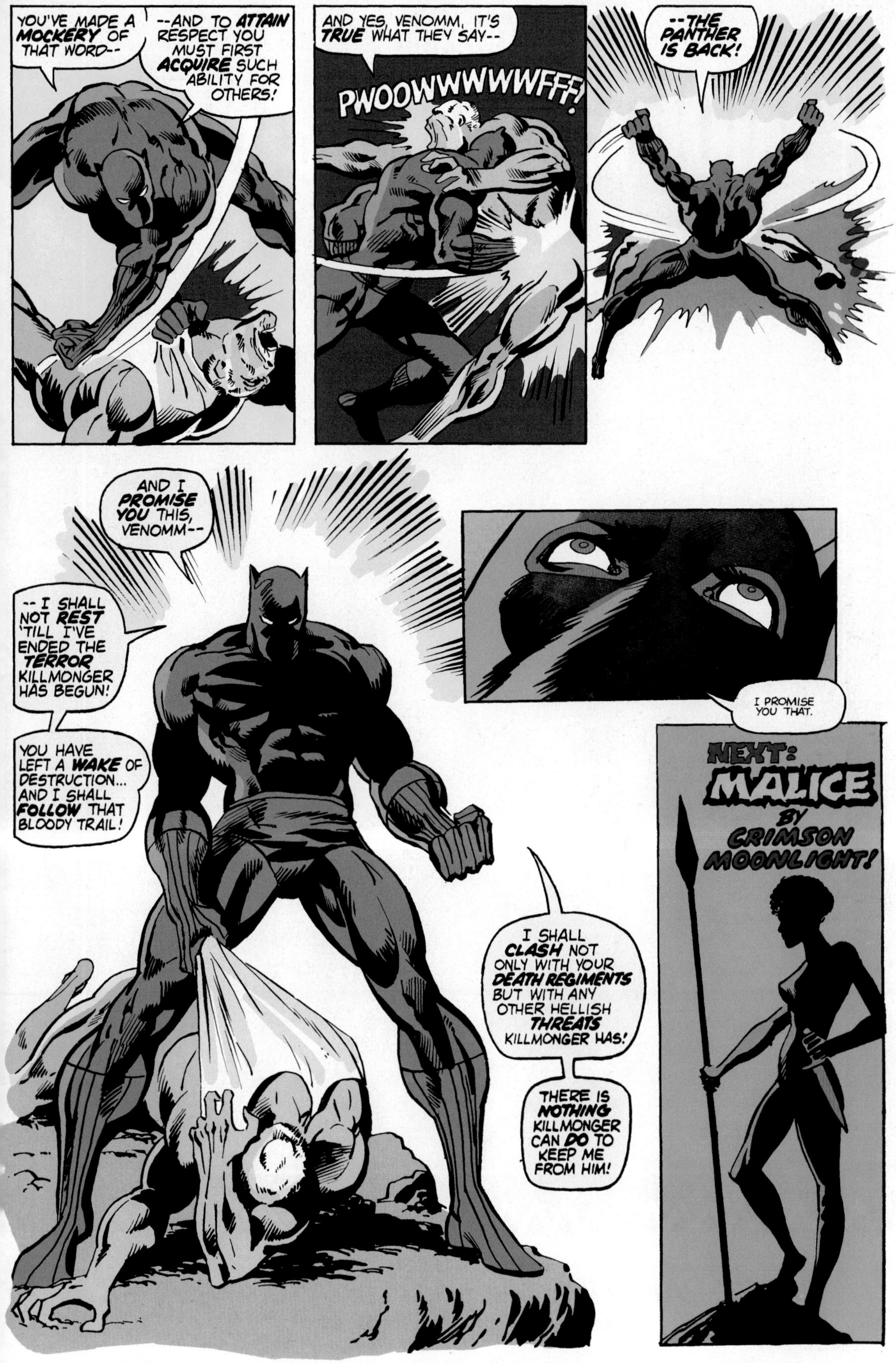

YOU'VE MADE A MOCKERY OF THAT WORD--
--AND TO ATTAIN RESPECT YOU MUST FIRST ACQUIRE SUCH ABILITY FOR OTHERS!
AND YES, VENOMM, IT'S TRUE WHAT THEY SAY--
PWOOWWWWWWFFF!
--THE PANTHER IS BACK!
AND I PROMISE YOU THIS, VENOMM--
-- I SHALL NOT REST 'TILL I'VE ENDED THE TERROR KILLMONGER HAS BEGUN!
YOU HAVE LEFT A WAKE OF DESTRUCTION... AND I SHALL FOLLOW THAT BLOODY TRAIL!
I SHALL CLASH NOT ONLY WITH YOUR DEATH REGIMENTS BUT WITH ANY OTHER HELLISH THREATS KILLMONGER HAS!
THERE IS NOTHING KILLMONGER CAN DO TO KEEP ME FROM HIM!
I PROMISE YOU THAT.
NEXT: MALICE BY CRIMSON MOONLIGHT!

BLACK PANTHER
WORLD OF WAKANDA

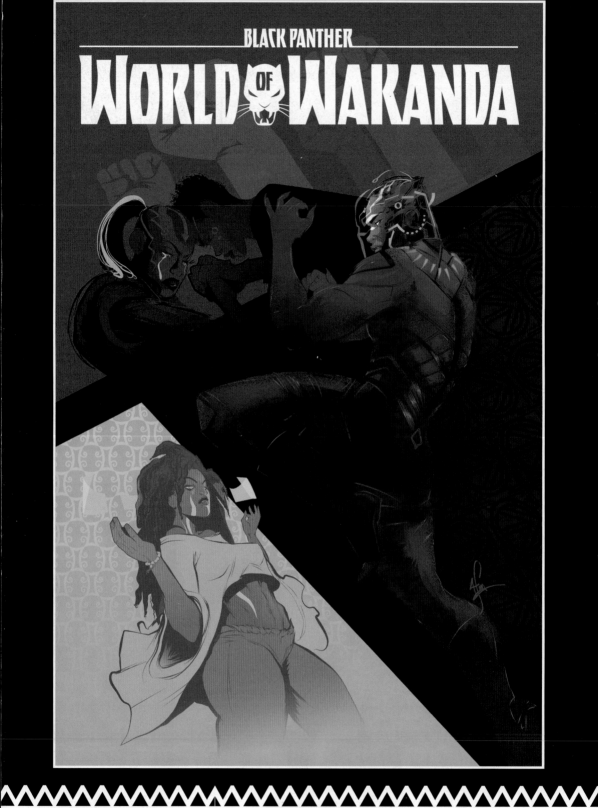

BONUS PREVIEW:

BLACK PANTHER: WORLD OF WAKANDA #1!

DAWN OF THE MIDNIGHT ANGELS - PART 1

WRITER: ROXANE GAY ● CONSULTANT: TA-NEHISI COATES ● ARTIST: ALITHA E. MARTINEZ
COLOR ARTIST: RACHELLE ROSENBERG ● LETTERER: VC'S JOE SABINO
COVER BY AFUA RICHARDSON

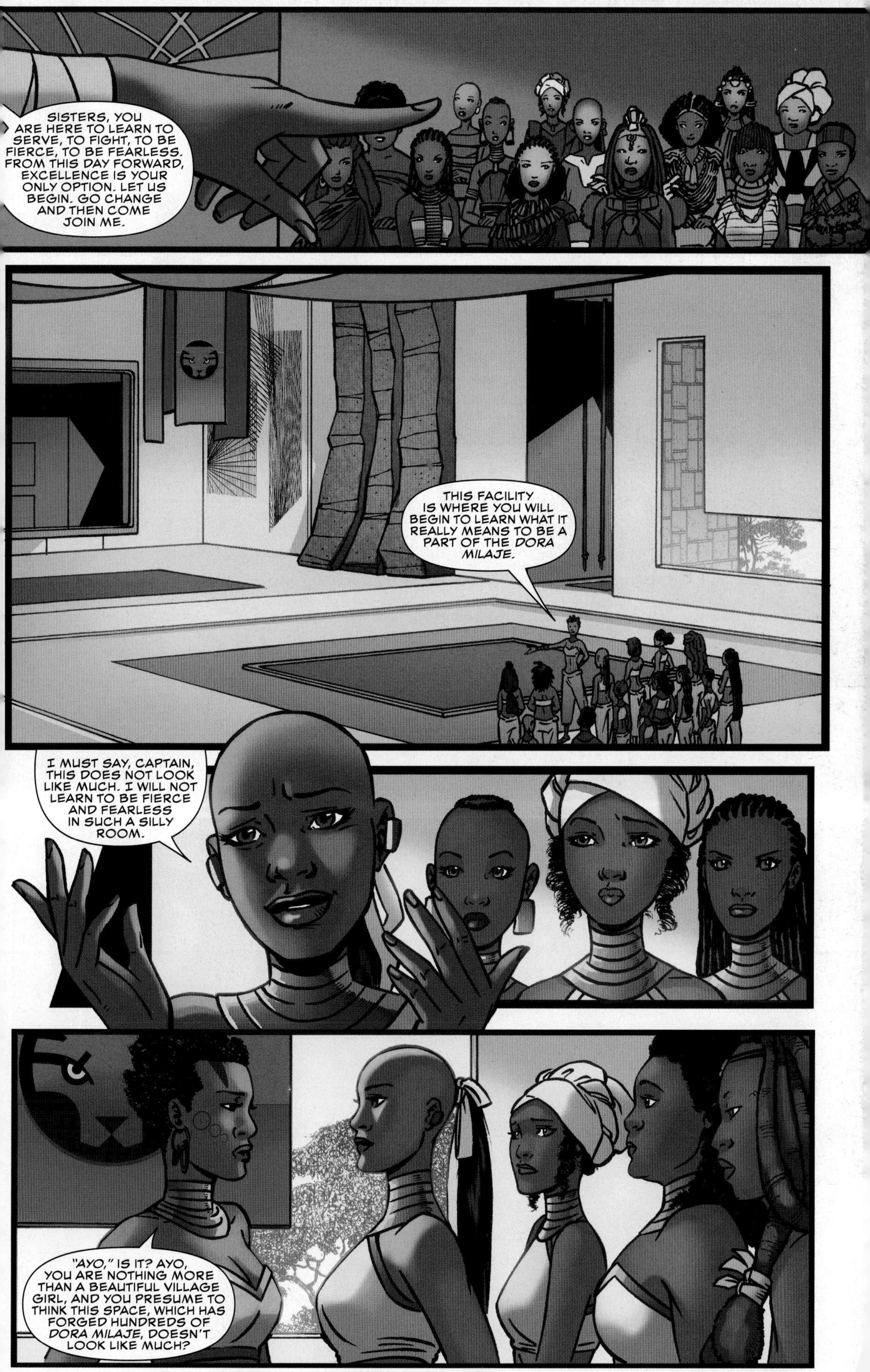
SISTERS, YOU ARE HERE TO LEARN TO SERVE, TO FIGHT, TO BE FIERCE, TO BE FEARLESS. FROM THIS DAY FORWARD, EXCELLENCE IS YOUR ONLY OPTION. LET US BEGIN. GO CHANGE AND THEN COME JOIN ME.
THIS FACILITY IS WHERE YOU WILL BEGIN TO LEARN WHAT IT REALLY MEANS TO BE A PART OF THE *DORA MILAJE*.
I MUST SAY, CAPTAIN, THIS DOES NOT LOOK LIKE MUCH. I WILL NOT LEARN TO BE FIERCE AND FEARLESS IN SUCH A SILLY ROOM.
"AYO," IS IT? AYO, YOU ARE NOTHING MORE THAN A BEAUTIFUL VILLAGE GIRL, AND YOU PRESUME TO THINK THIS SPACE, WHICH HAS FORGED HUNDREDS OF *DORA MILAJE*, DOESN'T LOOK LIKE MUCH?

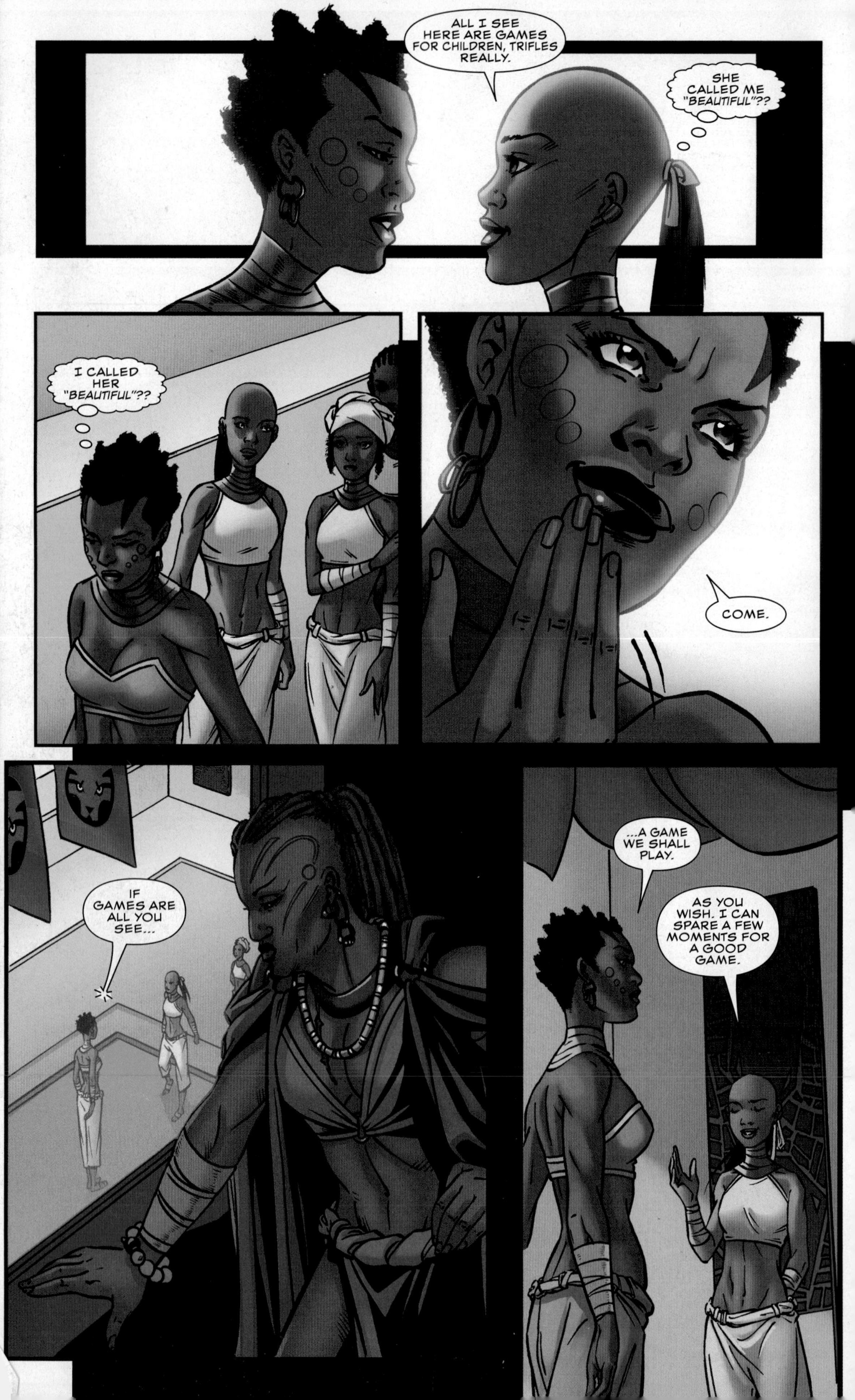
ALL I SEE HERE ARE GAMES FOR CHILDREN, TRIFLES REALLY.
SHE CALLED ME "BEAUTIFUL"??
I CALLED HER "BEAUTIFUL"??
COME.
IF GAMES ARE ALL YOU SEE...
...A GAME WE SHALL PLAY.
AS YOU WISH. I CAN SPARE A FEW MOMENTS FOR A GOOD GAME.

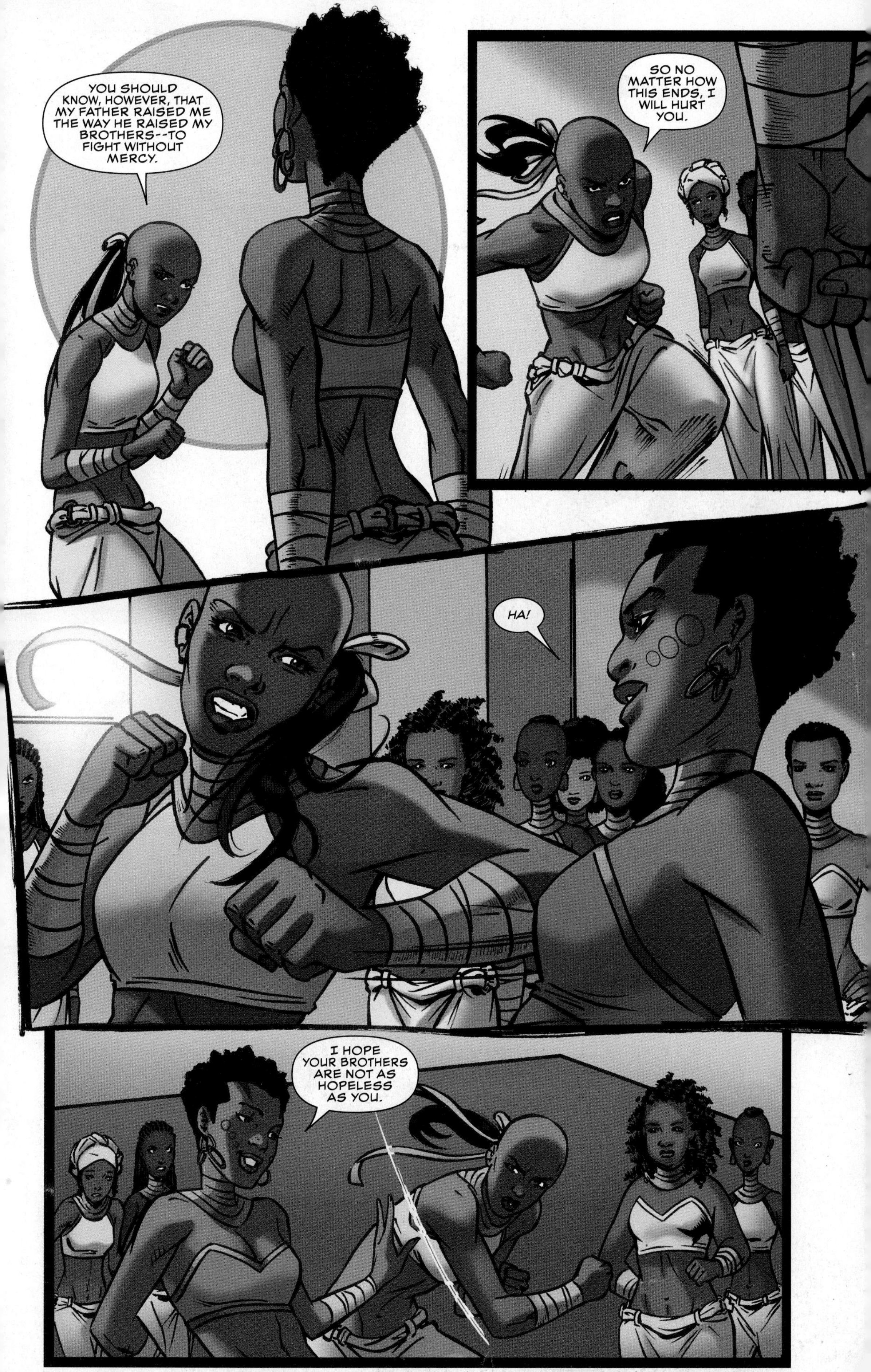
YOU SHOULD KNOW, HOWEVER, THAT MY FATHER RAISED ME THE WAY HE RAISED MY BROTHERS--TO FIGHT WITHOUT MERCY.
SO NO MATTER HOW THIS ENDS, I WILL HURT YOU.
HA!
I HOPE YOUR BROTHERS ARE NOT AS HOPELESS AS YOU.

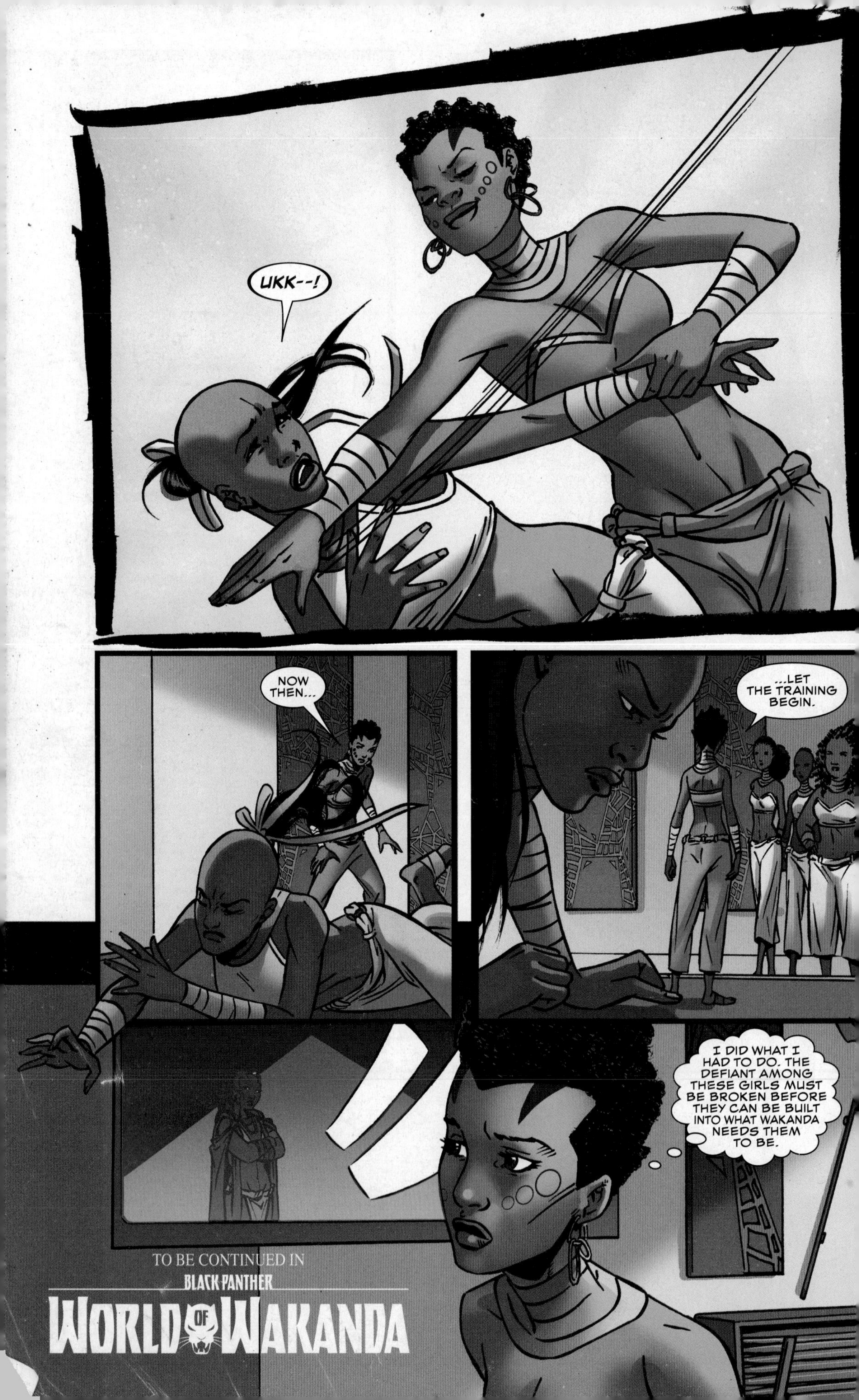
UKK--!
NOW THEN...
...LET THE TRAINING BEGIN.
I DID WHAT I HAD TO DO. THE DEFIANT AMONG THESE GIRLS MUST BE BROKEN BEFORE THEY CAN BE BUILT INTO WHAT WAKANDA NEEDS THEM TO BE.
TO BE CONTINUED IN
BLACK PANTHER
WORLD OF WAKANDA